Kant and the Problem of Metaphysics

MARTIN HEIDEGGER

# Kant and the Problem
# of Metaphysics

TRANSLATED BY JAMES S. CHURCHILL

FOREWORD BY THOMAS LANGAN

INDIANA UNIVERSITY PRESS

BLOOMINGTON

*To the memory of*
*Max Scheler*

# 1505373

## CONTENTS

v

# FOREWORD

"In contrast to the methods of historical philology, which
has its own problems, a dialogue between thinkers is bound
by other laws." Heidegger thus tells the reader in which spirit
he should approach *Kant and the Problem of Metaphysics.*
This is a "thoughtful dialogue," hence it is as much Heidegger
as Kant. Indeed the *Kantbuch* of 1929 is a model for the long
series of dialogues with the leading thinkers of the Western
tradition that form Heidegger's rethinking of the whole history of ontology. The "laws" governing such dialogue are
grounded in Heidegger's conception of Being and how Being
has come to be.

In the Introduction to *Sein und Zeit* the role of such dialogue
is explained in terms of a program for establishing an authentic,
a "fundamental" ontology. The question of "the Being of the
things that are" itself came to be at a definite moment in time,
with the questioning of the Greek philosophers in the gener-
ation before Socrates. The meaning of the question and the
answers given it were in the beginning indetermined, ambiguous,
pregnant with different sorts of possible interpretation. The
history of ontology, however, has been dominated by a chain
of evolving *metaphysical* answers, that is, answers all of the
sort that seeks beyond the sum total of things of our experience,
a ground in a super-thing—a Platonic Idea of the Good, an
Aristotelian Thought of Thought, St. Thomas' *Actus purus,*
Spinoza's Substance.

The meta-physical construction of ontology is necessarily

accompanied by a "conformity" theory of truth: Truth is conceived as the mind's conformity with the principles of a reality that is lying there before us, already constituted in itself, and inviting our submissive grasp of its reality. Latent in the metaphysical conception of Being and the conformity theory of truth are great tensions: the tension between the "here-below" and the "thingliest of things" beyond all experience, and between the *ob-jectum* "out-there" and the *sub-jectum* "in here" which must somehow go out of itself to enfold and possess this object.

The history of metaphysics has been that of the progressive domination of the object by the subject. After all, it is the subject who knows, and it is in the subject that the criteria of truth are to be found. Descartes takes the decisive step toward converting the object into the subject's "representation." By Kant's time, the way is prepared for the most serious inquiry into the rules governing the subject's placing (*stellen*) the representation (*Vor-stellung*) before (*vor*) himself. With this inquiry the whole historical destiny of metaphysics is fulfilled, although ironically it is saved by being *reversed*. Because the metaphysical tradition began with the unquestioned assumption that "Being" lies in a reality already constituted in itself before the human existent arrives on the scene and begins knowing it, a subject-object polarity was established. Then the gradual domination of the object by the subject leads ultimately to the realization that without the consciousness of the subject the object could not be. With this turn of events the whole question of Being is projected onto a radically new plane. The "Being" of things is now seen to be grounded in the possibility of experience. The search for "Being" is now directed not toward a "reality in itself" but toward the subjective roots of the transcendental horizons of consciousness. The quest for "Being" is no longer a search for the "thingliest of things"—the "cause" *meta-ta-phusika* responsible for there being any things in the first place; rather, it is a quest to understand how the existent can bring to be a world of meaning, a world of time, a history in which "things" can be with significance.

With Kant, then, the "question of Being" is at a particularly crucial crossroads. Kant opens the possibility of "transcendental inquiry" into the fundamental "ground" of Being. But has he succeeded in penetrating more deeply than the ancient subject-object split itself, has he plunged through to the authentic moment of the coming to be—neither a subjective nor an objective process, but the mating of the *Seienden* and the interpretative, time-projecting horizons of the human existent, a mating which brings into being the historical Thing? Heidegger's later dialogues with Hegel and Nietzsche and his laments over the destiny of the "planetary domination of the Technique" are eloquent evidence of his judgment of the historical position of Kant: With Kant the Western tradition has not yet come into full possession of a fundamental ontology that need not devolve either into the subjectivism of the Nietzschean "Will for the sake of Will," nor into the objectivism of "the Eternal Return of the Like;" neither into the totalitarian arbitrariness of a positivistic "Technique," nor into the transcendental Absolutism of Fichte. In Heidegger's dialogue with Hegel we are invited to gaze on perhaps the most tragic spectacle of all, a Being-revelation that is so close, ah yet so far! A monumental ambiguity is the result, making it impossible to know whether Being is only the creation of the human will or an Absolute that dips down into time through the medium of the human subject.

A fundamental ontology must dispel this ambiguity through a twofold program of inquiry into Being. The published part of *Sein und Zeit* begins the task of phenomenological inquiry into the human existent as "the place where Being comes to be in time." *Kant and the Problem of Metaphysics* begins the second aspect of the task, a rethinking of the whole course of that historical coming to be of "Being" and "Truth." The two enterprises—the "existential analytic" and the "recalling of the historical destiny" of the Western tradition—progressively illumine one another. *Sein und Zeit* would not have been possible if this historical evolution had not brought us to our present state. And we would not be at that point, that is to say the history would not be so comprehended and *therefore* advanced another step, if *Sein und Zeit* had not actually been carried out. *Kant and the Problem of Metaphysics* is, then, a collision of the vision of *Sein und Zeit* with the vision of the *Critique of Pure Reason,* the latter a vision without which *Sein und Zeit* would not have been possible, but one which *Sein und Zeit* had to transcend, giving the *Critique* in that very act its ultimate sense.

In *Kant and the Problem of Metaphysics* Heidegger is not, then, trying to say what Kant "really" said, nor what he "meant" to say. Rather, in this work we simply witness Heidegger in the very personal act of nourishing the enterprise of fundamental ontology on the wine of the first pressing of the *Critique.* Against the background of his conception of the history of ontology and with the basic discoveries of *Sein und Zeit* in mind, Heidegger wishes to profit as much as possible from the *Critique*'s transcendental analysis of the synthesis of imagination as foundation of a temporal horizon of significance. Heidegger wishes to liberate these discoveries from whatever hesitations, ambiguities, or later subjectivizing or absolutizing interpretations may keep them from full fruition. This fruition is the "fundamental ontology"—and *Kant and the Problem of Metaphysics* is an instrument of that peculiarly Heideggerian enterprise.

Is this work of interest then only to the student of Heidegger and not to the student of Kant? Were Heidegger's "fundamental ontology" based on a fantastic and absurd reconstruction of the history of philosophy, such would then be the lamentable case. That there are some unacceptable elements in Heidegger's reading of the history of our tradition is undeniable. But before anyone consigns the whole enterprise to the limbo of philosophical curiosities, let him, if he is a serious student of Kant, read the work here translated as evidence that there is much in what Heidegger says about our history, and that both his insights and his errors in this regard run on the deepest possible level of historical *explanation*. Before Heidegger applied the phenomenological ontology unveiled in *Sein und Zeit* to the *Critique of Pure Reason,* no one had so clearly seen the ontological mission of Kant's great work, the sense in which its anti-metaphysics is precisely fundamental *ontology*. Heidegger's Being-in-time vision illumines the Kantian doctrine of the temporal synthesis of the imagination as ground of the coming to be of the Thing, as it never has been before. And in this perspective, the First Edition's glimpse of the problem of the Nothingness of the "Thing in itself" is brought into stark relief, and the Second Edition's apparently deliberate backing away from it is dramatized so that the enigma it poses cannot be overlooked.

These are contributions of authentic Kantian commentary—of a dialogue with Kant on his own level. Criticism of *Kant and the Problem of Metaphysics* should march on this same level. Only the confrontation of ontology with ontology, and this in a way that can challenge a whole conception of history, is worthy of participation in this dialogue. It is in this sense that the *Kantbuch* is a model, not only for Heidegger's own subsequent dialogues, but for all "thoughtful dialogues between thinkers." Philosophical explanation is only worthy of our tradition when it moves with the current of Being itself.

THOMAS LANGAN

The purpose of *Kant and the Problem of Metaphysics,* according to Heidegger, is to explicate the *Critique of Pure Reason* "as a laying of the foundation of metaphysics as a problem of fundamental ontology" (p. 3). Metaphysics, Heidegger explains, can be divided into two distinct parts, (1) *metaphysica specialis,* which is concerned with the study of the particular spheres of essents,[1] i.e., God, nature, and man, within the essent in totality, and (2) *metaphysica generalis,* the object of which is the study of the essent "in general," i.e., ontology—or in Kant's terminology, "transcendental philosophy." [2]

It is the second of these branches to which Heidegger refers in the expression "laying of the foundation of metaphysics." Hence, "to lay the foundation of metaphysics . . . is to reveal the internal possibility of ontology" (p. 17). And since ontolog-

---

1. Since there is no form of the verb "to be" equivalent to Heidegger's *Seiend,* a term "alien to our everyday speech" (Martin Heidegger, *An Introduction to Metaphysics,* trans. Ralph Manheim [New Haven, 1959], p. 77), I have adopted Ralph Manheim's procedure in using the term "essent." This word, coined by Manheim, is "based on the fiction that *essens, essentia* is the present participle of sum" (*ibid.,* p. ix).

I have translated the words *Sein* and *sein* by "Being" and "being" respectively, although the fact that *sein* is an infinitive and "being" a participle occasionally makes for awkwardness. In addition, when the occasion demands it, I use "being" as an equivalent for *Wesen.*

2. *Critique of Pure Reason,* trans. Norman Kemp Smith (London, 1929), p. 662.

ical knowledge, i.e., the "precursory" (*vorgängig*) comprehension of the Being of essents, is "that which makes . . . ontic knowledge possible" (p. 15), to interpret the *Critique of Pure Reason* as a laying of the foundation of metaphysics is to interpret it as the establishment of the possibility of that which makes empirical (i.e., objective) knowledge possible.

As ontology is an inquiry concerned with the Being of things, so "fundamental ontology" is an inquiry concerned with the possibility of ontology. In other words, its object is the analysis of the comprehension of Being as that on which ontology itself depends; it is concerned to uncover the source of the "objectivity factor" as that without which objective experience would be impossible.

If the first *Critique* is a "laying of the foundation" of ontology (metaphysics), this foundation being the comprehension of Being itself as that which makes ontology possible, then the *Critique* is ultimately concerned with the "preparation" of this foundation, i.e., with determining from what and in what manner this foundation itself arises.

This foundation of the foundation, Heidegger asserts, is *Dasein*,[3] and the business of determining how the foundation

3. *Dasein,* the key term in Heidegger's technical vocabulary, is one which has thus far resisted successful translation. Translations such as M. Corbin's *réalité humaine* and Professor John Wild's *transience,* for example, fail to preserve the neutrality of *Dasein* and to convey the sense of place or situation inherent in *Da-sein.* On the other hand, translations such as Ralph Manheim's simple "being-there" seem also to be unsatisfactory. The *Da* of *Dasein* means both "here" and "there" or even "where," in short, place or situation in general. But the English "there" ("in that place") carries the implication of position in space, "there" as opposed to "here," and it is just this notion which Heidegger asserts in *Sein und Zeit* (p. 52ff.) does not apply to the mode of "being in" the world characteristic of *Dasein.*

In view of these and other objections, I have decided to leave

of metaphysics as the comprehension of Being is grounded in and arises from *Dasein* must proceed by an "existential [or as he expresses it in the *Kant-book,* an "ontological"] analytic of *Dasein.*" [4] The object of the *Critique of Pure Reason* is just such an analytic. But this is also the object of *Sein und Zeit,* namely, the "working out of the meaning of Being" by means of an existential analytic of *Dasein.* Thus, it is apparent that in stating that the object of *Kant and the Problem of Metaphysics* is to present the *Critique of Pure Reason* "as a laying of the foundation of metaphysics in order thus to present the problem of metaphysics as the problem of a fundamental ontology," Heidegger looks upon Kant as being engaged in the same task as that with which he himself is occupied in *Sein und Zeit,* namely, in showing how it is possible for man as a "finite being which as such is delivered up to the essent" to have a comprehension of Being by virtue of which this being "is able to bring forth the ontological structure [*Seinsverfassung*] of the essent" (p. 42), i.e., render objective experience possible.

Heidegger, then, has no quarrel with Kant's basic assumptions. Both accept the fundamental hypothesis of idealism—that the principles of order in experience are *a priori*—and both are necessarily concerned with the analysis of that which makes possible the objectivity-factor required by this hypothesis (pure reason in the one case, *Dasein* in the other). If Heidegger has a quarrel with Kant, it is that the latter was too much a prisoner of tradition to carry this analysis to its ultimate conclusion,

---

the term in the original German. The meaning of *Dasein* can perhaps best be conveyed by stating, as I have intimated, that it is roughly equivalent to Kant's "pure reason" although without the rationalistic overtones of this term.

4. *Sein und Zeit,* 6th ed. (Tübingen, 1949), p. 13; this and subsequent passages from *Sein und Zeit* are based on the "informal English paraphrase" of part of this book by Robert J. Trayhern, John Wild, Bert Dreyfus, and C. DeDeugd.

namely, that the basis of this objectivity-factor is temporality as the Being of *Dasein* or, in Kant's case, pure reason.

In general, Kant's critics fail to appreciate the enormous importance of time in the development of Kant's critical idealism. Heidegger is certainly an exception to this observation; indeed, it can be said that the over-all purpose of the *Kant-book* is to show how time, or to be more exact, temporality, is involved in every phase of Kant's thought. This purpose is evident not only on the basis of the content of this work but also on the basis of what Heidegger in effect says about it.

*Kant and the Problem of Metaphysics,* Heidegger informs us in the preface, arose "in the course of the elaboration of the second part of *Sein und Zeit*" (p. xxiii). The second part of this work (which has never appeared) was to have as its title, *The Fundamental Characteristics of a Phenomenological Destruction of the History of Ontology under the Guidance of the Problematic of Temporality,* and Section Two of Part One was to have the subtitle, *Kant's Doctrine of Schematism and of Time as the First Stage in the Elaboration of the Problem of Temporality.*[5]

By the term "destruction," Heidegger tells us, he does not mean either the "trivial business of relating ontological standpoints to one another" or the "shaking off" of the history of ontology, but rather, "the loosening up of a tradition that has grown rigid" and so conceals and denies access to those "original 'sources' from which the categories and concepts relative to Being were in part genuinely created." The primary concern of this destruction, which is really an uncovering, is to discover how and to what extent "the interpretation of Being has coincided thematically with the phenomenon of time." [6]

5. *Ibid.,* p. 39.
6. *Ibid.,* p. 22f.

Viewed in this light, i.e., as an exercise in the destruction of the history of ontology, the over-all pattern of the *Kant-book* becomes clear. It begins, in Section One, with a characterization of the ontological tradition which formed the background of Kant's thought. This tradition not only supplied the frame of reference for the first *Critique* as a laying of the foundation of metaphysics but also predisposed Kant in favor of the supremacy of reason and the understanding as opposed to such "lower" faculties as the imagination. This is why, according to Heidegger, even though the whole trend of the *Critique* points to the central function of the imagination insofar as the possibility of the ontological synthesis is concerned, Kant refused to recognize this and in the second edition reduced the imagination to a "function of the understanding" (p. 167).

Section Two is devoted to a detailed analysis of the *Critique of Pure Reason* as a laying of the foundation of metaphysics. In the course of this analysis, Heidegger brings out the importance of the imagination as the "formative center" of ontological knowledge by showing, particularly in his discussion of the transcendental deduction of the categories and the doctrine of schematism, that it is the imagination which creates the horizon of objectivity without which objective experience would be impossible.

Section Three, "The Laying of the Foundation of Metaphysics in Its Basic Originality"—wherein, according to Ernst Cassirer, Heidegger "no longer speaks as a commentator but as a usurper" [7]—contains the most controversial material of the *Kant-book*. In this section, Heidegger with "violence" wrests from Kant what he "intended to say" but "recoiled from" because he was a prisoner of tradition, namely, that not only is temporality the ground of the transcendental imagination, it

7. Ernst Cassirer, *Kant und das Problem der Metaphysik, Bemarkungen zu Martin Heideggers Kant-Interpretation, Kant-Studien,* XXXVI, No. 1/2 (1931), p. 17.

is also the basis of the "selfhood" of the self—pure practical reason as well as intuition, understanding, and the imagination.

Properly speaking, Section Three marks the end of Heidegger's interpretation of the first *Critique* as a laying of the foundation of metaphysics. What follows, in Section Four, Heidegger terms a "repetition" [*Wiederholung*] of the laying of the foundation of metaphysics.

In Heidegger's terminology, the "repetition" of a philosophical problem does not signify an abridgment or a summary of the problem, "but the disclosure of the primordial possibilities concealed in it. The development of these possibilities has the effect of transforming the problem and thus preserving it in its import as a problem" (p. 211).

The repetition of a problem, however, is possible only on the basis of a preceding "destruction." Only by first "loosening up a tradition that has grown rigid" and so making accessible the "original sources" of a problem can the possibilities inherent in this problem be developed in a repetition which both lets us see the problem as a problem and at the same time goes beyond it.

This movement, which might be described as a kind of dialectic, is exemplified in connection with the central problem of the *Critique of Pure Reason,* that of establishing the possibility of objective experience, or, as Heidegger expresses it, that of laying the foundation of metaphysics. In the first three sections of the *Kant-book,* Heidegger by a destruction of the history of ontology brings to light the hidden "foundation of the foundation" of metaphysics, i.e., temporality as the Being of *Dasein. Sein und Zeit* (the essentials of which are presented in Section Four of the *Kant-book*) is a repetition of this problem, in the course of which not only is the problem restated and redeveloped in terms of a comprehension of the Being of things but it is also transcended as a problem. That is, Heidegger goes beyond the problem of trying to account for objective experience by means of a comprehension of the Being of things to the problem of the meaning of Being in general and its relation to *Dasein*.

Nor has this movement, this going beyond, ceased with *Sein und Zeit*. On the contrary, as the works written after *Sein und Zeit* reveal, it is still going on. And if the trend of the past thirty years is any indication, its ultimate end seems to be the emergence of Being as such as a kind of Absolute.

Could it be that in going beyond Kant, Heidegger is "repeating" the history of immediate post-Kantian German philosophy and is illustrating within his own thought that the fundamental hypothesis of idealism leads straight to the Hegelian Absolute?

J. S. C.

## FROM THE AUTHOR'S PREFACE TO THE
## FIRST EDITION

In its essentials, the following interpretation was first presented in a four-hour course held during the winter semester of 1925–26. It was later repeated in lectures and series of lectures (at the Herder Institute in Riga in September, 1928, and in connection with the university courses held at Davos in March, 1929).

This interpretation of the *Critique of Pure Reason* arose in the course of the elaboration of the second part of *Sein und Zeit*.

This work is dedicated to the memory of Max Scheler. Its content was the subject of the last conversation in which the author was privileged once more to experience the unfettered power of his mind.

*Todtnauberg im bad. Schwarzwald, Whitsunday, 1929*

## AUTHOR'S PREFACE TO THE
## SECOND EDITION

This work, the first edition of which was published twenty years ago and immediately sold out, appears here unaltered. It is preserved in that form in which in a multitude of ways it has been effective and ineffective.

My critics have constantly reproached me for the violence of my interpretations, and the grounds for this reproach can easily be found in this work. From the point of view of an inquiry which is both historical and philosophical, this reproach is always justified when directed against attempts to set in motion a thoughtful dialogue between thinkers. In contrast to the methods of historical philology, which has its own problems, a dialogue between thinkers is bound by other laws. These laws are more easily violated; the possibility of going astray is more threatening, the shortcomings more frequent.

The extent to which I have gone astray in the present endeavor and the shortcomings thereof have become so clear to me in the period of time since its first publication that I refrain from making it a patchwork through the addition of supplements and postscripts.

Through their shortcomings, thinkers learn to be more persevering.

*Freiburg im Breisgau, June, 1950*

INTRODUCTION

# THE THEME AND ORGANIZATION OF THE INQUIRY

# THE THEME AND ORGANIZATION OF THE INQUIRY

The task of the following investigation is to explicate Kant's *Critique of Pure Reason* as a laying of the foundation [*Grundlegung*] [1] of metaphysics in order thus to present the problem of metaphysics as the problem of a fundamental ontology.

By fundamental ontology is meant that ontological analytic

1. The English term "ground" with its rich and varied meaning is generally equivalent to the German *Grund* except in one particular. It is not commonly used to denote a foundation in the sense of a foundation of a building. In Heidegger's usage, at least, the German *Grund* does include this sense. Furthermore, it is just this sense ("foundation" in the sense of the foundation of a building) which Heidegger suggests (page 4) in his use of the expression *Grundlegung*, "laying of the foundation." Therefore, I use the term "foundation" as an equivalent for *Grund* in the expression *Grundlegung* and otherwise "ground," "principle," or "basis," depending on the context. For example, on page 5 I have rendered *So ist die Grundlegung als Entwurf der inneren Möglichkeit der Metaphysik notwendig ein Wirksamwerdenlassen der Trägerschaft des gelegten Grundes* as "Thus, the laying of the foundation as the projection of the intrinsic possibility of metaphysics is necessarily a letting become effective of the supporting power of the established ground." (J. S. C.)

of man's finite essence which should prepare the foundation for the metaphysics "which belongs to human nature." Fundamental ontology is that metaphysics of human *Dasein* necessary if metaphysics in general is to be possible. Fundamental ontology is basically different from all anthropology, even philosophical anthropology. To analyze the idea of fundamental ontology means: To set forth the ontological analytic of *Dasein* as a prerequisite and to make clear to what purpose and in what manner, on what basis and under what presuppositions it puts the concrete question: "What is man?" But if an idea manifests itself chiefly through its own power to illuminate, the idea of fundamental ontology must exhibit and affirm itself in an explication of the *Critique of Pure Reason* as a laying of the foundation of metaphysics.

To this end, it is necessary first to clarify the meaning of the expression "to lay the foundation of . . ." Its meaning is best illustrated within the field of architecture. To be sure, metaphysics is not an actual edifice, yet it is present as a "natural disposition" in all men.[2] Accordingly, laying the foundation of metaphysics can mean either putting a foundation under this natural metaphysics or replacing one already laid by a new one. However, it is precisely the idea that it is a matter of providing a foundation for an edifice already constructed that must be avoided. Laying the foundation, rather, is the projection [*Entwerfen*] of the building plan itself in such a way as to indicate on what and how the structure will be grounded. On the other hand, laying the foundation of metaphysics is not the

2. *Critique of Pure Reason,* 2nd ed., p. 21. The first edition (A) and the second (B) are set over against one another in a masterly fashion in the text edited by Raymund Schmidt (Meiner's *Philosophische Bibliothek,* 1926). The following passages will be cited according to both A and B. (In subsequent citations, the page reference according to Kemp Smith's translation will be given after that according to Schmidt.)

mere fabrication of a system and its subdivisions but the tracing of the architectonic limits and design of the intrinsic possibility of metaphysics, i.e., the concrete determination of its essence. All essential determination is first achieved, however, in the revelation of the essential ground.

Thus, the laying of the foundation as the projection of the intrinsic possibility of metaphysics is necessarily a letting become effective of the supporting power of the established ground. If and how this takes place is the criterion of the basic originality and depth of a laying of the foundation.

If the following interpretation of the *Critique of Pure Reason* succeeds in bringing to light the basic originality of the origin of metaphysics, then this basic originality can be essentially understood only if from the outset it is brought into the concrete development of the act of origination, that is, if the laying of the foundation of metaphysics is repeated.

So far as metaphysics belongs to "human nature" and factually exists with human nature, it is always actualized in some form or other. Hence, a specific laying of the foundation of metaphysics never arises out of nothing but out of the strength and weakness of a tradition which designates in advance its possible points of departure. With regard to the tradition it implies, every laying of the foundation when compared with those which precede it is a transformation of the same problem. Thus, the following interpretation of the *Critique of Pure Reason* as a laying of the foundation of metaphysics must attempt to clarify these four points:

1. The point of departure of the laying of the foundation of metaphysics.

2. The carrying out of the laying of the foundation of metaphysics.

3. The laying of the foundation of metaphysics in its basic originality.

4. The laying of the foundation of metaphysics in a repetition.

5

# THE POINT OF DEPARTURE OF THE LAYING OF THE FOUNDATION OF METAPHYSICS

SECTION ONE

## THE POINT OF DEPARTURE OF THE LAYING OF THE FOUNDATION OF METAPHYSICS

The exposition of the way in which Kant conceived the point of departure for the laying of the foundation of metaphysics is equivalent to answering the question: Why for Kant does the laying of a foundation of metaphysics take the form of a *Critique of Pure Reason?* The answer must be forthcoming through a discussion of the following three questions: 1. What concept of metaphysics did Kant inherit? 2. What is the point of departure for the laying of the foundation of this traditional metaphysics? 3. Why is this laying of the foundation a *Critique of Pure Reason?*

### § 1. The Traditional Concept of Metaphysics

The horizon within which metaphysics appeared to Kant and within which his laying of the foundation had to begin may be characterized schematically by means of Baumgarten's definition: *Metaphysica est scientia prima cognitionis humanae principia continens:* [1] metaphysics is the science which contains

1. A. G. Baumgarten, *Metaphysica,* 2nd ed., 1743, § 1.

9

the first principles of that which is within the comprehension of human knowledge. In the concept of "the first principles of human knowledge" lies a peculiar and, to begin with, a necessary ambiguity. *Ad metaphysicam referuntur ontologia, cosmologia, psychologia, et theologia naturalis.*[2] The motives and the history of the development and stabilization of this school-concept of metaphysics cannot be presented here. However, a brief indication of what is presented therein should serve to break up the problematic content of this concept and thus prepare the way for an understanding of the basic significance of the Kantian point of departure of the laying of the foundation of metaphysics.[3]

It is well known that the meaning of the expression *meta ta physika* (as the collective name for those treatises of Aristotle which were classified as following those belonging to the

2. *Ibid.,* § 2.

3. After the precedent set by H. Pilcher's *Über Christian Wolffs Ontologie,* 1910, Kant's relation to traditional metaphysics has been of late more searchingly and more exhaustively investigated. See above all, the inquiries by H. Heimsoeth, *Die Metaphysischen Motive in der Ausbildung des Kritischen Idealismus, Kantstudien,* vol. XXIX (1924), p. 121ff.; further, *Metaphysik und Kritik bei Chr. A. Crusius, Ein Beitrag zur ontologischen Vorgeschichte der Kritik der Reinen Vernunft in 18. Jahrhundert (Schriften der Konigsberger Gelehrten Gesellschafft* III. *Jahr, Geisteswiss. Kl. Hft. 3,* 1926). In addition, the longer work by M. Wundt, *Kant als Metaphysiker. Ein Beitrag zur Geschichte der deutschen Philosophie in achtzehnten Jahrhundert,* 1924. R. Kroner provides an account of the Kantian philosophy in the light of the history of metaphysics after Kant in *Von Kant bis Hegel,* two volumes, 1921 and 1924. For the history of metaphysics in German idealism see also Nic. Hartmann, *Die Philosophie des deutschen Idealismus,* part I, 1923, part II, 1929. A critical evaluation of these works is not possible here. One thing should be noted, however; each of them from the beginning clings to the interpretation of the *Critique of Pure Reason* as "theory of knowledge" and treats of metaphysics and "metaphysical themes" only in a subsidiary way.

10

"Physics"), which was at first purely descriptive, later came to express a philosophical judgment concerning the content of these works. This change in meaning does not have the harmlessness which is attributed to it. Rather, it has forced the interpretation of these treatises in a particular direction and thereby has determined that what Aristotle discusses therein is to be understood as "metaphysics." Nevertheless, whether that which is contained in Aristotle's *Metaphysics* is "metaphysics" must be doubted. However, Kant himself still attempts directly to attribute a real meaning to the expression: "With reference to that to which the name 'metaphysics' refers, it is unbelievable that it arose by chance since it corresponds so exactly to the content of the science: since *physis* means nature, and since we can arrive at the concept of nature only through experience, that science which follows it is called metaphysics (from *meta* [*trans*], and *physica*). It is a science which, being outside the domain of physics, as it were, lies beyond it." [4]

The classificatory expression which occasioned this particular interpretation of Aristotle's writings itself arose from a difficulty concerning the comprehension of the treatises thus classified in the *corpus aristotelicum*. In the philosophy of the schools (logic, physics, ethics) which followed Aristotle, no discipline or framework could be found into which could be fitted what Aristotle pursued as *prōtē philosophia,* true philosophy, philosophy of the first rank; *meta te physika* is thus the title of a basic philosophical difficulty.

This difficulty has its origin in the obscurity which envelops the essentials of the problems and ideas discussed in the treatises. Insofar as Aristotle expresses himself on the subject, it is

4. M. Heinze, *Vorlesungen Kants über Metaphysik aus drei Semestern, Abhdlg. der K. Sächsisch. Ges. der Wissenschaften. Bd.* XIV, *phil.-hist. Kl.* 1894, p. 666 (*Sep.* S. 186). *Cf.* also: Kant, *Über die Fortschritte der Metaphysik seit Leibniz und Wolff, Works* (Cassirer) VIII, p. 301ff.

evident that there is a curious ambiguity in the definition of "first philosophy." It is knowledge of the essent [*des Seienden*] *qua* essent (*on ē on*) as well as knowledge of the highest sphere of essents (*timiōtaton genos*) through which the essent in totality is defined.

This dual characterization of *prōtē philosophia* does not contain two radically different trains of thought nor should one be weakened or rejected outright in favor of the other. Furthermore, we should not be over-hasty in reconciling this apparent duality. Rather, through an analysis of the problem of "first philosophy" we must throw light upon the reason behind this duality and the manner in which both determinations are connected. The task is all the more pressing in that the ambiguity mentioned did not first make its appearance with Aristotle but has dominated the problem of Being since the first beginnings of ancient philosophy.

In order to keep this problem of the essential determination of "metaphysics" in view, it can be said by way of anticipation that metaphysics is the fundamental knowledge of the essent as such and in totality. This "definition" is only to be considered, however, as an indication of the real problem, the question: Wherein lies the essence of the knowledge of the Being of essents? In what respect does this knowledge necessarily lead to a knowledge of the essent in totality? Why does this knowledge in turn lead to a knowledge of the knowledge of Being [*Seinserkenntnis*]? Thus, "metaphysics" remains the title of a fundamental philosophical difficulty.

Post-Aristotelian metaphysics owes its development not to the adoption and elaboration of an allegedly pre-existent Aristotelian system but to the failure to understand the doubtful and unsettled state in which Plato and Aristotle left the central problems. The formation of the school-concept of metaphysics mentioned above owes its development primarily to two considerations which, at the same time, have proved to be an ever-

12

growing obstacle in the way of taking up the original problem again.

The one consideration concerns the organization of metaphysics with respect to its content and arises from the devout Christian interpretation of the world. According to this, all that is not divine is created—the totality of creatures defining the universe. Among created things man has a special place inasmuch as everything is centered on the welfare of his soul and his own eternal existence. In keeping with the Christian belief concerning the world and existence, the essent in totality is divided into God, nature, and man, each of these realms having a particular discipline devoted to its study. These disciplines are theology, the object of which is the *summum ens,* cosmology, and psychology. Together they form the discipline called *metaphysica specialis.* In distinction from this, *metaphysica generalis* (ontology) has as its object the essent "in general" (*ens commune*).

The other consideration essential to the development of the school-concept of metaphysics concerns the mode of knowledge and the methodology involved. Since the object of metaphysics is both the essent in general and the highest essent, in which "everyone takes an interest" (Kant), it is a science of the highest dignity, the "queen of the sciences." Consequently, its mode of knowledge must be perfectly rigorous and absolutely binding. This requires that it conform to a corresponding cognitive ideal, "mathematical" knowledge. Because it is free from the contingencies of experience, mathematical knowledge is in the strictest sense rational and *a priori,* i.e., it is a pure, rational science. Thus, the knowledge both of the essent in totality (*metaphysica generalis*) and of its principal divisions (*metaphysica specialis*) becomes "a science established by mere reason."

Kant remained faithful to the purpose of this metaphysics; indeed, he strengthened it and shifted its center of gravity toward *metaphysica specialis*. This last he termed "true meta-physics," "metaphysics in its final purpose." [5] In view of the constant "failure" which has attended all undertakings in this science, their incoherence and their ineffectualness, all further attempts to extend the knowledge of pure reason must be held in abeyance until the question of the intrinsic possibility of this science is settled. Thus, the task arises of the laying of a foundation of metaphysics in the sense of the determination of its essence. How did Kant set about this essential delimitation of metaphysics?

## § 2. The Point of Departure for the Laying of the Foundation of Traditional Metaphysics

In metaphysics as the pure, rational knowledge of the essent "in general" and of the totality of its principal divisions there is accomplished a "passing beyond" that which experience can supply partially and in particular. In passing beyond the sensible, this mode of knowledge seeks to comprehend the super-sensible. "Its method [however, has] hitherto been merely a random groping, and, what is worst of all, a groping among mere concepts." [6] Metaphysics lacks a binding proof of its alleged insights. What gives metaphysics the intrinsic possibility of being what it claims to be?

A laying of the foundation of metaphysics in the sense of a delimitation of its intrinsic possibility must, above all, keep the final purpose of metaphysics in view, i.e., the determination of the essence of *metaphysica specialis*. It is *metaphysica specialis* which in a pre-eminent sense is knowledge of the supersensible essent. This question of the intrinsic possibility of such knowledge, however, is thrown back upon the more general question

5. *Über die Fortschritte* . . . , p. 238.
6. B XV, NKS, p. 21.

14

of the intrinsic possibility of the manifestation [*Offenbarmachen*] of the essent as such. The laying of the foundation is now the elucidation of a comportment [*Verhalten*] with regard to the essent, a comportment in which the essent reveals itself in itself [*sich dieses an ihm selbst zeigt*] so that all statements relative to it become verifiable.

But what does the possibility of such comportment entail? Is there a "clue" as to what makes it possible? Yes, the method of the scientist: "a light broke upon all students of nature. They learned that reason has insight only into that which it produces after a plan of its own, and that it must not allow itself to be kept, as it were, in nature's leading-strings, but must itself show the way with principles of judgment based upon fixed laws, constraining nature to give answer to questions of reason's own determining." [7] The "previously projected" plan of nature in general determines in advance the constitution of the Being [*Seinsverfassung*] of the essent to which it must be possible to relate all modes of questioning. This precursory [*vorgängige*] projection relative to the Being of the essent is inscribed in the basic concepts and axioms of the natural sciences. Hence, what makes the relation to the essent (ontic knowledge) possible is the precursory comprehension of the constitution of the Being of the essent, namely, ontological knowledge.[8]

The mathematical natural sciences provide a clue to the essential connection of the conditions which hold between ontic and ontological knowledge and in this exhaust their function in the laying of the foundation of metaphysics. For this reference to the connection of the conditions is not yet a solution of

7. B XIIIf., NKS, p. 20.
8. The distinction between the ontic (the empirical) and the ontological is a fundamental one for Heidegger. For a discussion of the validity of this distinction see: Karl Löwith, *Phenomenologische Ontologie und protestantische Theologie, Zeitschrift für Theologie und Kirche*, N.F. 11, 1930, p. 365ff. (J. S. C.)

15

the problem but only an indication of the direction in which the problem, understood in its fundamental generality, must first be sought. Whether it can be found only in this direction, or whether it can be found at all, i.e., whether the idea of *metaphysica specialis* can be developed in accordance with the concept of positive (scientific) knowledge—this is still to be decided.

The projection of the intrinsic possibility of *metaphysica specialis* has been led back beyond the question of the possibility of ontic knowledge to the question of that which makes this ontic knowledge possible. But this is precisely the problem of the essence of the precursory comprehension of Being, i.e., ontological knowledge in the broadest sense. The problem of the intrinsic possibility of ontology includes, moreover, the question of the possibility of *metaphysica generalis*. The attempt to provide a foundation for metaphysics is thus centered in the question of the essence of *metaphysica generalis*.

With such an approach to the laying of the foundation of metaphysics Kant is led immediately into a discussion with Aristotle and Plato. Now for the first time, ontology becomes a problem. Thereby the structure of traditional metaphysics undergoes its first and most profound shock. The vagueness and the obviousness with which *metaphysica generalis* hitherto treated of the "generality" of the *ens commune* disappears. The problem of the laying of the foundation of metaphysics for the first time demands a certain clarity with regard to the mode of generalization and the character of the passing beyond [*Überschritt*] proper to the knowledge of the constitution of the Being [of the essent]. Whether Kant himself ever became perfectly clear with respect to this problem remains a subordinate question. It is enough that he recognized the urgency of the problem and, above all, that he presented it. It is clear, moreover, that the primary objective of ontology is not a laying of the foundation of the positive sciences. Its necessity and its role are based

16

on a "higher interest" with which human reason is always concerned. However, because *metaphysica generalis* provides the necessary "preparation" [9] for *metaphysica specialis,* laying the foundation of the former necessarily transforms the essential determination of the latter.

To lay the foundation of metaphysics in totality is to reveal the internal possibility of ontology. Such is the true, i.e., the metaphysical (having metaphysics as its only theme), sense of that which, under the heading of Kant's "Copernican revolution," has been constantly misinterpreted. "Hitherto it has been assumed that all our knowledge must conform to objects. But all attempts to extend our knowledge of objects by establishing something in regard to them *a priori,* by means of concepts, have, on this assumption, ended in failure. We must, therefore, make trial whether we may not have more success in the tasks of metaphysics if we suppose that objects must conform to our knowledge. This would agree better with what is desired, namely, that it should be possible to have knowledge of objects *a priori,* determining something in regard to them prior to their being given." [10]

By this Kant means: not "all knowledge" is ontic, and where such knowledge is given, it is possible only through ontological knowledge. The "old" concept of truth as the "adequateness" (*adaequatio*) of knowledge to the essent is so little shaken by the Copernican revolution that the latter presupposes the former, indeed, confirms it for the first time. Ontic knowledge can be adequate to the essent (to "objects") only if the essent is already manifest beforehand as essent, that is, if the constitution of its Being is known. It is to this last knowledge that objects, i.e., their ontic determinability, must conform. The manifestation of the essent (ontic truth) depends upon the revelation of the constitution of the Being of the essent (ontologi-

9. *Über die Fortschritte* . . . , p. 302.
10. B XVI, NKS, p. 22.

17

cal truth).[11] However, ontic knowledge by itself can never conform "to" objects, because without ontological knowledge it
cannot have even a possible "to what" [*Wonach*] of the con-
formation.

It has thus become clear that the laying of the foundation of
traditional metaphysics begins with the question of the internal
possibility of ontology as such. But why does this laying of the
foundation become a *Critique of Pure Reason?*

### § 3. The Laying of the Foundation of Metaphysics as a Critique of Pure Reason

Kant reduces the problem of the possibility of ontology to
the question: "How are *a priori* synthetic judgments possible?"
The analysis of this formulation of the problem is carried out as
a critique of pure reason. The question of the possibility of
ontological knowledge requires a provisional characterization
of that knowledge. In this formulation of the problem, Kant,
following tradition, understands knowledge to be an act of judgment. But what kind of knowledge is found in ontological comprehension? Through it something is known, and what is thus
known belongs to the essent no matter how it may be experienced and determined. This known what-ness [*Wassein*] of the
essent is brought forth *a priori* in ontological knowledge before
all ontic knowledge, although precisely in order to serve the
latter. Knowledge that brings forth the quiddity [*Wasgehalt*] of
the essent, in other words, knowledge which reveals the essent
itself, Kant calls synthetic. Thus, the question of the possibility of ontological knowledge turns out to be the problem of
the essence of synthetic judgments *a priori*.

The instance capable of establishing the legitimacy of these

11. For a more complete discussion of Heidegger's concept of
truth, see *Sein und Zeit*, p. 212ff., and "On the Essence of Truth,"
in *Existence and Being*, p. 321ff. (J. S. C.)

material judgments concerning the Being of the essent cannot be found in experience, for experience of the essent is itself always guided by the ontological comprehension of the essent, which last becomes accessible through experience according to a determinate perspective. Ontological knowledge, then, is judgment according to principles which must be brought forth without recourse to experience.

Kant terms our faculty of knowledge according to *a priori* principles "pure reason." [12] "Pure reason is that faculty which supplies the principles of knowing anything entirely *a priori*." [13] If the principles supplied by reason constitute the possibility of *a priori* knowledge, then the revelation of the possibility of ontological knowledge must become an elucidation of the essence of pure reason. The delimitation of the essence of pure reason, however, is at the same time the differentiating determination of its dis-essence [*Unwesen*] and, hence, the limiting and restricting (critique) of pure reason to its essential possibilities. Thus, the laying of the foundation of metaphysics as the revelation of the essence of ontology is a *Critique of Pure Reason*.

It is ontological knowledge, i.e., the *a priori* synthesis, "for the sake of which alone our whole critique is undertaken." [14] Now that the problem which guides this establishment of metaphysics has been fixed, it is all the more imperative that this synthesis be more precisely defined. Not only does this expression, as Kant employs it, have many meanings,[15] these meanings are intermingled even in the formulation of the problem of the laying of the foundation of metaphysics itself. The question is concerned with the possibility of synthetic judgments *a priori*.

12. *Critique of Judgment,* Preface to the 1st ed., trans. J. H. Bernard (London, 1931), p. 1.
13. A 11, B 24, NKS, p. 58.
14. A 14, B 28, NKS, p. 60.
15. *Cf.* below, § 7, p. 42.

Now every judgment is, as such, an "I connect," namely, subject and predicate. *Qua* judgment, even analytic judgments are synthetic, although the basis of the connection of agreement between subject and predicate lies simply in the representation which forms the subject. Synthetic judgments, then, are "synthetic" in a double sense: first, as judgments as such, and, second, so far as the legitimacy of the "connection" (synthesis) of the representations is "brought forth" (synthesis) from the essent itself with which the judgment is concerned.

But in the problem of synthetic judgments *a priori* still another type of synthesis is concerned which must bring something forth about the essent not first derived from it through experience. This bringing forth of the determination of the Being of the essent is a precursory act of reference to the essent. This pure "reference-to . . ." (synthesis) first constitutes the direction and the horizon within which the essent is first capable of being experienced in the empirical synthesis. The possibility of this *a priori* synthesis must now be clarified. An investigation concerned with the essence of this synthesis Kant terms "transcendental." "I entitle *transcendental* all knowledge which is occupied not so much with objects as with the mode of our knowledge of objects insofar as this mode of knowledge is to be possible *a priori*." [16] Thus, transcendental knowledge does not investigate the essent itself but the possibility of the precursory comprehension of the Being of the essent. It concerns reason's passing beyond (transcendence) to the essent so that experience can be rendered adequate to the latter as its possible object.

To make the possibility of ontology a problem means: to inquire into the possibility, i.e., into the essence, of this transcendence which characterizes the comprehension of Being; in other words, it means to philosophize transcendentally. This is

16. A 11f., B 25, NKS, p. 59.

20

why when Kant wishes to characterize the problematic of traditional ontology, he makes use of the expression "transcendental
philosophy" [17] to denote the subject matter of *metaphysica
generalis* (*ontologia*). This is also why, in mentioning this traditional ontology, he speaks of the "transcendental philosophy of
the ancients." [18]

However, the *Critique of Pure Reason* does not provide a
"system" of transcendental philosophy but is a "treatise on the
method" [19] thereof. This expression does not signify a doctrine
relative to the procedural technique involved; on the contrary,
it indicates a complete determination of the "whole plan" and
of the "internal organization" of ontology. This laying of the
foundation of metaphysics, understood as the projection of the
intrinsic possibility of ontology, traces the "complete outline of
a system of metaphysics." [20]

The purpose of the *Critique of Pure Reason* is completely
misunderstood, therefore, if this work is interpreted as a "theory
of experience" or perhaps as a theory of the positive sciences.
The *Critique of Pure Reason* has nothing to do with a "theory
of knowledge." However, if one could admit the interpretation
of the work as a theory of knowledge, it would be necessary to
say that the *Critique* is not a theory of ontic knowledge but of
ontological. But even this interpretation, although far removed
from the usual interpretation of the aesthetic and transcendental
analytic, does not touch upon what is essential in the *Critique,*
that therein ontology as *metaphysica generalis,* i.e., as the essential part of metaphysics as a whole, is provided with a foundation and, for the first time, revealed for what it is in itself.
With the problem of transcendence, Kant does not replace

17. A 845, B 873f.; A 247, B 303; NKS, pp. 662, 264. *Cf.* also
*Über die Fortschritte,* pp. 238, 263, 269, 301.
18. B 113, NKS, p. 118.
19. B XXII, NKS, p. 25.
20. B XXIII, NKS, p. 15.

21

metaphysics by a theory of knowledge but brings into question the intrinsic possibility of ontology.

If truth pertains to the essence of knowledge, the transcendental problem of the intrinsic possibility of *a priori* synthetic knowledge becomes the question of the essence of the truth of ontological transcendence. It is a question of determining the essence of "transcendental truth which precedes all empirical truth and makes it possible." [21] "For no knowledge can contradict it without at once losing all content, that is, all relation to any object, and therefore all truth." [22] Ontic truth, then, must necessarily conform to ontological truth. This is the correct interpretation of the meaning of the "Copernican revolution." By this revolution, Kant thrusts the problem of ontology to the fore. Nothing can be presupposed in dealing with the problem of the possibility of primordial ontological truth, least of all the "fact" of the truth of the positive sciences. On the contrary, without appealing to such extraneous facts, the laying of the foundation must trace the *a priori* synthesis back to its original sources which permit that synthesis to be what it is (makes it possible in its essence).

From his clear insight into the originality of a laying of the foundation of metaphysics, Kant states of the *Critique of Pure Reason:* "The task is difficult and demands a reader resolved to think himself gradually into a system which is grounded in nothing regarded as given except pure reason itself, and thus tries to develop knowledge out of its original seeds without seeking the support of any fact." [23]

Thus, the task arises of showing how this development of the possibility of ontology from its sources is carried out.

21. A 146, B 185, NKS, p. 186.
22. A 62f., B 87, NKS, p. 100.
23. *Prolegomena:* "To any future Metaphysics that will be able to present itself as a science," trans. Peter G. Lucas (Oxford, 1949), p. 29.

# THE CARRYING OUT OF THE LAYING OF THE FOUNDATION OF METAPHYSICS

# THE CARRYING OUT OF THE LAYING OF THE FOUNDATION OF METAPHYSICS

In order to project the intrinsic possibility of ontological knowledge we must first have an insight into the dimension in which takes place the regression to the ground supporting the possibility of that which, in its essential constitution, we are seeking. Now, it is necessarily the fate of every real incursion into an hitherto unknown field that the dimensions of this field are only determined "little by little." It is in the course of such an advance itself that the direction of approach is first established and the way made feasible. If this first incursion is guided by the creative power that reveals the proper direction with an indefectible certitude, it is not less true that the field itself is at first neither clearly marked out nor free from obstruction. Indeed, every "critique requires knowledge of the sources, and reason must know itself." [1] And yet, it is only by the *Critique* that pure reason acquires with Kant this first knowledge of itself.

1. *Kant's Posthumous Works in Manuscript Form*, vol. V, *Metaphysics* (*Works*, ed. by the *Preuss. Akad d. Wissenschaften*, III, 51), 1928, No. 4892. *Cf.* B. Erdmann, *Reflexionen Kants zur kritischen Philosophie*, II, 217.

25

Because the subsequent interpretation has not yet regained the original power which projects the direction to be followed, it must make specifically sure in advance of the guiding insight and thus anticipate the principal stages of the internal movement of the whole of the laying of the foundation. Before the laying of the foundation of metaphysics can be carried out again, an insight into the dimension in which the regressive movement of this laying of the foundation takes place must be secured. This section, then, is divided as follows:

A. The Characterization of the Dimension in Which the Regression Necessary for the Development of the Laying of the Foundation of Metaphysics is Carried Out.

B. The Stages of the Carrying Out of the Projection of the Intrinsic Possibility of Ontology.

# A. The Characterization of the Dimension in Which the Regression Necessary for the Development of the Laying of the Foundation of Metaphysics Is Carried Out

The objective is the determination of the essence of ontological knowledge through the elucidation of its origin in the sources which make it possible. This requires, above all, clarity concerning the essence of knowledge in general and the locus and nature of its field of origin. In previous interpretations of the *Critique of Pure Reason,* the preliminary characterization of the dimension of origin of this work has either been unduly neglected or misinterpreted. This is why the efforts, uncertain to begin with, which have had as their object the determination of the purpose of this work have been unable to assimilate productively its fundamental tendency. Together with the characterization of the field of origin of the *Critique,* the particular way in which the origin is revealed must also be described.

# I. The Essential Attributes of the Field of Origin

## § 4. The Essence of Knowledge in General

Kant does not discuss the essential attributes of the field of origin thematically; rather, he takes them for granted in the sense of "self-evident presuppositions." This is all the more reason why the interpretation should not overlook the predeterminative function of these "assumptions." They may be summarized in the following thesis:

The fundamental source of the laying of the foundation of metaphysics is human pure reason, so that the human character of reason, i.e., its finitude, becomes essential for the problematic of the laying of the foundation. It is advisable, therefore, that in characterizing the field of origin we concentrate on the clarification of the essence of the finitude of human knowledge.

However, the finitude of human reason by no means consists merely and primarily in the fact that human knowledge exhibits many shortcomings: that it is unstable, inexact, liable to error, and so on. This finitude, rather, lies in the essential structure of knowledge itself. The factual limitation of reason is a consequence of its essence.

In order to disclose the essence of the finitude of knowledge, a general characterization of the essence of cognition is required. In this connection, what Kant states in the first sentence of the thematic discussion of the *Critique of Pure Reason* is

27

usually regarded all too lightly. "In whatever manner and by whatever means a mode of knowledge may relate to objects, *intuition* is that through which it is in immediate relation to them and from which all thought gains its material." [2]

In order to gain an understanding of the *Critique of Pure Reason,* the following must, as it were, be hammered in: Cognition is primarily intuition. From this it is at once clear that to interpret knowledge as judgment (thought) does violence to the decisive sense of the Kantian problem. Thinking is simply in the service of intuition. It is not something which exists merely beside and in "addition to" intuition, but by its intrinsic structure serves that to which intuition is primarily and constantly directed. If thinking is so essentially relative to intuition, then both intuition and thinking must have a certain affinity which permits their unification. This affinity, this descent from the same genus, finds expression in this: that both may be termed *"representation . . . (repraesentatio)*." [3]

Representation here has at first the broad, formal sense, according to which something indicates, announces, gives notice of, or presents something else. This act of representation can be such that it takes place "with consciousness." [4] It is characterized by an awareness that something announces itself and is announced (*perceptio*). Now, if in the act of representing something by something else, not only this act but also that which is represented in it is represented as such, i.e., "consciously," then such an act of representation refers to that which is presented in that act as such. Thus understood as "objective perception," knowledge is an act of representation.

Knowledge as representation is either intuition or concept (*intuitus vel conceptus*). "The former relates immediately to an object and is single, the latter refers to it mediately by

2. A 19, B 33, NKS, p. 65.
3. A 320, B 376f., NKS, p. 314.
4. *Ibid.*

means of a feature which several things may have in common." [5] According to the first sentence of the *Critique of Pure Reason,* quoted above, knowledge is a thinking intuition. Thought, i.e., the act of "representation in general," serves only to render the singular object, i.e., the concrete essent itself, accessible in its immediacy and for everyone. "Each of these two (intuition and thought) is certainly representation but not yet knowledge." [6]

One could conclude from this that there is a reciprocal and perfectly symmetrical relation between intuition and thought so that he could also say with equal right: Knowledge is intuitive thinking and therefore basically, and in spite of everything, an act of judgment.

In opposition to this, however, it must be maintained that intuition defines the true essence of knowledge, and that, despite the reciprocity of the relation between intuition and thought, it is in the first that the true center of gravity is to be found. This stands out clearly, not only because of Kant's statement, quoted above, with its underscoring of the word "intuition," but also because only through this interpretation is it possible to grasp what is essential in this definition, namely, the finitude of knowledge. This first sentence of the *Critique of Pure Reason* is, indeed, no longer a definition of cognition in general but the real definition of human knowledge. "On the other hand, in that which concerns man (in contrast to 'God or any other higher spirit') all knowledge consists of concept and intuition." [7]

The essence of finite human knowledge is elucidated by contrasting it with the idea of infinite, divine knowledge, i.e., *"intuitus originarius."* [8] Divine knowledge as knowledge, not as divine, is also intuition. The difference between infinite and

5. *Ibid.*
6. *Über die Fortschritte,* p. 312.
7. *Ibid.*
8. B 72, NKS, p. 90.

finite intuition consists only in this, that the former in its immediate representation of the individual, that is, the singular and unique essent taken as a whole, first brings it into being, that is, effects its coming forth (*origo*). Absolute intuition would not be absolute if dependent on an essent already on hand in adaption to which the object of intuition first became accessible. Divine cognition is that mode of representation which in the act of intuition first creates the object of intuition as such.[9] Seeing right through the essent in advance, such cognition intuits it immediately and has no need of thought. Thought as such, then, is in itself the seal of finitude. Divine cognition is "intuition, for all its knowledge must be intuitive, and not *thought,* which always involves limitations." [10]

But the decisive element in the difference between finite and infinite knowledge would not be understood and the essence of finitude overlooked if one were to say: Divine cognition is intuition alone, while human cognition, on the other hand, is a thinking intuition. The essential difference between these two types of knowledge lies primarily in intuition itself, because, strictly speaking, cognition is intuition. The finitude of human knowledge must first of all be sought in the finitude of the intuition proper to it. That a finite being must "also" think in order to possess knowledge is an essential consequence of the finitude of its intuition. Only in this way can the essentially subordinate role of "all thinking" be seen in its true light. Wherein, then, lies the essence of finite intuition and therefore the finitude of human knowledge in general?

## § 5. *The Essence of the Finitude of Knowledge*

To begin with, we can say negatively that finite knowledge is non-creative intuition. What is presented immediately and in its particularity must be already on hand. Finite intuition

9. B 139, 145, NKS, pp. 157, 161.
10. B 71, NKS, p. 90.

looks to the intuitable as something on which it is dependent and which exists in its own right. That which is intuited proceeds [*herleiten*] from such an essent and for that reason is also termed *intuitus derivatus,* "derivative." [11] Finite intuition of the essent is not able by itself to give itself an object. It must let this object be given. But not every intuition as such is receptive—only the finite is so. Hence, the finitude of intuition lies in its receptivity. Finite intuition cannot receive anything, however, unless the latter announces itself [*sich melden*], that is, the essence of finite intuition is such that it must be solicited [*angegangen*] or affected by a possible object.

Because the essence of knowledge lies primarily in intuition and because the finite essence of man is a central theme of the whole laying of the foundation of metaphysics, Kant proceeds immediately to enlarge upon the first sentence of the *Critique:* "But intuition takes place only insofar as the object is given to us. This again is only possible, to man at least, insofar as the mind is affected in a certain way." [12] The phrase "to man at least" was first inserted in the second edition. It only makes clearer that in the first edition finite knowledge is the theme from the beginning.

If human intuition as finite is receptive and if the possibility of its receiving something "given" presupposes affection, then organs capable of being affected—the organs of "sense"—are necessary. Human intuition, therefore, is not "sensible" because its affection takes place through "sense" organs. Rather, the converse is true: it is because our *Dasein* is finite—existing in the midst of the essent which already is and to which our *Dasein* is abandoned—that it must of necessity receive the essent, that is, offer it the possibility of giving notice of itself. These organs are necessary in order that the notification be able to get through. The essence of sensibility lies in the finitude of intuition. The organs which serve affection are sense

11. B 72, NKS, p. 90.
12. A 19, B 33, NKS, p. 65.

organs, therefore, because they belong to finite intuition, i.e., to sensibility. Thus, Kant was the first to arrive at an ontological, non-sensuous concept of sensibility. Consequently, if empirical, affective intuition of the essent does not necessarily coincide with "sensibility," then it follows that the possibility of a non-empirical sensibility remains essentially open.[13]

Knowledge is primarily intuition, i.e., an act of representation that immediately represents the essent itself. Now, if finite intuition is to be knowledge, it must be able to make the essent itself, insofar as it is manifest, accessible with respect to how and what it is to everyone and at any time. Finite beings capable of intuition must be able to agree in the actual intuition of the essent. But finite intuition as intuition is, at bottom, always bound to the particular which is being intuited at any given moment. However, that which is intuited becomes an object of knowledge only if everyone can make it intelligible to himself and to others and in that way communicate it. So, for example, this intuited particular, this piece of chalk, must admit of being determined as chalk or as a body in order that we may be able jointly to know this essent itself as the same for each of us. In order to be knowledge, finite intuition always requires such a determination of the intuited as this or that.

In such determination, that which is represented by intuition is further represented with reference to what it is "in general." However, this determination does not represent the general as such thematically; for example, it does not take the corporeality of a thing as an object. To be sure, the determinative representation of the thing intuitively represented orients itself toward the general, but it does this only that it may turn to the particular thing and determine it with respect to this orien-

13. "Sensible intuition is either pure intuition (space and time) or empirical intuition of that which is immediately represented, through sensation, as actual in space and time" (B 147, NKS, p. 162).

tation. This "general" representation, which as such serves intuition, makes that which is represented more representative [*vorstelliger*] in that it comprehends the many under the one and, on the basis of this com-prehension, "applies to many." Hence, Kant names this act of representation "representation by concepts" (*repraesentatio per notas communes*). The determinative act of representation appears, then, as "the representation (concept) of a representation (intuition)." In addition, this act is in itself an assertion of something about something (predication). "Judgment is, therefore, the mediate knowledge of an object, that is, the representation of a representation of it." [14] The "faculty of judging" is the understanding, and the act of representation proper to it makes intuition "capable of being understood."

If the judicative act of determination is essentially directed toward [*angewiesen auf*] intuition, thinking is always united with intuition in order to serve it. Through such a union (synthesis), thought refers mediately to the object which in the unity of a thinking intuition becomes manifest (true). In this way, the synthesis of thought and intuition effects the manifestation *qua* object of the essent encountered. Therefore, we call it the true-(manifest-) making (veritative) synthesis. It coincides with what has been described above as that which "brings forth" the determinateness, with regard to content, of the essent itself.

But thought which is united with intuition in the veritative synthesis is, as an act of judgment, a unification (synthesis) in another sense. Kant states: "A judgment is the representation of the unity of the consciousness of different representations, or the representation of the relation between them as far as they form a concept." [15] A judgment is a "function of

14. A 68, B 93, NKS, p. 105.
15. *Cf. I. Kants Logik. Ein Handbuch zu Vorlesungen*, ed. by G. B. Jäsche, *Works* (Cass.) VIII, § 17, p. 408.

33

unity," i.e., an act of representation of the unifying unity of a concept in its character as a predicate. This unifying act of representation we call the predicative synthesis.

The predicative synthesis does not coincide, however, with that act of unification in which the judgment presents itself as the connection of subject and predicate. This synthesis we call the apophantic.

Consequently, in the veritative synthesis which constitutes the essence of finite knowledge, the predicative synthesis and the apophantic synthesis are necessarily joined together in a structural unity of syntheses.

If one asserts that, according to Kant, the essence of knowledge is "synthesis," this assertion says nothing as long as the term "synthesis" remains indeterminate and ambiguous.

Finite intuition, since it is in need of determination, is dependent on the understanding. The understanding, in turn, is not only involved in the finitude of intuition, it is itself even more finite inasmuch as it lacks the immediacy of finite intuition. Its mode of representation is indirect; it requires a reference to something general by means of which, and according to which, the several particulars become capable of being represented conceptually. This detour (discursiveness), which is essential to the understanding, is the clearest index of its finitude.

Just as the metaphysical essence of finite intuition as receptivity retains the general, essential character of intuition, in that it is "giving," so also does the finitude of the understanding reveal something of the essence of absolute knowledge, i.e., of an "originative (creative) intuition." This [originative] type of intuition spontaneously and by its own act brings forth the essent capable of being intuited. Now, the understanding— bound as it is to finite intuition—is just as little creative as this [finite intuition]. It never produces the essent, yet, as distinguished from the receptivity of the act of intuition, it is in

34

a certain sense productive. To be sure, the act of judgment relative to the essent does not simply create the general character by means of which the intuited is conceptually represented. This general character, insofar as its real content is concerned, is derived from the object of intuition. Only the way in which this content as an inclusive unity applies to the many is the work of the understanding. 1505373

In producing [*herstellen*] the form of a concept, the understanding permits the content of the object to be put at our disposition [*beistellen*]. The representation [proposition—*vorstellen*] proper to the act of thought is revealed by this mode of "position" [*Stellen*]. The metaphysical essence of the thus "productive" understanding is indeed determined in part by this character of "spontaneity" [*von sich aus*], but this determination does not really get to the root of the matter.

Finite knowledge has been characterized up to now as a mode of intuition which is receptive and, hence, in need of thought. This elucidation of the notion of finitude was carried out with reference to the structure of cognition. Considering the fundamental importance of the notion of finitude to the problem of the laying of the foundation of metaphysics, the essence of finite knowledge must be examined from yet another side, namely, with reference to what is knowable in such knowledge.

If finite knowledge is receptive intuition, the knowable must show itself by itself. What finite knowledge is able to make manifest, therefore, must be an essent which shows itself, i.e., which appears, an appearance. The term "appearance" refers to the essent itself as the object of finite knowledge. More precisely, only for finite knowledge is there such a thing as an ob-ject [*Gegenstand*].[16] Only such knowledge is exposed to the

16. The literal meaning of *Gegenstand,* namely, "that which stands opposite to" should be compared with that of "object." (J. S. C.)

essent which already is. Infinite knowledge, on the other hand, cannot be confronted by any such essent to which it must conform. Such a "conforming-to . . ." would be a "dependence on . . ." and, consequently, a form of finitude. Infinite cognition is an act of intuition which lets the essent itself come forth [*entstehen lassen*]. Absolute cognition itself reveals the essent in the act of letting it come forth and possesses it "only" as that which arises from this very act, i.e., as e-ject [*Entstand*].[17] Insofar as the essent is manifest to absolute intuition, it "is" precisely in its coming-into-Being. It is the essent as essent in itself, i.e., not as object. Strictly speaking, then, we fail to hit upon the essence of infinite knowledge if we say its "object" is produced in the very act of intuition.

The essent "as it appears" [i.e., as a phenomenon] is the same as the essent in itself and only this. Indeed, only insofar as it is essent can it become an object, although only to finite knowledge can it be such. It manifests itself thereby in conformity with the manner and scope of the receptive and determinative power at the disposal of finite knowledge.

Kant used the expression "appearance" in a narrow and in a broad sense. Finite knowledge as intuition which is receptive and in need of thought makes the essent itself manifest in the form of "objects," [18] i.e., appearances in the broad sense (phenomena). "Appearance" in the narrow sense refers to what in the appearance (in the broad sense) is the exclusive correlate of the affection inherent in finite intuition when this is stripped of the elements supplied by thought (determination):

17. The meaning of the term *Ent-stand* is "that which stands forth," the prefix *ent* having the meaning "forth," "from," or "out of." Although the English prefix "e" does not have exactly this meaning, nevertheless, its meaning is close enough to that of the German *ent* to support the analogy—ob-ject: e-ject: *Gegenstand: Ent-stand*—and to convey the sense of *Ent-stand* intended. (J. S. C.)
18. A 235 (heading), B 249, NKS, p. 259.

36

the content of empirical intuition. "The undetermined object of an empirical intuition is entitled *appearance*." [19] To appear means to be "an object of empirical intuition." [20]

Appearances are not mere illusions but the essent itself. And the essent, on its side, is nothing other than the thing "in itself." The essent can be manifest without being known "in itself," i.e., *qua* e-ject. The dual characterization of the essent as thing in itself and as "appearance" corresponds to the relation in which it stands to infinite and finite knowledge respectively, as e-ject and ob-ject.

If it is true that in the *Critique of Pure Reason,* human finitude becomes the basis of all the problems relative to the laying of the foundation of ontology, then the *Critique* must lay special emphasis on this distinction between finite and infinite knowledge. This is why Kant said of the *Critique of Pure Reason* that it teaches "that the object is to be taken *in a twofold sense,* namely as appearance and as thing in itself." [21] In the strict sense of the term one should not speak of an "object," for to absolute knowledge no object can be given. In the *Opus postumum,* Kant states that the thing in itself is not something other than the appearance: "The distinction between the concept of thing in itself and that of appearance is not objective but merely subjective. The thing in itself is not another object but another aspect (*respectus*) of the representation with regard to *the same object*." [22]

From this interpretation of the concepts "appearance" and "thing in itself," an interpretation based on the distinction between finite and infinite knowledge, the meaning of the expressions "behind the appearance" and "mere appearance"

19. A 20, B 34, NKS, p. 65.
20. A 89, B 121, NKS, p. 123.
21. B XXVII, NKS, p. 28.
22. Kant's *Opus postumum,* presentation and critique by E. Adickes, p. 653 (italics by the author).

must now be clarified. This "behind" cannot mean that in spite of everything the thing in itself still confronts finite knowledge but in such a way that it is not apprehended in its entirety but, ghostlike, is now and then indirectly visible. Rather, the phrase "behind the appearance" signifies that finite knowledge as finite necessarily conceals and, indeed, from the first, conceals in such a way that not only is the thing in itself not completely accessible to such knowledge, it is not accessible to it at all. That which is "behind the appearance" is the same essent as the appearance, but because the appearance gives the essent only as ob-ject, it is basically impossible for it to let the essent be seen as e-ject. "According to the *Critique,* everything that manifests itself in an appearance is itself again appearance." [23]

Thus, it is a misunderstanding of the significance of the "thing in itself" to believe that it is necessary to prove through a positivistic critique that knowledge of it is impossible. Such attempts at proof suppose the thing in itself to be something which must be considered as an object within the sphere of finite knowledge but one whose factual inaccessibility can and must be demonstrated. Correlatively, in the expression "mere appearance," the "mere" does not signify a limitation and a diminution of the reality of the thing but serves only as the denial of the assumption that in finite knowledge the essent can be known in a manner appropriate to infinite knowledge. "In the world of sense, however deeply we enquire into its objects, we have to do with nothing but appearances." [24]

The essence of the distinction between appearance and thing in itself is revealed with particular clarity in the two meanings of the expression "outside us." [25] Both of these meanings refer

23. I. Kant, *Über eine Entdeckung nach der alle neue Kritik der reinen Vernunft durch eine ältere entbehrlich gemacht werden soll,* 1790, *Works* (Cass.) VI, p. 27.
24. A 45, B 62f., NKS, p. 84.
25. A 373, NKS, p. 348.

to the essent itself. *Qua* thing in itself, the essent is outside us since, being finite, we are excluded from the mode of infinite intuition pertaining to it. When, on the contrary, the expression refers to appearances, the essent is outside us because we ourselves are not this essent but yet have access to it. On the other hand, an examination of the distinction between finite and infinite knowledge in terms of the difference in character of what is known therein reveals that the concepts "appearance" and "thing in itself," which are fundamental to the *Critique,* can be made intelligible and the object of further investigation only if they are based explicitly on the problematic of the finitude of man. These concepts, however, do not refer to two levels of objects positioned one behind the other in "one" fixed and completely undifferentiated [field of] knowledge.

What is essential to the dimension within which the laying of the foundation of metaphysics takes place is revealed with this characterization of the finitude of human knowledge. At the same time, we have obtained a clearer indication of the direction which the regress to the sources of the intrinsic possibility of ontology must take.

## § 6. The Field of Origin of the Laying of the Foundation of Metaphysics

The interpretation of the essence of knowledge in general and of finite knowledge in particular has revealed that finite intuition (sensibility) as such is in need of determination by the understanding. On its side, the understanding, which is essentially finite, is dependent on intuition, for: "we can understand only that which brings with it, in intuition, something corresponding to our words." [26] When Kant states, however, that "Neither of these qualities is preferable to the other," [27]

26. A 277, B 333, NKS, p. 286.
27. A 51, B 75, NKS, p. 93.

he seems to be contradicting his previous assertions to the effect that the basic character of cognition is to be found in intuition. If thought is based structurally on intuition as the primary act of representation, then the fact that sensibility and understanding necessarily belong together does not preclude but rather implies the existence of an order of precedence. If one wishes to follow the intrinsic development of the Kantian problematic, this order of precedence should not be neglected when considering the mutual relationship of sensibility and understanding, nor should this relationship be reduced to an indifferent correlation of content and form.

Nevertheless, in order to ask the question concerning the field of origin of the possibility of finite knowledge, it seems sufficient to hold to the simple and reflexive duality of its elements. And all the more so since Kant himself expressly fixed the "springs" of our knowledge in "two fundamental sources of the mind." "Our knowledge springs from two fundamental sources of the mind; the first is the capacity of receiving representations (receptivity for impressions), the second is the power of knowing an object through these representations (spontaneity in the production of concepts)." [28] And with even greater emphasis, Kant states: "we have no [source of] knowledge besides these two (sensibility and understanding)." [29]

But this duality of the sources is not a simple juxtaposition, for only in a union of these sources prescribed by their structure can finite knowledge be what its essence demands. "Only through their union, however, can knowledge arise." [30] The unity of their union, however, is not the subsequential result of their coming together; rather that which unites them, this "synthesis," must let these elements spring forth in their togetherness and their unity. However, if the essence of finite

28. A 50, B 74, NKS, p. 92.
29. A 294, B 350, NKS, p. 298.
30. A 51, B 75f., NKS, p. 93.

40

knowledge is to be found in the original synthesis of the fundamental sources, and if the laying of the foundation of metaphysics inevitably must push on into the essential ground of finite knowledge, then with the first mention of the two "fundamental sources," it is to be expected that an allusion to their field of origin, i.e., to their original unity, is not far off.

Both in the introduction and in the conclusion to the *Critique,* Kant provides a characterization of the two fundamental sources that goes beyond their mere enumeration. "By way of introduction or anticipation we need only say that there are two stems of human knowledge, namely, *sensibility* and *understanding,* which perhaps spring from a common, but to us unknown, root. Through the former, objects are given to us; through the latter, they are thought." [31] "We shall content ourselves here with the completion of our task, namely, merely to outline the *architectonic* of all knowledge arising from *pure reason;* and in so doing we shall begin from the point at which the common root of our faculty of knowledge divides and throws out two stems, one of which is *reason.* By reason I here understand the whole higher faculty of knowledge, and am therefore contrasting the rational with the empirical." [32] "Empirical" denotes here the receptive element of experience, sensibility as such.

In these passages, the sources are envisaged as "stems" which spring from a common root. But, whereas in the first passage the "common root" is qualified by a "perhaps," in the second its existence is affirmed. However, in both passages there is only a bare mention of this root. Kant not only fails to pursue the matter further but declares that the root is "to us unknown." One thing of fundamental importance concerning the general character of the Kantian laying of the foundation of metaphysics is clear from this,. however; it does not lead to the clear and

31. A 15, B 29, NKS, p. 61f.
32. A 835, B 863, NKS, p. 655.

41

unconditional evidence of an axiom or first principle but in full
consciousness proceeds into and points toward the unknown.
It is a philosophical laying of the foundation of philosophy.

## II. The Manner in Which the Origin
## Is Revealed

### § 7. The Outline of the Stages of the Laying
### of the Foundation of Ontology

The establishment of metaphysics is the projection of the
internal possibility of the *a priori* synthesis. The essence of
this synthesis must be determined and the manner of its origin
from its field of origin set forth. The elucidation of the essence
of finite knowledge and the characterization of its fundamental
source have served to fix the dimension wherein the revelation
of the essential origin takes place. The question of the internal
possibility of *a priori* synthetic knowledge has gained precision
thereby and, at the same time, has become more complex.

The preliminary exposition of the problem of the establishment of metaphysics has yielded the following result: [33] Knowledge of the essent is possible only on the basis of a precursory,
experience-free knowledge of the ontological structure [*Seinsverfassung*] of the essent. But finite knowledge (and it is the
finitude of knowledge which is in question) is essentially a
receptive and determinative intuition of the essent. If finite
knowledge is to be possible, it must be based on a comprehension [*Erkennen*] of the Being of the essent that precedes
every receptive act. Finite knowledge requires, therefore, a
non-receptive (and apparently non-finite) mode of cognition,
a kind of creative intuition.

33. See above, § 2, p. 14.

Thus, the question as to the possibility of the *a priori* synthesis narrows down to this: How can a finite being which as such is delivered up to the essent and dependent on its reception have knowledge of, i.e., intuit, the essent before it is given without being its creator? Otherwise expressed, how must this finite being be constituted with respect to its own ontological structure if, without the aid of experience, it is able to bring forth the ontological structure of the essent, i.e., effect an ontological synthesis?

If the question of the possibility of the *a priori* synthesis is put in this way, and if all finite knowledge as finite is composed of the two elements mentioned above, i.e., is itself a synthesis, then this question of the possibility of the *a priori* synthesis acquires a peculiar complexity, for this synthesis is not identical with the above-named veritative synthesis which is concerned only with ontic knowledge.

Because the ontological synthesis is, as knowledge, already synthetic, the laying of the foundation must begin with an exposition of the pure elements (pure intuition and pure thought) of pure knowledge. Thus, it is a matter of elucidating the character proper to the primordial essential unity of these pure elements, i.e., the pure veritative synthesis. This synthesis must be such that it determines *a priori* the element of pure intuition. Hence, the content as well as the form of the concepts pertaining to this synthesis must precede all experience. This implies that the pure predicative synthesis which is an essential element of the pure veritative synthesis is one of a special kind. In consequence, the question of the essence of the "ontological predicates" must be central to the problem of the *a priori* (i.e., ontological) synthesis.

The question of the intrinsic possibility of the essential unity of a pure veritative synthesis, however, forces us even further back to the elucidation of the original ground of the intrinsic possibility of this synthesis. Through the revelation of the essence of the pure synthesis from its ground, we begin to understand in what sense ontological knowledge can be the condition which makes ontic knowledge possible. In this manner, the complete essence of ontological knowledge is delimited.

Accordingly, the laying of the foundation of ontology runs through five stages: (1) the essential elements of pure knowledge; (2) the essential unity of pure knowledge; (3) the intrinsic possibility of the essential unity of the ontological synthesis; (4) the ground of the intrinsic possibility of the ontological synthesis; (5) the complete determination of the essence of ontological knowledge.

## § 8. The Method by Which the Origin is Revealed

The preliminary characterization of the essential structure [*Wesensbau*] of finite knowledge has already revealed a wealth of supplementary substructures which function as modes of synthesis. So far as the pure veritative synthesis contains, in a certain sense, the idea of a seemingly non-finite knowledge, the question of the possibility of ontology for a finite being is further complicated. Finally, the indications given us concerning the nature of the field of origin of the fundamental sources of finite knowledge lead into the unknown.

Given the nature of the chief problem and the dimension wherein it must be worked out, it is not surprising that the method whereby the origin is revealed and the manner of regress to the field of origin remain at first indeterminate. Certainty and precision with regard to these matters can be attained only in the course of the advance into a region hitherto unknown and by the exposition of what is revealed therein. Indeed, the domain of the revelation of the origin of ontological knowledge is none other than that of the human mind [*Gemüt*] (*mens sive animus*). The exploration of this domain is a task usually assigned to "psychology." However, insofar as the

44

exploration concerns an analysis of "knowledge," the essence of which is commonly placed in the act of judgment (*logos*), "logic" must also be given a part in it. At first sight, in fact, it would appear that "logic" and "psychology" are to share this task, in other words, struggle for supremacy and in the process transform and extend themselves.

But if, on the one hand, one considers the uniqueness and originality of the Kantian investigation and, on the other, the questionable character of traditional "logic" and "psychology" neither of which is at all suited to such a problematic, it is readily apparent that any attempt to grasp the essentials of the Kantian laying of the foundation of metaphysics by means of the method of approach of either logic or psychology, or any superficial combination thereof, is hopeless. Furthermore, as soon as one understands the difficulties, both basic and methodological, which are involved in the determination of the essence of man as a finite being, it is clear that the term "transcendental psychology" is only an expression of bewilderment.

It remains, therefore, only to leave open the method whereby the origin is to be revealed without attempting prematurely to force it into the mold of some particular discipline, whether traditional or newly devised for the purpose. In leaving the nature of this method open, it is fitting to remember what Kant said of the *Critique of Pure Reason* immediately after its completion. "An inquiry of this kind will always remain difficult." [34]

It is necessary, however, to provide some indication of the basic character of the procedure involved in this laying of the foundation of metaphysics. The method of inquiry may be understood as an "analytic" in the broadest sense of the term. It concerns finite pure reason as that which by its essence makes the ontological analytic possible. This is why Kant refers to the *Critique of Pure Reason* as a "study of our inner nature." [35]

34. *Briefe an M. Herz,* 1781, *Works* (Cass.), IX, p. 198.
35. A 703, B 731, NKS, p. 570.

This revelation of the essence of human *Dasein* "to a philosopher is really a matter of duty."

The term "analytic" as it appears here does not signify a dissolution in the sense of a reduction, i.e., as if it were a matter of reducing pure finite reason to its elements. Rather, the term signifies a "dissolution" which loosens and lays bare the seeds [*Keime*] of ontology. It reveals those conditions from which springs an ontology as a whole according to its intrinsic possibility. In Kant's own words, such an analytic "is brought to light by reason itself;" it is that which "reason produces entirely out of itself." [36] This analytic, then, lets us see the genesis of finite pure reason from its proper ground.

The analytic contains, therefore, the anticipatory projection of the whole internal essence of finite pure reason. Only as one pursues the construction of this essence does the essential structure of ontology become visible. Thus revealed, this structure determines, at the same time, the disposition of the substructures necessary to it. This anticipatory projection of the totality which makes an ontology possible in its essence discovers metaphysics on that ground wherein it is rooted as a "visitation" [37] on human nature.

## B. The Stages of the Realization of the Projection of the Intrinsic Possibility of Ontology

At this point, the interpretation of the *Critique,* anew and with greater precision, must make certain of the leading problem. The object of the inquiry is the essential possibility of the ontological synthesis. Stated precisely, the question reads:

36. A XX, NKS, p. 14.
37. B XV, NKS, p. 21.

46

How can finite human *Dasein* in advance pass beyond (transcend) the essent when not only has it not created this essent but also is dependent on it in order to exist as *Dasein?* Thus, the problem of ontology is the question relative to the essence and the essential ground of the transcendence proper to the precursory comprehension of Being. The problem of the transcendental synthesis, i.e., of the synthesis constitutive of transcendence, can be put in this way: How must the finite essent that we call man be in his inmost essence in order that in general he can be open [*offen*] to the essent that he himself is not, which essent therefore must be able to reveal itself by itself?

The stages through which an answer to this question must pass have already been outlined above.[38] It is now a question of going through them one by one, without, however, pretending to provide an equally exhaustive interpretation of each. We shall follow thereby the inner movement of the Kantian laying of the foundation but without holding to the disposition and the formulation favored by Kant. It is advisable to go behind these in order to be able, by a more fundamental understanding of the internal character and development of the laying of the foundation, to pass judgment on the suitability, validity, and limits of the external architectonic of the *Critique of Pure Reason.*


*The First Stage of the Laying of the Foundation:*
*The Essential Elements of Pure Knowledge*

If the essence of *a priori* synthetic knowledge is to be brought to light, the elucidation of the standing [*des Bestandes*] of its necessary elements is first required. As a mode of cognition

38. *Cf.* § 7, p. 42.

47

the transcendental synthesis must be an intuition, and, as cognition *a priori,* it must be a pure intuition. As pure knowledge pertaining to human finitude, pure intuition must necessarily be determined by means of pure thought.

## a) Pure Intuition in Finite Knowledge

### § 9. The Elucidation of Space and Time as Pure Intuitions

Can such a thing as an act of pure intuition be found in the finite knowledge of the essent? What is sought is the possibility of the immediate, although experience-free, encountering of something singular [*Begegnenlassen eines Einzelnen*]. To be sure, as finite, the act of pure intuition is an act of representation that is receptive. But that which is to be received, if it is a matter of the cognition of Being and not of the essent, cannot be something already on hand that presents itself [*das sich gibt*]. On the contrary, the pure receptive act of representation must give itself something capable of being represented. Pure intuition, therefore, must be in a certain sense "creative."

What is represented in pure intuition is not an essent (no object, i.e., not something that appears) but yet not absolutely nothing. It is all the more necessary, then, to disclose both *what* is represented in, and only in, pure intuition, and *how* the mode of representation corresponding to it is to be delimited.

According to Kant, the pure intuitions are space and time. It is advisable first to show how space manifests itself in the finite knowledge of the essent and to determine that with respect to which alone its essence can be adequately represented.

In his disclosure of the essence of space and time, Kant, in each case, deals first with the negative characteristics of the phenomenon and only then with the positive characteristics from which the negative follow.

48

It is no accident that the essential characterization of space and time begins negatively. This characterization opens by denying that space and time have this or that property. This course is followed because the positive characteristics of space and time, even though in a certain sense unrecognized or even misunderstood, are essentially familiar to everyone. Spatial relations—the relations of *beside, above,* and *in back of*—are not localized "here" or "there." Space is not just another thing on hand; it is no empirical representation, that is, nothing that can be represented empirically. In order that any given thing may be able to reveal itself as extended in accordance with definite spatial relationships, it is necessary that space be already manifest before the receptive apprehension of the thing. Space must be represented as that "within which" any actual thing can be encountered. Space is a pure representation, i.e., that which is necessarily represented in advance in finite human cognition.

Insofar as this representation "applies to every" particular spatial relation, it seems to be a representation which "applies to many"—a concept. In turn, the essential analysis of that which under these circumstances is represented as space provides information about the corresponding act of representation. Space, Kant tells us—again speaking negatively—is not a "discursive" representation. The unity of space is not obtained by reference to the plurality of individual spatial relations and is not constructed by way of a comparison of these relations. This unity is not that of a concept but the unity of something which in itself is one and unique. The many spaces are only limitations of the one unique space. And the latter is not only the actually limitable; the limiting limits [*die einschränkenden Schranken*] themselves have the same essence, i.e., are spatial. Space as one and unique is wholly itself in each one of its parts. The representation of space is accordingly the immediate representation of a unique particular, an intuition, that is, if it be

49

true that the essence of intuition must be defined as *repraesentatio singularis*. More precisely, and in accordance with what has been said above, space is what is intuited in a pure intuition.

Pure intuition as intuition, however, must not only give that which is intuited immediately; it must give it as a whole. This act of pure intuition is no mere reception of a part; in such an act the whole is present with the part. "Space is represented as an infinite given magnitude." [39] To say that space is a magnitude does not mean that it is of such and such an extent [*Grosses*], nor does the expression "infinite magnitude" mean of "limitless extent." Rather, "magnitude" here means "extensiveness" [*Grossheit*] as that which makes being of such and such an extent (quantity) possible. "The quantum wherein alone all quantity can be determined is, with regard to the number of parts, indeterminate and continuous; such are space and time." [40]

To say that this "extensiveness" is "infinite," then, does not mean that space differs from its particular, determinate parts in the degree and richness of its composition but that it is infinitely, i.e., essentially, different. It precedes all its parts as the unique and limitable whole. Unlike the generality of a concept, this totality does not have the many particulars "under itself" but, as already co-intuited, "in itself," so that this pure intuition of the whole can deliver up the "parts" at any time. The representation of such "infinite" extensiveness is, therefore, an act of intuition which gives [itself its content]. If this unique whole is given at once and as a whole, then the act of representation in question originates that which is capable of being represented and in this sense may be termed an "original" act of representation.[41]

39. A 25, B 39, NKS, p. 69.
40. *Kant's Posthumous Works in Manuscript Form*, vol. V, No. 5846, *cf.* Erdmann, *Reflexionen*, II, 1038.
41. A 32, B 48; *cf.* also B 40, NKS, pp. 76 and 70.

50

Thus, in pure intuition there is indeed something intuited and in such a way that it is given only in and through the corresponding act of intuition itself. The something intuited is not, to be sure, a given essent, nor in the act of intuition is it apprehended as such. In handling things and in perceiving them, we undoubtedly "intuit" their spatial relations but, for the most part, do not intend these relations as such. That which is intuited in pure intuition is presented to us unobjectively and unthematically in a preliminary insight. This insight has in view that unique whole which makes coordination according to *beside, under,* and *in back of* possible. That which is intuited in this mode of intuition is not absolutely nothing.

From what has already been said, the following is clear: The further clarification of that which is "originally represented" in pure intuition will be possible only when we have succeeded in elucidating more precisely the sense in which pure intuition is "original," i.e., when we understand how it lets that which is intuited by it spring forth.

## § 10. Time as the Universal Pure Intuition

In pure intuition, we seek the first of the essential elements of ontological knowledge on which the experience of the essent is based. But space as pure intuition merely gives in advance the totality of those relations by means of which what affects the external sense is ordered. At the same time, however, we find "givens" of the "internal sense" which exhibit neither spatial forms nor spatial relations but manifest themselves as a succession of mental states [*Gemütes*] (representations, drives, moods). That which in experiencing these phenomena is held in view from the first, although unthematically and unobjectively, is pure succession [*Nacheinander*]. Time, therefore, is "the form of inner sense, that is, of our intuition of ourselves and of our inner state." [42] Time determines "the relation of representations

42. A 33, B 49, NKS, p. 77.

51

in our inner state." [43] Time "cannot be a determination of outer appearances; it has to do neither with shape nor position." [44]

The two pure intuitions, space and time, thus refer to two distinct regions of experience, and it seems impossible at first to find one pure intuition which is constitutive of all knowledge of the Being of the essent and which, therefore, permits the problem of ontological knowledge to be formulated in universal terms. Nevertheless, immediately after having assigned both pure intuitions to *two* regions of phenomena, Kant states the following thesis: "Time is the formal condition *a priori* of all appearance whatsoever." [45] Thus, time takes precedence over space. As universal pure intuition, it must be the dominant and essential element of pure knowledge and hence of transcendence as well, since it is pure knowledge which makes transcendence possible.

The following interpretation will reveal how time in the course of the development of the several stages of the foundation of metaphysics comes more and more to the fore and thereby reveals its proper essence in a more original way than is possible by means of the provisional characterization in the *Transcendental Aesthetic.*

How does Kant justify the precedence of time as the universal pure intuition? It may seem astonishing at first that Kant questions the role of external phenomena in the determination of time, especially when it is in these phenomena—in the motions of the stars and in natural events in general (growth and decay)—that everyday experience first discovers time, and in so immediate a way that time is equated with the "heavens." However, Kant does not absolutely reject the temporal determination of external phenomena, if it is true that time is meant to be the formal condition *a priori* of all phenomena. The one

43. A 33, B 50, NKS, p. 77.
44. A 33, B 49, NKS, p. 77.
45. A 34, B 50, NKS, p. 77 (italics are Heidegger's).

thesis denies intra-temporality [*Innerzeitigkeit*] to physical things, the other concedes it. How may these mutually opposed theses be reconciled?

When Kant limits time as pure intuition to the data of internal sense, i.e., to representations in the broadest sense, this limitation amounts actually to an extension of the domain within which time can function as the precursory mode of intuition. Among representations in general are those which as representations let essents be encountered which are not like the being that represents them. Hence, Kant's reflections take this course:

Because all representations as states of the faculty of representation fall immediately in time, what is represented as such in an act of representation also belongs in time. Thus, by means of a detour through the immediate intra-temporality of the act of representation we arrive at a mediate intra-temporality of that which is represented, i.e., those "representations" which are determined through external sense. Therefore, since external phenomena are only mediately intra-temporal, in one sense the determination of time applies to them, but in another it does not. The argument from the intra-temporality of the intuition of external phenomena as a psychical event to the intra-temporality of what is intuited therein is made easy for Kant because of the ambiguity of the terms *intuition* [*Anschauung*] and *representation* [*Vorstellung*]. These expressions refer both to states of consciousness and to what such states may have as objects.

We will not pass judgment at this time on the question as to whether this argument in support of the universality of time as pure intuition justifies the central ontological function of time attributed to it. We will also leave open for the present the further question as to whether space as pure intuition is deprived thereby of a possible central ontological function.[46]

If, in general, it is possible to establish the universality of

46. *Cf.* below § 35, p. 201.

time as pure intuition, such an attempt will succeed only if it can be shown that, although both space and time as pure intuitions belong "to the subject," time is implanted therein in a more fundamental way than is space. Time as immediately limited to the data of internal sense can be, ontologically speaking, more universal than space only if the subjectivity of the subject consists in being overt to the essent. The more that time is subjective, the more original and extensive is the freedom from limitation of the subject.

The universal ontological function that Kant assigned to time at the beginning of his laying of the foundation of metaphysics can be justified only if time itself in its ontological function, i.e., as the essential element of pure ontological knowledge, forces us to determine the essence of subjectivity more primordially than heretofore.[47]

The task of the *Transcendental Aesthetic* is the exposition of the ontological *aisthēsis* which makes it possible "to discover *a priori*" the Being of the essent. Insofar as intuition maintains the dominant role in all knowledge, "one of the factors required for solution of the general problem of transcendental philosophy"[48] has been attained.

Just as it is inadmissible to minimize in the slightest degree the role of pure intuition as an essential element of ontological knowledge, so one cannot hope to discover the basic function of an element of pure intuition by considering it in isolation. It is not a question of eliminating the transcendental aesthetic as a provisional statement of the problem but of keeping its problematic while, at the same time, rendering it more precise. Such must be the true objective of the laying of the foundation of metaphysics as carried out by Kant, provided that it is aware of its own task.

But first, by means of an inquiry which, as before, begins by

47. *Cf.* below § 34, p. 193.
48. B 73, NKS, p. 90f.

isolating its object, we must uncover the second essential element of pure, finite knowledge, namely, pure thought.

## b) The Role of Pure Thought in Finite Knowledge

### § 11. The Pure Concepts of the Understanding (Notions)

The other element in the finitude of human knowledge is thought which as determinative representation is directed toward what is intuited in intuition and thus is entirely at the service of the latter. The object of an intuition (which is always a particular) is determined as such and such in a "general representation," i.e., through concepts. Hence, the finitude of reflective [thinking] intuition is a mode of cognition through concepts, and pure cognition is pure intuition through pure concepts. These pure concepts must be exhibited if the complete essential structure of pure knowledge is to be secured. However, if one wishes to discover such pure concepts, a clarification of the meaning of this expression ["pure concept"] is necessary.

When one represents, for example, a linden, beech, or fir as a tree, the particular thing intuited is determined as such and such with reference to that which "applies to many." Although this property of "applying to many" describes a representation insofar as it is a concept, it does not characterize the primordial essence of the latter. The property of "applying to many" as a derived character is itself based on the fact that in every concept there is represented one element [das Eine] in which the several particulars agree. Conceptual representation lets the many come to agreement in this one. In conceptual representation, therefore, the unity of this one must be anticipatively kept in view so that it can serve as a standard for all statements capable of determining the many. This anticipative

55

keeping in view [*Heraussehen*] of the *one* in which the many can agree is the basic act of conceptualization. Kant calls it "reflection." It is that which "enables different representations to be comprehended in one act of consciousness." [49]

Such a reflection brings before itself a unity which as such embodies a many, so that with reference to this unity the many can be compared (comparison). At the same time, that which is not in accord with this *one* is disregarded (abstraction, in the Kantian sense). What is represented in conceptual representation is "*one* representation so far as it can be contained in different objects." [50] A concept is not merely a presentation of something that happens to be common to many things; rather, it is this being-common-to insofar as it is common [*dieses Zukommende, sofern es zukommt*], i.e., in its unity. What is so represented is the concept; hence, Kant says rightly: "It is a mere tautology to speak of general or common concepts." [51]

Because a representation becomes a concept in the fundamental act which anticipatively holds in view the *one* which is common to the *many,* i.e., according to Kant in reflection, concepts are also said to be reflective representations, in other words, concepts which arise from reflection. The conceptual character of a representation—the fact that what is represented therein has the form of an element common to many—always arises from reflection. However, insofar as the content of the determinative unity is concerned, this arises, for the most part, from an empirical act of intuition which compares and abstracts. Hence, the origin of the content of such empirical concepts is not a problem.

Insofar as a pure concept is concerned, however, what is sought is a "reflected" concept, the content of which can in no wise be derived from the phenomena. Therefore, its content

49. *Logikvorlesung,* VIII, § 6, p. 401.
50. *Ibid.,* VIII, § 1, note 1, p. 399.
51. *Ibid.,* note 2.

56

must be obtainable *a priori*. Concepts, the content of which is given *a priori*, Kant terms *notions, conceptus dati a priori*.[52]

Are there such concepts, and are they to be found already prepared in human understanding? How is the understanding able to produce a content when it is only an empty connective function dependent on an intuition which itself supplies a content? And, finally, can such a content, represented as given, be found in the understanding if, as is supposed to be the case, the understanding is cut off from all intuition? If the understanding in itself is to be the origin not only of the form of every concept but also of the content of certain concepts, then this origin can only lie in the fundamental act of conceptualization itself, i.e., in reflection.

Every determination of something as something (judgment) contains "the unity of the act of bringing various representations under one common representation."[53] This act of reflective unification is possible only if it is itself guided by a precursory reference to a unity in the light of which all unification becomes possible. The act of representation, quite apart from whatever concept arises from its action, is already the precursory act of representation of a unity which as such guides and directs the work of unification. Accordingly, if the act of reflection itself is a representation of unity, this means that the act of representation of unity belongs to the essential structure of the fundamental act of the understanding.

The essence of the understanding is primordial comprehension. In the structure of the action of the understanding as a mode of unification that is representational, there lie already prepared representations of the directive unity. These represented unities form the content of the pure concepts. This content is, in each case, a unity by means of which a unification becomes possible. The act of representation of this unity is in

52. *Ibid.*, § 4, p. 401; further A 320, B 377, NKS, p. 314.
53. A 68, B 93, NKS, p. 105.

itself, by reason of its specific content, already conceptual *a priori*. A pure concept does not need to be endowed with a conceptual form; fundamentally it is itself this form.

Pure concepts, therefore, do not result from an act of reflection. They are not reflective concepts but those which belong, from the first, to the essential structure of reflection. They are representations which act in, with, and for reflection; they are *reflecting* concepts. "All concepts in general, no matter whence comes their material, are reflective, i.e., representations raised to the logical relation of general applicability. But there are concepts the entire sense of which is nothing other than to be constitutive of such and such a reflection, under which the actual representations as they occur can be subsumed. They may be called concepts of reflection (*conceptus reflectentes*), and since every act of reflection takes place in the judgment, they must, as the foundation of the possibility of judging, be in themselves, and in an absolute way, the pure activity of the understanding which in the judgment is applied to the relation." [54]

Hence, there are pure concepts in the understanding as such, and the "analysis of the faculty of understanding" must bring to light these representations which are co-constituents of the essential structure of reflection.

## § 12. The Notions as Ontological Predicates (*Categories*)

The pure understanding in itself provides a manifold—the pure unities of the possible modes of unification. And if these possible modes of unification (judgments) form a closed continuity, i.e., the complete nature of the understanding itself, then there lies concealed in the understanding a multiplicity of pure concepts organized into a systematic whole. This totality

54. Erdmann, *Reflexionen*, II, 554, *Kant's Posthumous Works in Manuscript Form*, vol. V, No. 5051.

is the system of those predicates which function in pure knowledge, that is, assert something about the Being of the essent. The pure concepts have the character of ontological predicates which of old have been termed "categories." The table of judgments, then, is the source of the categories and their table.

This origin of the categories has been often, and always will be, doubted. The principal objection is centered on the questionable character of the original source itself, on the table of judgments as such, and on the sufficiency of its supporting principles. In point of fact, it is not from the essence of the understanding that Kant develops the multiplicity of functions exercised in the judgment. He submits a table already complete which is organized according to the four "principal moments" of quantity, quality, relation, and modality.[55] Furthermore, Kant does not show if, or in what respect, these four moments are grounded in the essence of the understanding. Indeed, whether they can be formally established at all must be doubted.

Hence, we must remain uncertain as to the character of this table of judgments. Kant himself seemed unsure of the nature of this table, for he called it at one time a "transcendental table"[56] and at another a "logical table of judgments."[57] If this is so, does not the objection which Kant raised against Aristotle's table of categories apply also to his own?

But this is not the place to decide whether the many adverse criticisms of the Kantian table of judgments are justified or whether they even so much as hit upon its basic defect. Rather, we must see that such a critique of the table of judgments, if presented as a critique of the original source of the categories, has by that token already failed completely to come to grips with the main problem. Not only are the categories not actually derived from the table of judgments, they cannot be so derived,

55. *Logikvorlesung*, § 20, p. 408.
56. A 73, B 98, NKS, p. 108.
57. *Prolegomena*, § 21.

and for this reason: In the present stage of the discussion in question wherein the elements of knowledge are examined in isolation, the essence and the idea of the categories are not capable of receiving any determination. Indeed, they cannot even be made a problem.

If, as a matter of principle, the question as to the source of the categories cannot yet arise, then the table of judgments insofar as the preparation of the question of the possibility of ontological knowledge is concerned must have a function other than that indicated above.

It seems easy to satisfy the requirements laid down by the first stage of the foundation of metaphysics. For what could be more obvious than the elements of pure knowledge, i.e., pure intuition and pure concept, when they are set side by side? But in so isolating these elements, we must never lose sight of the fact that it is finite pure knowledge that is the object of our inquiry. As has been stated above, this means that the second element, pure thought, is essentially at the service of intuition. Hence, the property of being dependent on intuition is not an accidental and superficial characteristic of pure thought but an essential one. When pure concepts are initially apprehended as notions, the second element of pure knowledge is by no means obtained in its elementary form. On the contrary, it is deprived of the decisive moment of its essence, namely, its relation to intuition. The idea of the pure concept *qua* notion is only a fragment of the second element of pure knowledge.

As long as pure understanding is not considered with regard to its essence, i.e., its pure relation to intuition, the origin of the notions as ontological predicates cannot be disclosed. The table of judgments, therefore, is not the "origin of the categories" but simply "the method of discovery of all pure concepts of the understanding." It should lead us to the complete totality of pure concepts, but it cannot disclose the full essence of the pure concepts as categories. Whether the table of judgments as Kant introduced and presented it can discharge even this limited function of outlining a systematic unity of the pure concepts of the understanding must here remain open.

It is now clear from what has been set forth that the more radically one attempts to isolate the pure elements of finite pure knowledge, the more apparent becomes the impossibility of such an isolation and the more evident becomes the dependence of pure thought on intuition. Thus, the artificiality of the first point of departure of this characterization of pure knowledge is revealed. Pure concepts can be determined as ontological predicates only if they are understood in the light of the *essential unity* of finite pure knowledge.

## *The Second Stage of the Laying of the Foundation: The Essential Unity of Pure Knowledge*

Taken separately, the pure elements of pure knowledge are: time as universal pure intuition and the notions as that which is thought in pure thinking. But they cannot be adequately understood even as elements when considered in isolation; still less can their unity be obtained by a supervenient combination of the isolated members. The problem of the essential unity of pure knowledge gains in acuity provided that one does not remain satisfied with the negative consideration that this unity cannot be a merely subsequential bond linking the two elements.

The finitude of knowledge manifests an original and intrinsic dependence of thought on intuition or, conversely, a need for the latter to be determined by the former. The mutual dependence of these elements emphasizes the fact that their unity cannot be "later" than the elements themselves but must be established "earlier" in them and serve as their foundation. This

61

unity unites the elements in so original a way that they first arise as elements in this unification and are maintained in their unity by means of it. Despite the fact that he proceeds from the isolated elements, to what extent does Kant succeed in making this primordial unity visible?

The first characterization of the original essential unity of the pure elements, and one which prepares the way for all further clarification, is given by Kant in the third section of the first chapter of the *Analytic of Concepts,* more precisely, in the part that is headed *The Pure Concepts of the Understanding of Categories.*[58] The comprehension of these paragraphs is the key to the comprehension of the *Critique of Pure Reason* as a laying of the foundation of metaphysics.

Because the notions pertaining to the finitude of knowledge are essentially bound to pure intuition and because this bond between pure intuition and pure thought contributes to the formation of the essential unity of pure knowledge, the essential delimitation of the categories as such is at the same time the elucidation of the intrinsic possibility of the essential unity of ontological knowledge. It is now a matter of presenting Kant's answer to the question as to the essential unity of pure knowledge through the interpretation of the section mentioned above. But first, the question itself must be made more precise.

## § 13. The Question of the Essential Unity of Pure Knowledge

If the elements of finite pure knowledge are essentially dependent on one another, then this dependence alone stands in the way of any attempt to interpret their unity as the result of their supervenient combination. However, the isolation of these elements has concealed and made unrecognizable both the fact

58. A 76–80, B 102–105; in B designated as § 10, NKS, pp. 111–3.

and the manner of their dependence on the unity that underlies them. Even when an analysis is carried out with the resolve to uncover this original unity, the complete apprehension thereof is not guaranteed. On the contrary, because of the rigor with which the isolation has been carried out, and because of the peculiar character of the second element, a character made even more prominent by this isolation, it is to be expected that the work of this isolation cannot be completely undone so that, in spite of everything, the unity will not be expressly developed from its proper origin.

That the unity is not the result of a simple colligation of the elements but that which, in unifying them, originates them is indicated by the term "synthesis" which is applied to it.

In the full structure of finite knowledge, the many syntheses involved are necessarily intermingled.[59] To the veritative synthesis belongs the predicative of which, in turn, the apophantic is an intrinsic part. Which of these syntheses is meant when the essential unity of pure knowledge is in question? Apparently it is the veritative synthesis, for it concerns the unity of intuition and thought. The other syntheses, however, are necessarily included in it.

But the essential unity of pure knowledge is supposed to be constitutive of the total unity joining all structural syntheses. Hence, in the question of the essential unity of pure knowledge, the veritative synthesis enjoys a priority only insofar as the problem of synthesis is concentrated therein. This does not exclude the possibility, however, that this problem is oriented just as necessarily on the other forms of synthesis.

The question of the essential unity of ontological knowledge bears, moreover, on the problem of the pure veritative synthesis. It is, at bottom, a question about the original unification of pure universal intuition (time) and pure thought (the notions). Now, pure intuition has in itself—as the representation of a unified

59. *Cf.* above, § 7, p. 42, § 9, p. 48.

63

whole—a unifying character. Hence, Kant speaks rightly of a "synopsis" in intuition.[60] At the same time, the analysis of the notion as a "reflective concept" has shown that pure thought as the representation of pure unity is in itself originally a source of unity, and in this sense is "synthetic."

The problem of the pure veritative or ontological synthesis is reduced, then, to this question: What is the primordial (veritative) "synthesis" of pure synopsis and the pure reflective (predicative) synthesis like? It can be seen from the very form of this question that the synthesis which we are seeking must be of a special kind if it is to unite entities which in themselves are synthetic. The synthesis in question, therefore, must from the first be equal to the forms of synthesis and synopsis to be unified; it must produce them in the act of bringing them to unity.

## § 14. The Ontological Synthesis

The question of the essential unity of pure intuition and pure thought is a consequence of the previous isolation of these elements. Thus, the nature of their unity may be designated in advance by showing how the structure of each of these elements is such as to require the other. They reveal articulations [*Fugen*] [61] which indicate in advance the possibility of their fitting

60. A 95, NKS, p. 127.
61. The literal meaning of *"Fuge"* is "joint" or "seam" in the sense of that which is the result of the fitting together of mortises and tenons. It is a variant of the term *Fug,* a word which conveys the meaning of "suitableness," "fitness," but which in modern German is almost obsolete save in the expression *mit Fug und Recht* ("with full right"). These expressions are employed by Heidegger as early as *Sein und Zeit* (*cf.* p. 52ff.) along with the verbs *fügen, einfügen,* and *verfügen.* In a kind of linguistic evolution typical of Heidegger (e.g., the words *Geschick* and *Existenz*), the root expression *Fug* has in his later works come to be a technical term,

together. Hence, the veritative synthesis not only dovetails these articulations by fitting the elements together, it is also that which first makes these articulations "fit" to be joined.

Kant introduces the general characterization of the essential unity of pure knowledge with the following consideration: "Transcendental logic, on the other hand, has lying before it a manifold of *a priori* sensibility presented by transcendental aesthetic, as material for the concepts of pure understanding. In the absence of this material those concepts would be without any content, therefore entirely empty. Space and time contain a manifold of pure *a priori* intuition, but at the same time are conditions of the receptivity of our mind—conditions under which alone it can receive representations of objects, and which therefore must also always affect the concept of these objects. But if this manifold is to be known, the spontaneity of our thought requires that it be gone through in a certain way, taken up, and connected. This act I name *synthesis*." [62]

The dependence of pure intuition and pure thought on one another is first introduced here in a form which is remarkably superficial. Strictly speaking, "transcendental logic" does not have "lying before it" the pure temporal manifold. Rather, this mode of presentation of the manifold belongs to the essential structure of pure thought as analyzed by transcendental logic. Correspondingly, the transcendental aesthetic does not supply the pure manifold; pure intuition is by nature "that which supplies" and furthermore for the sake of pure thought.

What is thus supplied is more rigorously characterized by Kant as an "affection," although it must be remembered that affection through the senses is not here intended. Insofar as this affection "always" pertains to pure knowledge, it signifies that

the meaning of which, namely, "commanding or overpowering order" is far removed from that of the original. *Cf. Introduction to Metaphysics*, p. 160f. (J. S. C.)

62. A 76f., B 102, NKS, p. 111.

our pure thought is always placed before the time which affects it. How this is possible is not immediately clear.

In connection with this essential dependence of our pure thought on the pure manifold, the finitude of our thought "demands" that this manifold be accommodated to thought itself insofar as the latter is determinative by means of concepts. But in order that pure intuition be determinable through pure concepts, its manifold must be freed from dispersion, i.e., run through and collected. This reciprocal adaption takes place in the operation which Kant generally terms "synthesis." The two pure elements conform to one another spontaneously in this synthesis, which fits the corresponding articulations together and thus constitutes the essential elements of pure knowledge.

This synthesis is the affair neither of intuition nor of thought. Mediating, as it were, "between" the two, it is related to both. Hence, it must share the fundamental character of the two elements, i.e., it must be an act of representation. "Synthesis in general, as we shall hereafter see, is the mere result of the power of the *imagination,* a blind but indispensable function of the soul, without which we should have no knowledge whatsoever, but of the existence of which we are scarcely ever conscious." [63]

This indicates from the first that everything in the essence of pure knowledge that has a synthetic structure is brought about by the imagination. But at present it is a question, particularly and above all, of the essential unity of pure knowledge, i.e., of the "pure synthesis." It is pure "if the manifold is not empirical but is given *a priori.*" [64] Hence, pure synthesis fits in with that which as synopsis unifies in pure intuition.

But, at the same time, this synthesis requires a reference to a directive unity. Therefore, as an act of unification that is representative, the pure synthesis must represent in advance and as such, i.e., in a general way, the unity which pertains to it.

63. A 78, B 103, NKS, p. 112 (italics are Heidegger's).
64. A 77, B 103, NKS, p. 111.

By this general representation of its specific unity, the pure synthesis raises the unity which it represents to the level of a concept and thereby gives unity to itself. Thus, in pure intuition, the pure synthesis acts in a manner purely synoptic and, at the same time, in pure thought in a manner purely reflective. From this, it is evident that the unity of the complete essence of pure knowledge is composed of three parts. "What must first be given—with a view to the *a priori* knowledge of all objects—is the *manifold* of pure intuition; the second factor involved is the *synthesis* of this manifold by means of the imagination. But even this does not yet yield knowledge. The concepts which give *unity* to this pure synthesis, and which consist solely in the representation of this necessary synthetic unity, furnish the third requisite for the knowledge of an object; and they rest on the understanding." [65]

Of these three elements, the pure synthesis of the imagination holds the central position. This is not meant in a superficial sense, as if in the enumeration of the conditions of pure knowledge the imagination simply fell between the first and the third. Rather, this central position has a structural significance. In it, the pure synopsis and the pure synthesis meet and fit in with one another. This fitting in with one another Kant expresses by establishing the self-sameness [*Selbigkeit*] of the pure synthesis in the syn-thetic character [*Syn-haften*] of the intuition and the understanding.

"The same function which gives unity to the various representations *in a judgment* also gives unity to the mere synthesis of various representations *in an intuition;* and this unity, in its most general expression, we entitle the pure concept of the understanding." [66] By this self-sameness proper to the synthetic function, Kant does not mean the empty identity of a formal and universally operative mode of combination but

65. A 78f., B 104, NKS, p. 112.
66. A 79, B 104f., NKS, p. 112.

the primordial, rich totality of a complex activity which, as intuition and thought, at once unifies and imparts unity. This is to say, at the same time, that the modes of synthesis mentioned earlier, namely, the formal, apophantic synthesis of the judicative function and the predicative synthesis of conceptual reflection, belong together in the unity of the essential structure of finite knowledge as the veritative synthesis of intuition and thought. Hence, self-sameness means here an essential, structural togetherness [*Zusammengehörigkeit*].

"The same understanding, through the same operations by which in concepts, by means of analytical unity, it produced the logical form of a judgment, also introduces a transcendental content into its representations, by means of the synthetic unity of the manifold in intuition in general." [67] That which is now revealed as the essential unity of pure knowledge is far removed from the empty simplicity of a first principle. On the contrary, it is revealed as a multiform action, although one which remains obscure in its character as an action as well as in the complexity of its modes of unification. This characterization of the essential unity of ontological knowledge cannot be the conclusion but, rather, the right way to begin the laying of the foundation of this knowledge. This laying of the foundation has the task of bringing the pure synthesis as such to light. But because this synthesis is an action, it can be made manifest in its essence only by tracing it back in its coming into being. Now, we see for the first time, and by virtue of that which forces itself on us as the theme of the laying of the foundation, why a laying of the foundation of ontological knowledge must become a revelation of the origin of the pure synthesis, i.e., why this synthesis must be revealed in its coming into being as such.

The foundation of metaphysics has now reached the point

67. A 79, B 105, NKS, p. 112f.

68

"where matters are by their very nature deeply veiled." [68] **If** we have no reason here to complain of this obscurity, then our need to pause for a methodological reflection on the present state of the laying of the foundation and on the further course to be pursued is all the greater.

### § 15. The Problem of the Categories and the Role of Transcendental Logic

The problem of the essential unity of ontological knowledge first provides a basis for the determination of the essence of the categories. If a category is not only, or even in its primary sense (as the name indicates), a mode of "assertion," *schēma tou logou,* and if it can satisfy its true nature, which is that of a *schēma tou ontos,* then it must not function merely as an "element" (notion) of pure knowledge; on the contrary, in it must lie the knowledge of the Being of the essent. Knowledge of Being, however, is the unity of pure intuition and pure thought. The pure intuitivity of the notions, therefore, becomes decisive for the essence of the categories.

The "metaphysical exposition" of pure intuition is the task of the *Transcendental Aesthetic.* The elucidation of the other element of pure knowledge, pure thought, devolves on the *Transcendental Logic,* in particular, on the *Analytic of Concepts.* The problem of the essential unity of pure knowledge has led the inquiry beyond the isolation of the elements. The pure synthesis, therefore, is the act neither of pure intuition nor of pure thought. It follows, then, that the explication of the origin of the pure synthesis which we are about to begin cannot be carried out within the compass either of transcendental aesthetic or transcendental logic. Accordingly, the problem posed by the categories belongs to neither discipline.

68. A 88, B 121, NKS, p. 133.

But within what discipline does the discussion of the central problem of the possibility of ontology fall? This question was never considered by Kant. He assigned to the *Analytic of Concepts* not only the explication of pure concepts as elements of pure knowledge but the determination and justification of the essential unity of pure knowledge as well. In this way, logic came to have a unique priority over aesthetic even though it is intuition which is the primary element in knowledge as a whole.

This oddity requires an explanation if the problematic of the succeeding stages of the laying of the foundation of metaphysics is to remain clear. This explanation is especially necessary in view of the fact that the usual interpretation of the *Critique of Pure Reason* succumbs constantly to the temptation to understand this work as a "logic of pure knowledge." This remains true even when intuition and, hence, the transcendental aesthetic are granted a relative right.

All things considered, the priority of transcendental logic in the whole of the laying of the foundation of *metaphysica generalis* is, in a certain sense, justified. But precisely because of this, the interpretation must free itself from the Kantian architectonic and make the idea of transcendental logic problematic.

First of all, we must make clear to ourselves in what respect Kant was justified in presenting in the *Analytic of Concepts* not only the discussion of the two elements of pure knowledge but also the problem of their unity.

If the essence of pure thought consists in its reference to intuition with a view to serving the latter, then, when properly conceived, an analytic of pure thought must introduce this reference as such into the development of its problematic. That this takes place with Kant thus proves that the finitude of thought is the theme of the analytic. If the primacy of transcen-

70

dental logic is understood in this sense, it in no wise effects a diminution of the role of the transcendental aesthetic, to say nothing of its complete elimination. On the other hand, if the reason for the priority accorded to transcendental logic is understood, this priority disappears, not to the benefit of the transcendental aesthetic but to that of a formulation of the question which takes up again, on a more original basis, the central question of the essential unity of ontological knowledge and its justification.

Because Kant assigned the discussion of the conditions and principles of the use of pure concepts to the *Analytic of Concepts,* the relation of pure thought to pure intuition expressed under the heading of "the use of pure concepts" comes necessarily to be the theme of the exposition. Nevertheless, the element of thought remains the point of departure for the formulation of the question of the essential unity of pure knowledge. The tendency to proceed in this way is constantly reinforced because of the fact that the categories, which at bottom contain the problem of essential unity, are always presented as notions under the heading of pure concepts of the understanding. To this must be added that Kant found it necessary, in view of his primary orientation on the element of thought, to refer to traditional formal logic as that which passes judgment on thought in general. In this way, that which, when transposed to the transcendental level, leads to the problem of the pure concepts as categories acquires the character of a logical, albeit logico-transcendental, exposition.

Finally, this orientation on the *logos* and on *ratio,* in conformity with the meaning of these terms in Western metaphysics, enjoys from the first a priority in the laying of the foundation of metaphysics. This priority is expressed in Kant's designation of the laying of the foundation as a *Critique of Pure Reason.*

71

Furthermore, in order to organize and present this "complicated web of human knowledge," [69] which for the first time was to become manifest through his analytic, Kant had need of a definite framework which a logic of pure knowledge, newly devised, could most easily borrow from formal logic.

As self-evident as this dominant and many-sided role of "logic" in the *Critique of Pure Reason* may be, the following interpretation of the later and decisive stages of the laying of the foundation of ontology must go beyond the architectonic which governs the external succession of the problems and their presentation in order to bring to light the internal development of the problematic which led Kant to adopt this form of presentation.

## The Third Stage of the Laying of the Foundation: The Intrinsic Possibility of the Essential Unity of the Ontological Synthesis

The answer, apparently firmly established, to the question of the essential unity of ontological knowledge is progressively transformed when one tries to determine this unity with greater precision and finally becomes the problem of the possibility of such a unification. In the pure synthesis, pure intuition and pure thought must be able to meet one another *a priori*.

But what and how must this pure intuition itself be in order to satisfy the requirements of such a unification? It is now a question of presenting the pure synthesis in such a way as to reveal how it is able to unify time and the notion. The presentation of the original formation of the essential unity of ontological knowledge is the meaning and the purpose of that which Kant termed the *Transcendental Deduction of the Categories*.

69. A 85, B 117, NKS, p. 121.

72

Therefore, if the basic intention of the *Deduction* is to be found in the analytical exploration of the fundamental structure of the pure synthesis, its true content cannot appear if it is presented as a *quaestio juris*. The *quaestio juris,* then, may not be taken as a guide for the interpretation of the central doctrine of the Kantian critique. On the contrary, it is necessary to explain, with respect to the fundamental orientation of the *Deduction,* why the latter is presented in the form of a *quaestio juris* and what the significance of this mode of presentation is.

For reasons that will be given below,[70] the present interpretation will be confined exclusively to the development of the *Transcendental Deduction* as it appears in the first edition. Kant repeatedly stressed the "difficulty" of the deduction and sought to "remedy" its "obscurity." The diversity and complexity of the relations involved in the problem of the deduction, properties which become increasingly apparent as the content of this problem is made precise, prevented Kant from the very beginning from remaining content with a single point of departure for the deduction and a single way of carrying it out. But despite the diversity of his approach to the problem of the deduction, Kant still found his labors immense and unceasing. Often it is only on the way thereto that the objective pursued by the deduction is clearly perceived and expressed. And what should first be disclosed in the course of the deduction is often anticipated in a simple "preliminary observation." The intrinsic complexity of the problem also frequently gives rise to the circumstance that certain relationships, the clarification of which occasions special difficulty, are overemphasized, this overemphasis in turn leading to an overestimation of their real significance. This applies particularly to the discussion of pure thought as it bears on the essential unity of pure knowledge taken as a whole.

70. *Cf.,* below, § 31, p. 166.

The present interpretation will not follow in detail all the tortuous paths of the *Transcendental Deduction* but will lay bare the original character and development of the problematic. To this end, it is necessary first to make sufficiently clear the true objective of the transcendental deduction with regard to the chief problem of the laying of the foundation of metaphysics.

## § 16. The Explication of the Transcendence of Finite Reason as the Basic Purpose of the Transcendental Deduction

A finite cognitive being is able to relate itself to an essent which it itself is not and which it has not created, only if this essent can by itself come forward to be met. However, in order that this essent can be encountered as the essent that it is, it must be "recognized" in advance as essent, i.e., with respect to the structure of its Being. But this implies that ontological knowledge, which in this circumstance is always pre-ontological, is the condition of the possibility that an essent as such can, in general, become an ob-ject for a finite being.[71] All finite beings must have this basic ability, which can be described as a turning toward . . . [orientation toward . . .] which lets something become an ob-ject.

71. The literal translation of *entgegenstehen,* namely, "to take up a position opposite to" often results in locutions which are extremely awkward. Hence, except in those passages where a literal translation is clearly required, I translate the term by "become an ob-ject" or "ob-jectification" and *Entgegenstehenlassen* by "letting become an ob-ject" or "act of ob-jectification." The use of the hyphen here is intended to convey the sense of activity implicit in the word "object" and its German equivalent *Gegenstand.* It should be noted, however, that this activity which Heidegger seeks to emphasize by his use of *entgegenstehen* is prior to that act of objectification referred to in theory of knowledge. (J. S. C.)

74

In this primordial act of orientation, the finite being first pro-poses to itself a free-space [*Spielraum*] within which something can "correspond" to it. To hold oneself in advance in such a free-space and to form it originally is nothing other than transcendence which marks all finite comportment [*Verhalten*] with regard to the essent. If the possibility of ontological knowledge is based upon the pure synthesis, and if it is ontological knowledge which makes the act of ob-jectification possible, then the pure synthesis must manifest itself as that which organizes and supports the unified totality of the intrinsic, essential structure of transcendence. Through the elucidation of the structure of the pure synthesis the inmost essence of the finitude of reason is revealed.

Finite knowledge is receptive intuition. As such, it requires determinative thinking. On this account, pure thought lays claim to a central role in the problem of ontological knowledge, although without prejudice to—indeed, because of—the priority which intuition enjoys in all knowledge.

To what service is pure thinking called in its subsidiary function? What is its task relative to that which makes the essential structure of transcendence possible? It is just this question relative to the essence of pure thought—although when put in this way it appears to isolate this element anew—that must lead to the core of the problem of the essential unity of ontological knowledge.

It is no accident that Kant, in the *Transition to the Transcendental Deduction of the Categories,*[72] alludes to the finitude, which he clearly perceives, of our act of representation and especially to that act as an act of pure knowledge, "for we are not here speaking of its causality by means of the will." On the contrary, the question is: What power is the act of representation as such able to exercise relative to the essent to which it relates itself? Kant states that the "representation

72. A 92f., B 124f., NKS, p. 125f.

75

in itself" "cannot produce its object so far as its existence is concerned." Our mode of cognition is not ontically creative; it is not able of itself to bring the essent before itself. Midway in the discussion of the *Transcendental Deduction,* Kant emphasizes that "outside our knowledge we have nothing which we could set over against this knowledge as corresponding to it." [73]

If our cognition as finite must be a receptive intuition, then it is not sufficient merely to establish this fact, for the problem now arises: What does the possibility of this by no means self-evident reception of the essent entail?

Obviously this: that the essent by itself can come forward to be met, i.e., appear as ob-jective [*Gegenstehendes*]. However, if the presence of the essent is not subject to our control, then our being dependent on its reception requires that the essent have in advance and at all times the possibility of becoming an ob-ject.

A receptive intuition can take place only in a faculty which lets something become an ob-ject in an act of orientation toward . . . , which alone constitutes the possibility of a pure correspondence. And what is it that we, by ourselves, let become an ob-ject? It cannot be something essent. If not an essent, then a Nothing [*Nichts*].[74] Only if the act of ob-jectification is a holding oneself into Nothing [*Sichhineinhalten in das Nichts*] can an act of representation within this Nothing let, in place of it, something not nothing, i.e., an essent, come

73. A 104, NKS, p. 134.

74. *Nichts* is usually translated as "nothingness" or "negativity," but in view of the fact that Heidegger introduces it in contexts wherein it can only be translated as "nothing" (for example, "What is to be investigated is the essent—and nothing else; only the essent —and nothing more; simply and solely the essent—and beyond that nothing. But what about this nothing?" *What is Metaphysics, op. cit.,* p. 358), it seems only consistent to continue to so translate it, capitalizing the word to avoid confusion. (J. S. C.)

forward to be met, supposing such to be empirically manifest. Naturally, this Nothing of which we speak is not the *nihil absolutum*. What it has to do with the act of ob-jectification remains to be discussed.

Since Kant so clearly places finitude in the perspective of transcendence, there is no need, under the pretext of avoiding an alleged "subjective idealism," of invoking that "return to the object" about which so much noise is made today, a noise unaccompanied by an adequate comprehension of the problem. In truth, a consideration of the essence of finitude inevitably forces us to a consideration of the question of the conditions governing the possibility of a precursory orientation toward the object, i.e., to a consideration of the question of the nature of the ontological turning toward the object necessary for this.

Thus, in the transcendental deduction, i.e., in connection with the clarification of the intrinsic possibility of ontological knowledge, Kant is the first to propound the decisive question: "At this point we must make clear to ourselves what we mean by the expression 'an object of representations.' " [75] It is a matter of investigating the nature of that which confronts us in the act of ob-jectification. "Now we find that our thought of the relation of all knowledge to its object carries with it an element of necessity; the object is viewed as that which prevents our modes of knowledge from being haphazard or arbitrary, and which determines them *a priori* in some definite fashion." [76] In this act of letting something take up a position opposite to . . . as such, is manifested something "which is opposed" [*was dawider ist*].

Kant refers to an immediate datum in order to make this opposition understandable and does not neglect to character-

75. A 104, NKS, p. 134.
76. *Ibid.* The expression *"was dawider ist"* ("which is opposed") which appears in the original disappears in Smith's translation. (J. S. C.)

ize its unique structure more closely. It should be noted, however, that it is not a question here of a character of resistance inherent in the essent or of the pressure of sensation on us, but of the precursory resistance of Being. The objectivity of objects "carries with it" something which constrains ("something of necessity"). Through this constraint all that is encountered is in advance forced into an accord [*Einstimmigkeit*], with reference to which also a manifestation of what is encountered as not in accord is first possible. This precursory and constant drawing together into unity [*Zusammenzug auf Einheit*] involves the [anticipative] pro-position of unity. The act of representation of a representative and unifying unity characterizes the essence of that type of representation which Kant names a concept. This designates "a consciousness" in the sense of an act of representation of unity.[77] The act of objectification is, therefore, the "primordial concept" [*Urbegriff*] and, insofar as conceptual representation is assigned to the understanding, is the fundamental activity of the understanding. The latter as a complete totality contains in itself a diversity of modes of unification. Consequently, the pure understanding is revealed as the faculty which makes the act of ob-jectification possible. The understanding as a totality gives in advance all that is opposed to the haphazard. Representing unity originally and precisely as unifying, the understanding presents to itself a form of constraint which in advance imposes its rule on all possible modes of togetherness. "The representation of a universal condition according to which a certain manifold can be posited in uniform fashion is called a *rule*."[78] The concept "may, indeed, be quite imperfect or obscure. But a concept is always, as regards its form, something universal which serves as a rule."[79]

77. A 103f., NKS, p. 134.
78. A 113, NKS, p. 140.
79. A 106, NKS, p. 135.

78

Now, the pure concepts (*conceptus reflectentes*) are those which have such normative unities as their sole content. They serve not only to furnish us with rules, but, as pure acts of representation, they provide, first of all and in advance, the normative as such. Thus, it is in connection with his explanation of the act of ob-jectification that Kant first arrives at the primordial concept of the understanding. "We may now characterize it as the *faculty of rules*. This distinguishing mark is more fruitful and approximates more closely to its essential nature." [80]

Now, if it is the understanding which makes the act of objectification possible, and if it is the understanding which has the power of regulating all that the "intuition" brings forth, is it not then defined as the supreme faculty? Has not the servant changed into the master? And what are we to think of the subsidiary function of the understanding, a function which up to now has been regarded as essential, as the true index of its finitude? Supposing his explication of the understanding as the faculty of rules to be descriptive of its essence, has Kant, in the decisive stages of the problematic of the transcendental deduction, forgotten that the understanding is finite?

However, inasmuch as it is the finitude of reason which gives rise to and defines the whole problem of the possibility of metaphysics as such, this supposition must be rejected. But how then may the now dominant role of the understanding be reconciled with its subordination? Can it be that in its dominance, as that which ob-jectifies the rules of unity, it is basically a subordination? Can it be that in this function the understanding reveals its deepest finitude, since, in letting something become an ob-ject, it betrays, in a most primordial form, the neediness of a finite being?

As a matter of fact, the understanding is—in its finitude— the supreme faculty, i.e., finite to the highest degree. And if

80. A 126, NKS, p. 147.

it is, then the dependence of the pure understanding on intuition should come most clearly to light in the fundamental act of the understanding, namely, in the act of ob-jectification. Naturally, the intuition concerned must be pure rather than empirical.

It is only insofar as the pure understanding as understanding is the servant of pure intuition that it can remain the master of empirical intuition.

But pure intuition itself—it above all—bears witness to a finite essence. It is only in their structural unity that the finitude of pure intuition and pure thought is fully expressed, this finitude being revealed as transcendence. However, if the source of the unity of the elements of pure knowledge is the pure synthesis, then the disclosure of the total synthetic structure of this synthesis is revealed as that which alone leads us to the objective of the transcendental deduction, i.e., to the elucidation of transcendence.

## § 17. The Two Ways of the Transcendental Deduction

The determination of the problematic of ontological knowledge has revealed the inner meaning of the transcendental deduction. The transcendental deduction is the analytical revelation of the total structure of the pure synthesis. At first sight, this interpretation of the transcendental deduction does not seem to correspond to its verbal concept. The interpretation seems even to contradict Kant's own specific explication of what is implied by the deduction. But before coming to a decision about this, we must first trace the development of the deduction and in this way present it concretely. To this end, our interpretation will be confined to the *Third Section* [81] of

81. A 115–128, NKS, p. 141–9.

the *Deduction of the Pure Concepts of the Understanding,* in which Kant discusses the elements of the deduction "in systematic interconnection." [82]

The heading of this section expresses clearly that the problem of the intrinsic possibility of ontological knowledge is nothing other than the revelation of transcendence. According to this heading, the deduction treats *Of the Relation of the Understanding to Objects in General, and the Possibility of Knowing Them a priori.* However, if one wishes to understand the twofold way along which Kant takes the deduction, it is necessary again to remind ourselves of its objective.

The essent is accessible to a finite being only on the basis of a precursory act of ob-jectification which at the same time is orientation toward that something. This [activity] admits in advance all entities capable of being encountered into the horizon of unity which forms the condition of all possible modes of togetherness [*Zusammengehörigkeit*]. The unity which unifies *a priori* must anticipate the encounterable. What is encountered is itself, however, already included in advance in the horizon of time pro-posed by pure intuition. The anticipatory, unifying unity of the pure understanding must itself, therefore, also have been united beforehand with pure intuition.

This totality composed of pure intuition and pure understanding, united in advance, "constitutes" the free-space within which all essents can be encountered. It is advisable to show, relative to this totality of transcendence, how (i.e., here conjointly) pure understanding and pure intuition are dependent on one another *a priori.*

This proof of the intrinsic possibility of transcendence can be conducted in two ways.

First, the presentation can begin with the pure understanding and through the elucidation of its essence reveal its intrinsic

82. A 115, NKS, p. 141.

dependence on time. The first way begins, as it were, "from above" with the understanding and leads down to the intuition. (A 116–120.) (NKS, pp. 141–44.)

The second way proceeds "from below," [83] beginning with the intuition and goes up to the pure understanding. (A 120–128.) (NKS, pp. 144–149.)

Each of the two ways achieves the revelation of the "two extremes, namely, sensibility and understanding [which] must stand in necessary connection with each other." [84] What is essential here is not the connecting of the two faculties but the structural elucidation of their essential unity. The decisive factor is that which enables them to be so connected. It is necessary, therefore, in each of the two ways to trace down this central, unifying factor and to bring it to light as such. The revelation of the pure synthesis takes place by means of this repeated passage between both extremes. It is now a question of presenting at least the main points of the twofold course of the deduction.

*a*) THE FIRST WAY

The necessary dependence of pure understanding on pure intuition must be revealed in order that the unity which mediates between them, the pure synthesis, can be made manifest in its mediative capacity. This requires that the pure understanding as the point of departure of the first way be interpreted in such a way that from its structure its dependence on a pure synthesis and, thereby, on a pure intuition becomes visible.

Consequently, the *Deduction* is something quite other than a logical, deductive operation by means of which the existence of the relations mentioned above between the understanding

83. A 119, NKS, p. 143.
84. A 124, NKS, p. 146.

on the one hand and the pure synthesis and pure intuition on the other can be inferred. Rather, from its very beginning the deduction has in view the totality of finite, pure knowledge. The explicit presentation of the relations structurally constitutive of the totality progresses from one element to the other while maintaining this inclusive point of view. Every statement in the *Transcendental Deduction* remains incomprehensible unless from the first one keeps the finitude of transcendence unwaveringly in view.

The character of being in opposition [*Dawider*], which makes the act of ob-jectification possible, is manifested in an anticipatory pro-position [*Vorweghalten*] of unity. In this act of representation of unity, the act appears to itself as bound to unity, i.e., as that which maintains its self-identity even in the pure action of representing unity as such.[85] Manifestly, "something" can confront this act of representation only if the act of representation of unity as such is itself confronted by the unifying unity as regulative. It is only because the act turns toward itself in this way that what is encountered is able to "concern us." [86]

The representation of unity as an act of pure thought necessarily has the character of an "I think." The pure concept as consciousness of unity in general is necessarily pure self-consciousness. This pure consciousness is not actually present and operative only on certain occasions but must constantly be possible. It is essentially an "I can." "This pure original unchangeable consciousness I shall name *transcendental apperception*." [87] The act of representation of unity which lets something become an ob-ject is based on this apperception "*as a faculty*." [88] Only as the constant "I can" is the "I think" able

85. A 108, NKS, p. 136.
86. A 116, NKS, p. 141.
87. A 107, NKS, p. 136.
88. A 117, fn., NKS, p. 142.

to let the being in opposition of unity become ob-jectified, if it is true that the act of binding [*Bindung*] is possible only with reference to a mode of behavior essentially free. The pure understanding in originally pro-posing unity to itself acts as trancendental apperception.

But what is represented in the unity which the transcendental apperception pro-poses? Is it perhaps the essent in totality presented all at once in the sense of the *totum simul* intuited by *intuitus originarius?* But this pure thinking is finite and, in consequence, incapable of setting the essent opposite to itself solely by means of its own act of representation, to say nothing of representing the totality of the essent all at once and as a unity. The unity represented first waits for the essent to come forward and in this way makes possible the encountering of [different] objects which manifest themselves at the same time. As non-ontic, this unity has the essential tendency to unify that which is not yet unified. This is why Kant, after the explication of transcendental apperception, states of the unity represented by it: "This synthetical unity presupposes or includes a synthesis." [89]

In characteristic fashion, Kant hesitates to define with precision the structural relations involved in the unity of the unifying synthesis. In any case, the latter belongs necessarily to the former. The unity is by nature unifying. This implies that the act of representation of unity takes place as an act of unification which, in order to realize its complete structure, requires an anticipation of unity. Kant does not hesitate to say that the transcendental apperception "presupposes" the synthesis.

Now, it has already been established in the second stage of the laying of the foundation that all synthesis is the product of the imagination. Accordingly, the transcendental apperception has an essential relation to the pure imagination. As

89. A 118, NKS, p. 142.

84

pure, the latter cannot re-present something already empirically given, in relation to which this faculty would be merely reproductive; rather, as pure imagination it is necessarily constitutive *a priori,* i.e., purely productive. Kant also calls the pure productive imagination "transcendental." "Thus the principle of the unity of pure (productive) synthesis of imagination, prior to [before] apperception, is the ground of the possibility of all knowledge, especially of experience." [90]

What is the significance here of the phrase "before all apperception"? Does Kant mean to assert that the pure synthesis precedes the transcendental apperception in the order of the establishment of the possibility of a pure knowledge? This interpretation would coincide with the assertion above, namely, that the apperception "pre-supposes" the pure synthesis.

But does this "before" have yet another significance? In fact, Kant employs the expression in a way which first gives the whole statement an essential sense and one so decisive that the interpretation mentioned above is at the same time included in it. At one point, Kant speaks "of an object for [before] a quite different intuition." [91] In this passage, to replace the "before" [*vor*] by "for" [*für*] would not only be useless but would also serve to weaken the text, especially when one remembers the Latin expression *coram intuitu intellectuali* which Kant likewise employs.[92] Only if one takes the "before" in the phrase cited to mean *coram* does the nature of the structural unity of transcendental apperception and pure imagination come to light. Consequently, the representation of unity has essentially in view a unifying unity, i.e., this act is in itself unifying.

However, the pure synthesis must unify *a priori.* Therefore,

90. A 118, NKS, p. 143.
91. A 287, NKS, p. 293. *Cf. Nächtrage zur Kritik* (from *Kant's Posthumous Works,* ed. by B. Erdmann), 1881, p. 45.
92. A 249, NKS, p. 266.

what it unifies must be given to it *a priori*. Now the universal, pure intuition which is *a priori*, receptive, and productive is time. Hence, pure imagination must be essentially related to time. Only in this way is pure imagination revealed as the mediator between transcendental apperception and time.

This is why Kant prefaces all discussion of the transcendental deduction by a "general observation which . . . must be borne in mind as being quite fundamental."[93] It states that all "modifications of the mind . . . are . •. . finally subject to time. . . . In it they must all be ordered, connected, and brought into relation."[94] One may be surprised at first that neither in the first nor in the second way of the transcendental deduction does Kant discuss explicitly and in detail the essential relation between time and pure imagination. Rather, the entire analysis is centered on the task of bringing to light the essential relation of pure understanding to the pure synthesis of the imagination. It is by means of this relation that the true nature of the understanding, namely, its finitude, is most clearly revealed. The understanding is what it is only insofar as it "presupposes or involves" the pure imagination. "This *unity of apperception in relation to the synthesis of imagination* is the *understanding;* and this same unity with reference to the *transcendental synthesis* of the imagination, the *pure understanding.*"[95]

### b) THE SECOND WAY

The necessary dependence of pure intuition on pure understanding, i.e., the unity which mediates between them, the pure synthesis, must be revealed as a mediator. Hence, the

93. A 99, NKS, p. 131.
94. *Ibid.*
95. A 119, NKS, p. 143.

second way begins with the following words: "We shall now, starting from below, namely, with the empirical, strive to make clear the necessary connection in which understanding, by means of the categories, stands to appearances." [96]

Even here, where it would seem advisable to set forth explicitly the pure condition of the receptivity of finite knowledge, Kant does not linger for a discussion of pure intuition (time) but proceeds immediately to the proof that although "sensibility" is receptive, it "has nothing" in itself corresponding to a connection [*Verbundenheit*] between phenomena. However, this connection must be capable of being experienced in finite cognition, since a finite being never has the essent as a *totum simul;* rather, as Kant states explicitly, what is encountered is found "separately and singly." [97] Therefore, if the essents encountered are to be able to reveal themselves as connected, it is necessary that "connection" in general be understood in advance. To re-present connection in advance means that one must first form, by representing it, the notion of relation in general. But this power of "forming" relations originally is pure imagination itself.

According to the "general observation," [98] the medium wherein joining and forming connections is possible is time as the universal pure intuition. The possibility of encountering an essent capable of revealing itself in its ob-jective [*gegenstehenden*] connectedness must have its basis in the imagination as that which is essentially related to time. In the pure act of forming determinate relations, the pure imagination proposes a mode of unification that is normative and opposed in advance to the arbitrary reception of what is encountered. This horizon of normative connection [*Bindung*] contains the pure "affinity"

96. *Ibid.*
97. A 120, NKS, p. 144.
98. A 99, NKS, p. 131.

of appearances. "That the affinity of appearances . . . should only be possible by means of this transcendental function of imagination is indeed strange but is none the less an obvious consequence of the preceding." [99]

Every act of connection, and particularly the pure act of forming unity in general, incorporates a preliminary act of representation of unity. If the pure synthesis is to function *a priori,* this act of representation itself must be *a priori* and must take place in such a way that it constantly accompanies all formation of unities as that which is invariably one and the same. This identity [*dieses Selbst*] which is "unchanging and permanent" is the ego of transcendental apperception. As time pertains to all empirical intuition, so also is the precursory formation of affinity in the pure imagination necessary to this same intuition as that which lets the essent be encountered in the order proper to it. But to pure imagination, however, "must be added" pure apperception, if reception is to be capable of being sustained by a pure act of orientation, i.e., by an act of ob-jectification. [100]

Now, the first way has revealed that the transcendental apperception which, through the essential mediation of the pure imagination, must be joined to pure intuition does not exist in isolation, and, therefore, it is not coupled to the pure imagination merely because the latter occasionally has need of it. On the contrary, the transcendental apperception, inasmuch as it is an act of representation of unity, must in turn have at hand a unity which is formed by an act of unification. Thus, in the second way as well as in the first, everything leads to the emphasis on the imagination in its role as a mediator. "A pure imagination, which conditions all *a priori* knowledge, is thus one of the fundamental faculties of the human soul. By its means we bring the manifold of intuition on the one side [and]

99. A 123, NKS, p. 146.
100. A 124, NKS, p. 146.

88

into connection with the condition of the necessary unity of pure apperception on the other." [101]

Thus, the triplicity of the three elements—pure intuition, pure imagination, and pure apperception—is no longer that of a mere juxtaposition of faculties. Through the revelation of the mediating function of the pure synthesis, the transcendental deduction has established the intrinsic possibility of the essential unity of pure knowledge. This constitutes the pure act of objectification and, by this means, first makes manifest a horizon of objectivity in general. And because pure knowledge in this way first opens up the free-space necessary for a finite being, i.e., the space in which "all relation of being or not being" [102] occurs, this knowledge must be termed ontological.

However, the understanding as that which bears witness to human finitude has a special part to play in the deduction. In the course of the various steps which make up the one or the other of the two ways, the understanding loses its priority and by this very loss manifests its essence, which consists in having to be grounded in the pure synthesis of the imagination, a synthesis which is bound to time.

## § 18. The External Form of the Transcendental Deduction

For what reason does the transcendental deduction, the purpose of which is the elucidation of transcendence, assume the form of a *quaestio juris?* By what right and within what limits

---

101. *Ibid.* The elimination of the "and" proposed by Erdmann and Riehl robs the exposition—which is put in a way that is perhaps difficult—of its decisive sense, according to which, the transcendental imagination on the one hand unifies pure intuition in itself and on the other unites the latter with pure apperception [Smith also eliminates the "and"].

102. A 110, NKS, p. 138.

does this mode of propounding the question take a "juridical" form, which to be sure appears only in the first introduction of the transcendental deduction and not in the course of its development?

Kant did not employ the term "deduction" in its philosophical sense of *deductio* as opposed to *intuitus*,[103] but in the sense in which a "jurist" would understand the term. In the course of a lawsuit "rights" are asserted and "claims" denied. Such a legal action necessarily involves two factors: first, the establishment of the actual facts and the points under dispute (*quid facti*), and second, the exposition of that which the law recognizes as the underlying right (*quid juris*) in the case. Jurists call a "deduction" the exposition of the conditions necessary to the establishment of a right.

Why, at this point, does Kant present the problem of the possibility of metaphysics in the form of such a juridical deduction? Does a "legal action" underlie the problem of the intrinsic possibility of ontology?

It has already been shown how, for Kant, the question of the possibility of *metaphysica generalis* (ontology) arises from the question of the possibility of the traditional *metaphysica specialis*.[104] The object of *metaphysica specialis* is the rational knowledge (knowledge by pure concepts) of the super-sensible essent. In these pure concepts (categories) lies the pretension to ontic knowledge *a priori*. Does this pretension have any foundation?

The discussion with traditional metaphysics considered with respect to "its final purpose" and relative to its proper possibility has become a legal action. Pure reason must "institute a process;" the witnesses must be examined. Kant speaks of a "tribunal." [105] The legal action thus included in the problem of

103. Descartes, *Regulae ad directionem ingenii, Opera,* ed. by Adam et Tannery, tom. X, p. 368sqq.
104. *Cf.* above § 2, p. 14ff.
105. A 699, B 697; A 703, B 731; NKS, p. 549, p. 553.

ontological knowledge requires a deduction, i.e., a demonstration of the possibility, insofar as pure concepts are concerned, of referring *a priori* to objects. Since the right to use these concepts which are not derived from experience cannot be defended by appealing to the fact of their actual use, they "always demand a deduction." [106]

The legitimacy of the categories must be decided by the elucidation of their essence. As pure representations of unities in a finite act of representation they are essentially dependent on the pure synthesis and, hence, on pure intuition. Put in another way, the solution of the problem, which is formulated simply as *quaestio juris,* is to be found in the disclosure of the essence of the categories. They are not notions but pure concepts which, by means of the pure imagination, are rendered essentially relative to time. Endowed with such a nature, they constitute transcendence. They contribute to the act of objectification. Because of this they are, from the first, determinations of objects, i.e., of the essent itself insofar as it is encountered by a finite being.

Through the explication of the essence of the categories as elements or articulations [*Fugen*] necessary to transcendence, their "objective reality" is demonstrated. However, in order to understand the problem of the objective reality of the categories as a problem of transcendence, it is necessary that one should not take the Kantian term "reality" [*Realität*] in the sense given it by modern "theory of knowledge," according to which "Reality" signifies what Kant denoted by the term *Dasein* or "existence." Rather, "reality" means, according to Kant's exact translation, "fact-hood" [*Sachheit*] and alludes to the quiddity [*Wasgehalt*] of the essent which is delimited through *essentia*. When Kant brings the objective reality of the categories into question, what he is asking is this: In what respect can the real content (reality) of what is represented in a pure concept be a determination of that which is ob-jectified in finite

106. A 85, B 117, NKS, p. 121.

knowledge, i.e., of the essent *qua* object? The categories are objectively real insofar as they belong to ontological knowledge which "produces" [forms] the transcendence of a finite being, that is, the letting something take up a position opposite to. . . .

Thus, it is evident that if one fails to interpret the expression "objective reality" from the point of view of the pure synthesis of the transcendental imagination as that which forms the essential unity of ontological knowledge, if one confines himself exclusively to the notion of "objective validity," an expression which Kant employs only in the preliminary formulation of the transcendental deduction as a juridical question, and if, in addition, one interprets "validity" to mean the logical validation of a judgment, an interpretation contrary to the sense required by the Kantian problematic—then the decisive problem is entirely lost to view.

The problem of the "origin and the truth" [107] of the categories, however, is the problem of the possible manifestation of the Being of the essent in the essential unity of ontological knowledge. If this question is to be conceived concretely and grasped as a problem, then the *quaestio juris* should not be understood as a question of validation. Rather, the *quaestio juris* is only a way of expressing the necessity of an analytic of transcendence, i.e., of a pure phenomenology of the subjectivity of the subject, and furthermore, of the subject as finite.

If the fundamental problem for which the traditional *Metaphysica specialis* provided the occasion is thus resolved by the transcendental deduction, has not the laying of the foundation already attained its objective in the stage just discussed? At the same time, does not what has now been stated justify the current opinion which holds, with respect to the interpretation of the *Critique of Pure Reason,* that the transcendental deduction is the central point of discussion within the positive part of *The Transcendental Doctrine of Elements?* What need, then, is there

107. A 128, NKS, p. 149.

92

of an additional stage of the laying of the foundation of ontological knowledge? What is it that requires an even more primordial regression to the ground of the essential unity of
ontological knowledge?

## The Fourth Stage of the Laying of the Foundation: The Ground of the Intrinsic Possibility of Ontological Knowledge

The intrinsic possibility of ontological knowledge is revealed
through the specific totality of the constitution of transcendence.
Its binding medium [*zusammenhaltende Mitte*] is the pure
imagination. Kant not only finds this result "strange," but also
stresses more than once the obscurity which inevitably engulfs
all discussion of the transcendental deduction. At the same
time, the laying of the foundation of ontological knowledge
strives—over and above a simple presentation of transcendence
—to elucidate this transcendence in such a way that it can be
developed into a systematic whole (transcendental philosophy =
ontology).

Now, the transcendental deduction has raised to a problem
the totality of ontological knowledge considered in its unity.
Given the decisive importance of finitude and the dominance of
the logical (rational) approach to the problems of metaphysics,
the understanding—or more precisely, its relation to pure imagination as the unifying medium—comes to the fore.

However, if all knowledge is primarily intuition and if finite
intuition is characterized by receptivity, then for an explication
of transcendence that is completely valid the relation of the
transcendental imagination to pure intuition and also that of
pure understanding to pure intuition must be explicitly discussed. Such a task demands that the transcendental imagina-

93

tion be presented in its unifying function and that thereby the constitution of transcendence and its horizon be exhibited in its most intimate development. Kant undertakes the revelation of the essential ground of ontological knowledge in the section which adjoins the transcendental deduction and is entitled: *The Schematism of the Pure Concepts of the Understanding.*[108]

This reference to the position occupied by the chapter on schematism within Kant's system and in the sequence of the stages of the laying of the foundation in itself reveals that these eleven pages of the *Critique of Pure Reason* form the heart of the whole work. Without doubt, the decisive importance of the Kantian theory of schematism first becomes obvious only on the basis of the interpretation of the content of this doctrine. This interpretation must let itself be guided by the fundamental problem of the transcendence of a finite being.

But, as before, Kant first introduces the problem in a form which is rather superficial, linking it to the question of the possible subsumption of phenomena under the categories. The justification of this procedure, in conformity with the treatment of the *quaestio juris,* must first await a working out of the internal dynamic of the problem of transcendence.

## § 19. *Transcendence and Sensibilization* [Versinnlichung]

If the essent is to be directly manifest to a finite being as something already on hand, then this being must be able to receive it. In order to be possible, reception demands something on the order of an act of orientation which cannot be arbitrary but must be of such a nature as to make possible the precursory encountering of the essent. But if the essent is to be capable of offering itself, the horizon within which it is encountered must itself have an offering-character [*Angebotcharakter*]. This act

108. A 137–148, B 176–187, NKS, pp. 180–8.

of orientation must in itself be an anticipatory proposition of something which has the nature of an offer.

If the horizon of ob-jectification is to be capable of fulfilling its function, this offering-character must have a certain perceptibility. By "perceptible" we mean that which is capable of being immediately received by intuition. Hence, the horizon in its character as a perceptible offer must present itself in advance and constantly as pure aspect [*Anblick*]. It follows that the act of ob-jectification of the finite understanding must offer objectivity as such in an intuitive manner, i.e., that the pure understanding must be based upon a pure intuition that sustains and guides it.

But what is necessary in order that the horizon of the precursory act of orientation be made perceptible? A finite being must have the power of making the horizon intuitive, i.e., of "forming" spontaneously the aspect of that which is capable of offering itself. However, if as the transcendental deduction indicates, pure intuition (time) stands in an essential relation to the pure synthesis, then the pure imagination brings about the formation of the aspect characteristic of the horizon. Not only does the pure imagination "form" the intuitive perceptibility of the horizon, in that it "creates" this horizon by the free turning-toward, but also in this act it is "formative" [*bildend*] in yet a second sense, namely, in that it provides for the possibility of an "image" [*Bild*] in general.

The expression "image" is to be taken here in its most basic sense, according to which we say that a landscape presents a beautiful "image" (aspect) or that a group presents a pitiful "image" (aspect). And in the course of the second way of the deduction which proceeds from the internal connection of time and pure imagination, Kant has already stated of the imagination that it "has to bring . . . into the form of an image." [109]

In the occurrence of this double formation of an image (the

109. A 120, NKS, p. 144.

95

production of an aspect) the ground of the possibility of transcendence first becomes visible. This occurrence also renders intelligible the aspect-character necessary to the essence of transcendence, this essence being precursory, ob-jective, and of the nature of an offer. But transcendence is, in truth, finitude itself. If in the act of ob-jectification, transcendence is to render intuitive the horizon formed in this way, finite intuition being equivalent to sensibility, then to offer an aspect is to make the horizon sensible. The horizon of transcendence can be formed only in a sensibilization.

The act of ob-jectification is, considered from the point of view of the pure understanding, an act of representation of unities which, as such, regulate all modes of unification. Transcendence is formed, therefore, in the sensibilization of pure concepts. And since transcendence consists in a precursory act of orientation, this sensibilization must likewise be pure.

Pure sensibilization takes place as a "schematism." Pure imagination in forming the schema gives in advance the aspect (image) of the horizon of transcendence. That the reference to such a sensibilization is not sufficient, if one does not first know its essence, follows from the very idea of sensibilization, quite apart from the fact that this sensibilization can never actually be exhibited.

Sensibility for Kant means finite intuition. Pure sensibility must be an act of intuition such that it receives its object in advance, before all empirical reception. But the act of finite intuition as such is not able to create the essent intuited. Hence, sensibilization must be a reception of something which is formed in the very act of reception itself, i.e., it must be an aspect which, however, does not present the essent.

What, then, must be the character of that which is intuited in pure sensibility? Can it have the nature of an "image"? What is the meaning of this term "image"? How is the aspect, the pure schema, "formed" in pure imagination, to be distinguished from an image? And finally, and in spite of everything, in what sense can the schema be called an "image"? Without a preliminary interpretation of these phenomena relative to sensibilization, the notion of schematism as the basis of transcendence remains wrapped in complete obscurity.

## § 20. Image and Schema

In general, sensibilization denotes the manner in which a finite being is able to make something intuitive, i.e., is able to procure an aspect (image) of something. The significance of the aspect or image differs according to the nature of what is presented and the mode of this presentation.

Ordinarily, the term "image" means: the aspect of a definite essent so far as it is manifest as something actually present. This essent offers an aspect [of itself]. In a secondary sense, "image" can also mean an aspect which reproduces something either now or no longer given; in still another sense, the term in question can refer to an aspect which provides a model for something yet to be produced.

In addition, the term "image" can have the very broad meaning of "aspect in general" wherein it is not stated whether something essent or non-essent is thereby made intuitable.

In fact, Kant uses the expression "image" in all three of these senses: as an immediate aspect of an essent, as a given reproductive aspect of an essent, and finally as an aspect of something in general. But these different senses of the word "image" are not expressly distinguished from one another. Indeed, it is even doubtful whether the different significations and modalities [of the word] which have just been enumerated are sufficient to clarify that which Kant discusses under the heading of schematism.

The most common mode of procuring an aspect (forming an image) is the empirical intuition of that which reveals itself. In this case, what reveals itself always has the character of an immediately intuited particular (a "this-here"). To be sure, this does not exclude the possibility of intuiting a plurality of "this-here's" which together constitute a richer "this-here," for example, this landscape as an individual totality. The landscape is called a view [aspect] (image), *species,* just as if it viewed us. An image, therefore, is always an intuitable "this-here." On this account, every image having the character of a reproduction, for example, a photograph, is only a copy of that which reveals itself immediately as the "image."

The expression "image" is also frequently employed in this second sense of reproduction. This thing here, this given photograph *qua* this thing immediately presents an aspect; it is an image in the first and broader sense of the term. But in revealing itself, it also reveals that which it reproduces. According to this second sense, to procure an "image" no longer signifies merely the immediate intuition of an essent but such activities, for example, as taking a photograph or purchasing one.

From such a reproduction, it is possible to make a new reproduction, e.g., one may photograph a death mask. This second reproduction immediately represents the death mask and thus reveals the "image" (the immediate aspect) of the deceased himself. The photograph of the death mask as the reproduction of a reproduction is itself an image but only because it provides an "image" of the dead, i.e., shows how the dead person appears or, rather, appeared. Sensibilization, according to the meanings of the expression "image" thus far differentiated, sometimes refers to the mode of immediate empirical intuition and sometimes to the mode of immediate apprehension of a reproduction presenting the aspect of an essent.

But a photograph is also capable of showing how something resembling a death mask appears in general. The death mask is also able to reveal in its turn how in general the face of a corpse appears. But a particular corpse can also reveal this.

98

The mask itself is also able to show how a death mask in general looks, just as the photograph is able to reveal not only the object photographed but also how a photograph in general looks.

But what do all these aspects (images in the broadest sense) of this dead man, of this mask, and of this photograph reveal? Which "appearances" (*eidos, idea*) do they furnish us? What do they make sensible? They reveal how something appears "in general" through the *one* which applies to many. But the unity which applies to many is what the representation represents according to the modality of concepts. These aspects, then, are to provide for the sensibilization of concepts.

But sensibilization in this sense can no longer mean the procuring of an immediate aspect or intuition of a concept. A concept as a represented universal may not be represented by a *repraesentatio singularis,* which is what an intuition always is. This is why a concept by its very essence cannot be put into an image.

But in general, what does the sensibilization of a concept signify? What pertains thereto? How does the aspect of an essent either empirically present or represented or reproduced share in such a sensibilization?

We say, for example, that this house which we perceive reveals how a house appears in general, consequently that which we represent in the concept "house." But in what way does the aspect of this house reveal the *how* of the appearance of a house in general? The house itself, indeed, presents a definite aspect. But we do not have to lose ourselves in this particular house in order to know exactly how it appears. On the contrary, this particular house is revealed as such that, in order to be a house, it need not necessarily appear as, in fact, it does appear. It reveals to us "only" the "how" of the possible appearance of a house.

It is this "how" of the possibility of the actual appearance

99

which we represent to ourselves in connection with this particular house. A house can appear thus. By its appearance, this actual house has restricted the range of possible appearances to one particular appearance. But the result of this "decision" interests us just as little as the result of those which turn upon the actual appearance of other houses. What does interest us is the range of possible modes of appearance as such: more precisely, that which delimits this range, i.e., that which regulates and predetermines how, in general, something must appear in order to be able, as a house, to present an aspect corresponding to its nature. This predetermination of the rule is not a description which simply enumerates the "characteristics" which one finds in a house but is a "distinguishing characteristic" [*Auszeichnen*] of the whole of that which is intended by "house."

But what is thus intended can, in general, be so intended only if it is represented as something which regulates the possible insertion of this complex [the house] into an empirical aspect. The unity of a concept, insofar as it is unifying, that is, applies to many, can be represented only by the representation of the way in which the rule prescribes the insertion of this pattern into a possible aspect. If, in general, a concept is that which serves as a rule, then conceptual representation is the supplying, in advance, of the rule insofar as it provides an aspect corresponding to the specific way in which it regulates. Such a representation is referred by a structural necessity to a possible aspect and hence is in itself a particular mode of sensibilization.

Sensibilization does not give an immediate, intuitive aspect of a concept. The immediate aspect which is necessarily called forth with it is, properly speaking, not intended as such but appears as the possible object of the presentation whose mode of regulation is represented. The rule is made manifest in the empirical aspect precisely according to the mode of its regulation.

Sensibilization, however, does not give us an immediate aspect of the concept as unity. This unity is not even thematically intended as the content of an autonomous representation. What this conceptual unity can and must be as unifying, it manifests only as regulative. This unity is never apprehended in itself and, furthermore, it is perceived as essentially determining the regulation only if it is not considered in itself but in the exercise of its regulative function. In not considering this unity in itself in this way, we do not lose sight of it; on the contrary, by apprehending the exercise of this function we are able to perceive the unity as regulative.

The representation of the regulative action as such is true conceptual representation. What has hitherto been so termed, namely, the representation of a unity which applies to many, was only an isolated element of the concept which, with regard to its function as the rule which governs the specific act of sensibilization just described, remains concealed.

However, if what is thematically represented in sensibilization is neither the empirical aspect nor the isolated concept, but the "index" of the rule which is the source of the image, then this index must be examined more closely. The rule is represented in the *how* of its regulation, that is, according to the manner in which, in regulating the presentation, it inserts itself in, and imposes itself on, the aspect which presents the presentation. The act of representation of the *how* of the regulation is the free (i.e., not bound to a definite representation) "construction" [*Bilden*] of a sensibilization. The latter, in the sense just described, is the source of the image.

Such sensibilization takes place primarily in the imagination. "This representation of a universal procedure of imagination in providing an image for a concept I entitle the schema of this concept." [110] The formation of a schema insofar as it is accomplished as a mode of sensibilization is called *schematism*. To be sure, the schema is to be distinguished from the image,

110. A 140, B 179f., NKS, p. 182.

but it is also related to the latter, i.e., the schema necessarily possesses the character of an image. This character has its own nature. It is neither only a simple aspect (an "image" in the first sense) nor a reproduction (an "image" in the second sense). It will be called, therefore, the schema-image.

## § 21. Schema and Schema-Image

A more precise characterization of the schema-image will serve to clarify both its relationship to the schema and, at the same time, the nature of the relation of the concept to the image.

The formation of schemata is the sensibilization of concepts. What is the relation between the aspect of an essent immediately represented and that which is represented of it in the concept? In what sense is this aspect an "image" of the concept? This question will be discussed with respect to two kinds of concepts, namely, those which are sensible and empirical (e.g., the concept of a dog) and those which are sensible and pure, the mathematical concepts (e.g., the concept of a triangle or of a number).

Kant stressed that an "object of experience" (the aspect accessible to us of a thing actually on hand) "or an image of such a thing" (an actual reproduction or copy of an essent) never "attains" [111] the empirical concept of the thing. Not attaining the concept means, first of all, not presenting it "adequately." But this does not mean that no adequate reproduction of the concept is possible. With reference to the corresponding concept, an empirical aspect of an essent can, in general, have no reproductive function. This inadequacy pertains rather to the schema-image, which, in the proper sense of the term, is the image of the concept. To be sure, the empirical aspect contains everything in the concept, if not more. But the aspect does not contain its object in the manner in which the concept represents

111. A 141, B 180, NKS, p. 182.

it, i.e., as the one which applies to many. The content of the empirical aspect is presented as being one thing among many, i.e., as particularized by that which is thematically represented as such. This particular has renounced the possibility of being just anything and, by this means, has become a possible example for the one which regulates the indifferent many. In this act of regulation, however, the general acquires its own specifically articulated determination and is in no way to be contrasted with the particular as being an indeterminate and confused "everything and anything."

The representation of the rule is the schema. As such, it necessarily remains relative to a possible schema-image to which no particular thing can claim to be the only possible [example]. "The concept 'dog' signifies a rule according to which my imagination can delineate the figure of a four-footed animal in a general manner, without limitation to any determinate figure such as experience, or any possible image that I can represent *in concreto* actually presents." [112] That the empirical aspect is not adequate to its empirical concept is an expression of the positive structural relation of the schema-image to the schema. This relation makes the schema-image a possible presentation of the rule of presentation represented in the schema. This means, at the same time, that beyond the representation of this regulative unity the concept is nothing. What in logic is termed a concept is based upon the schema. The concept "always refers directly to the schema." [113]

Kant states of the empirical object that it is "even less" adequate to its concept than is the "image" of the pure sensible concept to this concept itself. Can we conclude from this, then, that the schema-images of the mathematical concepts are adequate to their concepts? Obviously, one should not in this case think of this adequacy in the sense of a reproduction. The

112. *Ibid.*
113. A 141, B 180, NKS, p. 182f.

schema-image of a mathematical construction is valid whether or not it is empirically exact or crudely sketched.[114]

Obviously, Kant is thinking about the fact that a mathematical schema-image, e.g., a given triangle, must be either acute, right, or obtuse. These suffice to exhaust the possibilities of a triangle, whereas the possibilities are much more numerous when it is a matter of the presentation of a house. On the other hand, the range of presentability of an acute or a right triangle is more extensive. Hence, by its limitation such a schema-image approaches nearer to the unity of a concept, while by its greater extension it approaches nearer to the generality of this unity. But, however it may be, the image still has the appearance of a particular, while the schema-image has "as its intention" the unity of the general rule governing all possible presentations.

What is essential concerning the schema-image first becomes clear from the following: The image does not derive its intuitive character [*Anblickscharakter*] uniquely or in the first place from the content of this image. Rather, this intuitive character results both from the fact that the schema-image comes into being and from the way in which it comes into being from a possible presentation which is represented in its regulative function, thus bringing the rule within the sphere of a possible intuition.

Only when the expression "image" is understood in this sense of schema-image may five points . . . . . taken one after the others be called "an image of the number five." [115] The number itself never assumes the aspect of these five points, and also it never assumes that of the symbol "5" or the symbol "V." Doubtless, these symbols are in another way aspects of the number in question, but it should be noted that although the symbol "5" delineated in space has nothing in common with the number, the aspect of the five points . . . . . is numerable

114. *Über eine Entdeckung, ibid.*, p. 8, note.
115. A 140, B 179, NKS, p. 182.

through the number five. To be sure, this series of points does not manifest the number merely because it can be run through and because we are apparently able to take the number from it but because this series coincides with the representation of the rule of the possible presentation of this number.

However, we do not first apprehend this number by reason of this coincidence; rather, we possess this number beforehand —as we do all numbers—in the "representation of a method whereby a multiplicity, for instance a thousand, may be represented in an image in conformity with a certain concept." [116] The possibility of the image is already formed in the act of representing the rule of presentation. This possibility itself, not the isolated aspect of a multiplicity of points, is the true aspect, the aspect structurally inherent in the schema, the schema-image. Whether or not it is possible to take in at a glance a series of points, either actually set down or merely imagined, is without importance insofar as the "perception" of the schema-image is concerned.

This is also why mathematical concepts are never based on immediately perceptible images but on schemata. "Indeed, it is schemata, not images of objects, which underlie our pure sensible concepts." [117]

The analysis of the image-character of the schema-image of empirical as well as pure sensible concepts has led us to the following conclusion: The sensibilization of concepts is a completely specific operation which yields images of a particular kind. Sensibilization as productive of schemata can neither be understood by analogy with the usual "putting into an image" nor can it be traced back to this idea. Such a reduction is so little feasible that, on the contrary, sensibilization in the sense first described—the immediate, empirical perception of things and the formation of empirical reproductions of these things—

116. A 140, B 179, NKS, p. 182.
117. *Ibid.*

can take place only on the basis of a possible sensibilization of concepts in the manner in which this is accomplished in schematism.

All conceptual representation is essentially schematism. Now, all finite cognition is, as thinking intuition, necessarily conceptual. Necessarily contained, therefore, in the immediate perception of a given thing, for example, this house, is the schematizing, preliminary insight [*Vorblick*] into such a thing as a house in general. It is by means of this re-presentation [*Vorstellung*] alone that what is encountered can reveal itself as a house, i.e., can present the aspect of a given house. Thus, schematism takes place necessarily because our cognition is fundamentally a finite cognition. This is why Kant must state, "This schematism . . . is an art concealed in the depths of the human soul." [118] Hence, if schematism belongs to the essence of finite knowledge, and if finitude is centered in transcendence, then transcendence must take place as a schematism. Therefore, Kant must necessarily be concerned with a "transcendental schematism" as soon as he tries to bring to light the intrinsic possibility of transcendence.

## § 22. *The Transcendental Schematism*

The general characterization of schematism as a specific mode of sensibilization has shown that schematism belongs necessarily to transcendence. On the other hand, the characterization of the total structure of ontological knowledge, which last necessarily is intuition, has led to the following insight: Sensibilization belongs necessarily to transcendence and this sensiblization must be pure. We have affirmed that this pure sensibilization takes place as a schematism. It is a question now of confirming the assertion by proving that the necessary, pure sensibilization of the understanding and its concepts (notions) is brought about

118. A 141, B 180, NKS, p. 183.

in a transcendental schematism. The nature of this schematism will be brought to light by the revelation of the manner in which it takes place.

The function of the mode of sensibilization which forms schemata is to procure an image for a given concept. What is intended by the concept has, therefore, an ordered relation to some intuitivity [*Erblickbarkeit*] and first becomes perceptible through this intuitive character. The schema puts itself, i.e., puts the concept, into an image. The pure concepts of the understanding which are thought in the pure "I think" require an essentially pure intuitivity, if that which stands opposite as the result of the pure act of ob-jectification is to be perceptible as such. Pure concepts must be grounded in pure schemata which procure an image for these concepts.

But Kant says expressly: "On the other hand, the schema of a *pure* concept of understanding can never be reduced to any image whatsoever." [119] If to be put into an image belongs to the nature of a schema, then the expression "image" in the sentence quoted above must signify a definite type of image to the exclusion of all others. It is immediately evident that it can only be a question here of the schema-image. Thus, to deny the possibility of forming the schemata of notions into images means merely to deny that the presentable aspect, whose rule of presentation is represented in the schema of the notion, can ever be drawn from the domain of the empirically intuitive. If "image" is taken to mean "empirical aspect" in the broadest sense of the term, then obviously the schema of a notion cannot be put "into an image." Even the aspects which are associated with the mathematical construction of concepts are, as images of "quantities," limited to a particular realm of objectivity. Moreover, the notions as fundamental concepts cannot be put into such images. These notions represent those rules by means of which objectivity in general is formed as the precursory

119. A 142, B 181, NKS, p. 183.

107

horizon which makes the encountering of objects possible. In the phrase cited, the term "image" signifies those schema-images which are attached to the schemata of empirical and mathematical concepts. The schemata of the pure concept of the understanding cannot be put into such images.

The elucidation of the intrinsic possibility of ontological knowledge in the transcendental deduction has yielded the following: Pure concepts through the mediation of the pure synthesis of the transcendental imagination are essentially related to pure intuition (time), and this relation is reciprocal. Up to now, only the essential necessity of the relation between the notions and time has been discussed. However, the internal structure of this relation as that which is constitutive of the fundamental articulation of transcendence has not yet been clarified.

As pure intuition, time is that which furnishes an aspect prior to all experience. This is why the pure aspect (for Kant, the pure succession of the *now*-sequence) which presents itself in such pure intuition must be termed a pure image. And in the chapter on schematism, Kant himself states: "The pure image of . . . all objects of the senses in general [is] time." [120] Moreover, the same idea is expressed further on in a passage no less important where Kant defines the essence of the notion. The notion is "the pure concept, insofar as it has its origin in the understanding alone (not in the pure image of sensibility)." [121]

Thus, even the schema of a pure concept of the understanding can very well be put into an image, provided that the term "image" be taken in the sense of "pure image."

As a "pure image" time is the schema-image and not merely the form of pure intuition corresponding to the pure concepts of the understanding. Consequently, the schema of the notions has a special character. As a schema in general it represents

120. A 142, B 182, NKS, p. 183.
121. A 320, B 377, NKS, p. 314.

108

unities, and it represents them as rules which bear upon a possible aspect. According to the transcendental deduction, the unities represented in the notions have an essential and necessary relation to time. The schematism of the pure concepts of the understanding, therefore, must necessarily introduce these concepts into time as the rules thereof. But time, as the transcendental aesthetic shows, is the representation of a "single object." [122] "Different times are but parts of one and the same time; and the representation, which can be given only through a single object, is intuition." [123] Hence, time is not only the necessarily pure image of the schemata of the pure concepts of the understanding but also their only possibility of [presenting] a pure aspect. This unique possibility of presenting an aspect reveals itself to be nothing other than time and the temporal.

Now, if the closed multiplicity of the pure concepts of the understanding is to have its image in this unique possibility of presenting an aspect, this unique pure image must be capable of being formed in a multiple way. The schemata of the notions derive their image from time taken as a pure aspect by introducing them in time under the form of rules. The schemata thus develop the unique possibility of a pure aspect into a multiplicity of pure images. In this sense, the schemata of the pure concepts of the understanding "determine" time. "The schemata are thus nothing but *a priori* determinations of time in accordance with rules," [124] or, more simply, "transcendental determinations of time." [125] As such, they are a "transcendental product of the imagination." [126] This schematism forms transcendence *a priori* and, therefore, is termed "transcendental schematism."

122. A 31f., B 47, NKS, p. 75.
123. A 31f., B 47, NKS, p. 75.
124. A 145, B 184, NKS, p. 185.
125. A 138, NKS, p. 181.
126. A 142, B 181, NKS, p. 183.

The ob-jectification of that which offers itself as ob-ject, i.e., that which is in opposition, takes place in transcendence and in this way: Ontological knowledge as schematizing intuition renders distinguishable and, hence, receivable *a priori* the transcendental affinity of the rule of unity under the image of time. Because of its pure schema-image, the transcendental schema necessarily possesses an *a priori* correspondence-character. In consequence, the interpretations of the individual pure schemata as transcendental determinations of time must exhibit the character which is constitutive of this correspondence.

Now, Kant borrows the systematic unity of the pure concepts of the understanding from the table of judgments and, accordingly, gives the definitions of the schemata of the individual pure concepts of the understanding to the table of notions. Corresponding to the four moments of the division of the categories (quantity, quality, relation, and modality), the pure aspect of time must exhibit four possibilities of taking form, namely, "the *time-series,* the *time-content,* the *time-order,* and lastly, the *scope of time.*" [127] These characters of time are not so much developed systematically through an analysis of time itself as they are fixed in time following "the order of the categories." [128] The interpretation of the individual schemata [129] begins with a relatively detailed analysis of the pure schemata of quantity, reality, and substance and then becomes ever more concise until it finally ends with mere definitions.

In a certain sense, Kant has a right to such a summary presentation. If the transcendental schematism determines the essence of ontological knowledge, then the systematic elaboration of ontological concepts in the presentation of the system of synthetic principles *a priori* must necessarily hit upon the structure of schematism and bring to light the corresponding tran-

127. A 145, B 184f., NKS, p. 183.
128. *Ibid.*
129. A 142ff., B 182ff., NKS, p. 183ff.

scendental determinations of time. This in fact takes place, although only within certain limits.[130]

It is easy to see that the more light one throws on the structures essential to the transcendental schematism and, in general, all that pertains to transcendence as a whole, the better he is able to find his way in the obscurity which envelops these primordial structures "in the depths of the human soul." Without doubt, the nature of schematism in general, and of transcendental schematism in particular, has been determined with sufficient precision. However, one of Kant's own remarks reveals that this inquiry can be pursued further. "That we may not be further delayed by a dry and tedious analysis of the conditions demanded by transcendental schemata of the pure concepts of understanding in general, we shall now expound them according to the order of the categories and in connection with them." [131]

Is it only the dryness and tediousness of this analysis that deters Kant from a further determination? The answer to this question cannot be given as yet.[132] When it is given, it will also explain why the present interpretation refrains from any attempt to develop concretely the Kantian definitions of the pure schemata. However, in order to show that the Kantian doctrine of the transcendental schematism is no artificial theory but has its origin in the phenomena themselves, an interpretation—brief and rough, to be sure—of the transcendental schema of a particular category, that of substance, will be given.

"The schema of substance is the permanence of the real in time." [133] For the full elucidation of the schematism of this schema, it is necessary to refer to the *First Analogy,* i.e., the *Principles of Permanence of Substance.*

Substance as a notion signifies first of all only "that which

130. A 158ff., B 197ff., NKS, p. 194ff.
131. A 142, B 181, NKS, p. 183.
132. See below, § 35, p. 201.
133. A 144, B 183, NKS, p. 84.

111

underlies" (the subsistent).[134] Its schema must be the representation of subsistence so far as this schema is presented in the pure image of time. But time as the pure *now*-sequence is ever now. That is, in every *now* it is now. Time thus manifests its own constancy. As such, time is "non-transitory and abiding" "while all else changes." [135] More precisely: time is not one permanent thing among others, but by virtue of the essential character just mentioned—that it is now in every *now*—it provides the pure aspect of permanence in general. As this pure image (an immediate, pure "aspect") it presents the subsistent in pure intuition.

This function of presentation does not become entirely clear unless the full content of the notion of substance is considered, something Kant neglects to do here. Substance is a category of "relation" (between subsistence and inherence). It signifies that which subsists for an "accident." Time, therefore, forms the pure image of substance only if it presents this relation in the pure image.

But time exists as a *now*-sequence precisely because, flowing across each *now,* it remains a *now* even while becoming another *now*. As the aspect of the permanent, it offers at the same time the image of pure change in permanence.

Even this rough interpretation of the transcendental schema of substance, an interpretation which at best cannot uncover the primordial structure, reveals that that to which the notion of substance refers can be given a pure image *a priori* in time. By this means, objectivity, so far as substance belongs to it as a constitutive element, becomes visible and perceptible *a priori* in the act of ob-jectification. Thanks to this schematism, the notion as schematized is held in view in advance so that in this precursory view of the pure image of permanence, an essent can manifest itself to experience as that which remains invariable through change. "To time, itself non-transitory and

134. A 182ff., B 224ff., NKS, p. 212ff.
135. A 143, B 183, NKS, p. 184.

abiding, there corresponds in the field of appearance what is non-transitory in its existence" (i.e., in the given essent).[136]

Consequently, the transcendental schematism is the basis of the intrinsic possibility of ontological knowledge. It creates the object which takes up a position opposite to . . . in this pure act of ob-jectification and in such a way that what is represented in pure thought is necessarily given in an intuitive form in the pure image of time. As that which presents something [gebende] a priori, time bestows in advance on the horizon of transcendence the character of a perceptible offer. But this is not all. As the sole, pure, universal image, time gives the horizon of transcendence a precursory inclusiveness [Umschlossenheit]. This unique, pure, ontological horizon is the condition of the possibility that an essent within it can have this or that particular overt and ontic horizon. Time not only gives transcendence a precursory unifying cohesion but as the pure self-giving [sich Gebende] offers it, in general, something on the order of a check [Einhalt]. Times makes perceptible to a finite being the "opposition" of ob-jectivity, which opposition belongs to the finitude of that act of orientation by which transcendence takes place.

## § 23. Schematism and Subsumption

In the preceding pages the Kantian doctrine of the schematism of the pure concepts of the understanding was interpreted in the light of the intrinsic development of transcendence. Now, in his laying of the foundation of metaphysics, Kant not only strives to develop a problematic which renews itself at every step but also when introducing a decisive element of his doctrine confines himself to the most possible of the known formulations capable of presenting the problem. Thus, the transcendental deduction begins as a "legal action" within traditional metaphysics. This

136. A 143, B 183, NKS, p. 184.

action is decided by the proof that the notions must be categories, i.e., that they must belong essentially to transcendence itself if they are to be capable of the determination *a priori* of essents which are empirically accessible. At the same time, however, the condition of the "use" of these concepts is fixed.

To make use of concepts signifies in general; to apply them to objects or—from the point of view of the objects—to bring them "under" concepts. Traditional logic calls this use of concepts "subsumption." The use of pure concepts as transcendental determinations of time *a priori,* i.e., the achievement of pure knowledge, is what takes place in schematism. In fact, seen from this point of view, the problem of schematism may be explained, to begin with at least, by reference to subsumption. But it must be remembered that, from the first, it is a question here—in ontological knowledge—of ontological concepts and therefore of a specific, that is, ontological "subsumption."

But from the very first characterization of ontological knowledge,[137] Kant has not neglected to draw our attention to the fundamental difference between "bringing under concepts" [*unter Begriffe bringen*] (that which concerns objects) and "reducing to concepts" [*auf Begriffe bringen*] (that which concerns the pure synthesis of the transcendental imagination). "The reduction to concepts" of the pure synthesis takes place in the transcendental schematism. It "forms" [*bildet*] the unity represented in the notion in order to make it the essential element of pure objectivity, i.e., that objectivity which can be perceived *a priori.* Only in the transcendental schematism are the categories formed as categories. If the latter are the true "fundamental concepts" [*Urbegriffe*] then the transcendental schematism is primordial and authentic conceptualization as such.

Therefore, if Kant begins the chapter on schematism with a reference to subsumption, it is because he wishes to introduce transcendental subsumption as the central problem in order

137. *Cf.* A 78ff., B 104ff., NKS, p. 111ff.

114

to show that the question of the intrinsic possibility of primordial conceptuality arises in the essential structure of pure knowledge.

Empirical concepts are derived from experience and on that account are "homogeneous" with the content of the essent which they determine. Their application to objects, their use, poses no problem. "But pure concepts of understanding being quite heterogeneous with empirical intuitions, and indeed with all sensible intuitions, can never be met with in any intuition. For no one will say that a category, such as that of causality, can be intuited through sense and is itself contained in appearance. How, then, is the *subsumption* of intuitions under pure concepts, the *application* of a category to appearances, possible?" [138] It is in raising the question of the possible use of the categories that their true essence first becomes a problem. These concepts lay before us the question of the possibility of their "formation" in general. This is why speaking of the subsumption of phenomena "under the categories" is not a solution of the problem but conceals the very question at issue, namely, that of the sense in which one may speak here of subsumption "under concepts."

If the Kantian formulation of the problem of schematism as a problem of subsumption is taken simply in the sense of an introduction to the problem, then this formulation provides a clue as to the central purpose and essential content of the chapter on schematism.

To represent conceptually means to represent "in general." The "generality" of the act of representation becomes a problem as soon as the formation of concepts as such is called into question. But if the categories as ontological concepts are not homogeneous with the empirical objects and their concepts, then the "generality" of the categories is not merely that of a higher degree of abstraction, that possessed by a superior, or even a supreme, ontic "genus." [139] What, therefore, is the character of the "generality" enjoyed by ontological, i.e., meta-

138. A 137f., B 176f., NKS, p. 180.
139. *Cf. Sein und Zeit,* p. 3 (J. S. C.).

physical concepts? But this is really the question: What is the meaning of the term *generalis* in the characterization of ontology as *metaphysica generalis?* The problem of the schematism of the pure concepts of the understanding is a question concerning the inmost essence of ontological knowledge.

If Kant, in the chapter on schematism, poses the problem of the conceptuality of the fundamental concepts and resolves it with the help of the essential definition of these concepts as transcendental schemata, it is evident that the doctrine of the schematism of the pure concepts of the understanding is the decisive stage of the laying of the foundation of *metaphysica generalis.*

To a certain extent, however, Kant is justified in relying on the idea of subsumption to furnish a preliminary explication of the transcendental schematism. Consequently, Kant may also be permitted to derive from this idea an indication as to the possible solution of the problem and to provide a provisional characterization of the idea of transcendental schematism [in terms of subsumption]. If the pure concept of the understanding is completely heterogeneous with the phenomena but still determines the latter, then there must be a mediating agency which surmounts this heterogeneity. "This mediative representation must be pure, i.e., void of all empirical content, and yet at the same time, while it must in one respect be *intellectual*, it must in another be *sensible*. Such a representation is the *transcendental schema.*" [140] "Thus, an application of the category to appearances becomes possible by means of the transcendental determination of time, which, as the *schema* of the concepts of the understanding, mediates the subsumption of the appearances under the category." [141]

Thus, even the most immediate and superficial form of the problem of schematism, i.e., when it is considered as a problem

140. A 138, B 177, NKS, p. 181.
141. A 139, B 178, NKS, p. 181.

116

of subsumption, reveals the innermost significance of the transcendental schematism. There is not the slightest reason to complain unceasingly about the alleged incoherence and confusion of the chapter on schematism. If, in the *Critique of Pure Reason,* there is one passage weighed word by word and rigorously organized, it is certainly this part of the whole work. Because of its importance, this organization is reproduced explicitly below:

1) The introduction to the problem of schematism under the guidance of the traditional idea of subsumption (A 137, B 176; A 140, B 179; NKS, pp. 180–182: "The schema in itself is . . .").

2) The preliminary analysis of the structure of the schema in general and the schematism of the empirical and mathematical concepts (to A 142, B 161, NKS, p. 180: "On the other hand, the schema of a *pure* concept of the understanding . . .").

3) The analysis of the transcendental schema in general (to A 142, B 182, NKS, p. 183: "The pure image of all magnitudes . . .").

4) The interpretation of the particular transcendental schemata under the guidance of the table of categories (to A 145, B 184, NKS, p. 185: "We thus find that the schema of each category . . .").

5) The characterization of the four classes of categories relative to the corresponding four possibilities of the pure formation [*Bildbarkeit*] of time (to A 145, B 184, NKS, p. 119: "It is evident therefore . . .").

6) The definition of transcendental schematism as the "true and only condition" of transcendence (to A 146, B 185, NKS, p. 119: "But it is also evident . . .").

7) The critical application of the definition of the essence of the categories, a definition based on the idea of schematism (to the end of the chapter).

Far from being "confused," the chapter on schematism is

perfectly clear in its construction. It does not "generate confusion" but with a wonderful certainty leads to the heart of the whole problematic of the *Critique of Pure Reason*. This only becomes evident, however, when the finitude of transcendence is comprehended as the ground of the intrinsic possibility (i.e., of the necessity) of metaphysics so that the interpretation can be established on this basis.

To be sure, however, Kant wrote in his last years (1797): "In general, schematism is one of the most difficult points. Even Herr Beck cannot find his way about therein. —I hold this chapter to be one of the most important." [142]

## The Fifth Stage of the Laying of the Foundation: The Complete Determination of the Essence of Ontological Knowledge

In the preceding stages we have reached, with the transcendental schematism, the ground of the intrinsic possibility of the ontological synthesis, and we have thereby attained our objective. If we now add a fifth stage, this does not mean that we intend to pursue the laying of the foundation still further, but that it is necessary to take explicit possession of the ground thus won, with regard to the possible construction [of metaphysics].

To do this, we must comprehend the unity of the stages just traversed, not merely by adding them together, but by an autonomous and complete determination of the essence of ontological knowledge. Kant lays down this decisive determination in "the highest principle of all synthetic judgments." [143] How-

142. *Kant's Posthumous Works in Manuscript Form, op. cit.,* Vol. V, No. 6359.
143. A 154–158, B 193–197, NKS, pp. 191–4.

ever, if ontological knowledge is nothing other than the primordial formation of transcendence, the highest principle must contain the central determination of the essence of transcendence. That this is the case must now be shown. From the ground thus won, we shall obtain a prospect of the additional problems and consequences of the Kantian laying of the foundation of *metaphysica generalis*.

### § 24. The Highest Synthetic Principle as the Complete Determination of the Essence of Transcendence

This central part of the doctrine is also introduced by Kant in the form of a critical attitude taken with regard to traditional metaphysics. The latter lays claim to a knowledge of the essent "by means of pure concepts," that is, by thought alone. The specific essence of pure [*blossen*] thought is delimited by general logic. Pure thought is the connection of subject and object (in the act of judgment). Such connection only explicates what is represented as such in the connected representations. It must be purely explicative and nothing more because in it "We have merely played with representations." [144] In order to be what it is, pure thought must "remain" with what is represented as such. Without doubt, even in this isolation it has its own rules, namely, the principles, of which the first is the "principle of contradiction." [145] Pure thought is not knowledge; it is only an element, although a necessary one, of finite knowledge. However, provided it is taken only as an element of pure knowledge, it is possible to begin with pure thought and to show that it refers necessarily to something which in a primary sense determines knowledge in its totality.

Insofar as the predicate is an element of pure knowledge, it

144. A 155, B 195, NKS, p. 193.
145. A 150ff., B 189ff., NKS, p. 189ff.

119

is not so much a question of its relation to the subject (the apophantic-predicative synthesis) as of its "relation" (more precisely, the whole subject-predicate relationship) to "something altogether different." [146] This "something different" is the essent itself, with which knowledge—and therefore the judicative relation pertaining to it—must be "in accord." Knowledge, therefore, must "go beyond" that with which pure thought, as isolated in itself, must necessarily "remain." This "relation" to the totally different, Kant terms "synthesis" (the veritative synthesis). Knowledge as such is synthetic, since what is known is always something "totally different." But since the predicative-apophantic connection in pure thought can also be termed a synthesis, it is advisable to distinguish it, as has been done previously, from the synthesis which pertains specifically to knowledge, this synthesis being essentially that which brings forth (namely, the totally different).

This going-beyond to the "totally different," however, requires an immersion [Darinnensein] in a "medium" [147] within which this "totally different," that the knowing being itself is not and over which it is not master, can be encountered. That which constitutes the going-beyond, which orients [the knowing being] and makes this encounter possible, is described by Kant in the following terms: "There is only one whole in which all our representations are contained, namely, inner sense and its *a priori* form, time. The synthesis of representations rests on imagination, and their synthetic unity, which is required for judgment, on the unity of apperception." [148]

Here reappears that triplicity of elements which was introduced in the second stage of the laying of the foundation with the first characterization of the essential unity of ontological

146. A 154, B 193f., NKS, p. 192.
147. A 155, B 194, NKS, p. 192.
148. A 155, B 194, NKS, p. 192.

knowledge. The third and fourth stages have shown, however, how these three elements form a structural unity whose formative medium is the transcendental imagination. What is formed there is transcendence. If Kant, in order to provide a definitive explication of transcendence, recalls this triplicity, these elements may no longer be presented according to the order, still obscure, in which they were introduced in the second stage, but in the clarity of a structure which is finally revealed in the transcendental schematism. And if this fifth stage seems merely recapitulative, it also leads to our taking express possession of the essential unity of transcendence, which was only indicated as a problem in the second stage. This transcendence henceforth will become transparent to us, since it will be apprehended on the basis of its possibility.

Thus, Kant concentrates the entire problem of the essence of the finitude of knowledge in the concise formula of "the possibility of experience." [149] The term "experience" denotes the finite, receptive, intuitive knowledge of the essent. The essent must be given to knowledge as the ob-ject. However, the term "possibility" has in the expression "possibility of experience" a characteristic ambiguity.

The term "possible" in "possible experience" can be understood in terms of the distinction between "possible" and "real." But in the "possibility of experience," "possible" experience is no more a problem than is the "real;" both the one and the other are considered with regard to that which makes them possible in advance. The expression "possibility of experience" refers, therefore, to that which makes finite experience possible, i.e., experience which is not necessarily but contingently real. The possibility which renders this "contingent" experience possible is the *possibilitas* of traditional metaphysics and is identical with *essentia* or *realitas*. "Real definitions are derived from the

149. A 156ff., B 195ff., NKS, p. 193ff.

121

essence of the thing, from the primary ground of its possibility." They "serve to obtain knowledge of the thing relative to its intrinsic possibility." [150]

Hence, the "possibility of experience" denotes primarily the unified totality of that which makes finite knowledge essentially possible. "The *possibility of experience* is, then, what gives objective reality to all our *a priori* modes of knowledge." [151] Consequently, the possibility of experience is identical with transcendence. To delimit the latter in its full essence means to determine "the conditions of the possibility of experience."

"Experience," understood as the act and not the content of experience, is an act of receptive intuition which must let the essent be given. To give an object means to present it immediately in intuition.[152] But what is the significance of this? Kant answers: "that the representation through which the object is thought relates to actual or possible experience." [153] But this relating-to means that in order for an object to be capable of being given, there must take place in advance an orientation toward that which is capable of being "called up." This precursory orientation takes place as the transcendental deduction revealed and the transcendental schematism explained in the ontological synthesis. This act of orientation toward . . . is the condition of the possibility of experience.

But the possibility of finite knowledge requires a second condition: knowledge is knowledge only when it is true. Truth, however, means "agreement with the object." [154] There must, therefore, be encountered in advance something on the order of a with-what [*Womit*] of the possible agreement, i.e., something

150. *Logikvorlesung,* § 106, note 2, *loc. cit.,* VIII, p. 447; *cf.* also B 302, note, A 596, B 624, note, NKS, p. 503.
151. A 156, B 195, NKS, p. 193.
152. A 156, B 195, NKS, p. 193.
153. *Ibid.*
154. A 157, B 196f., NKS, p. 194.

which regulates and provides a standard. It is necessary from the first that the horizon of the ob-jective be overt and perceptible as such. This horizon is the condition of the possibility of the object relative to its being able to take up a position opposite to. . . .

Consequently, the possibility of finite knowledge, that is, the act of experiencing that which is experienced as such, stands under two conditions. These two conditions together must delimit the complete essence of transcendence. This delimitation can be expressed in one proposition which states the ground of the possibility of synthetic judgments, i.e., judgments characteristic of finite knowledge. This is a proposition which as such is valid for all "judgments."

What is the definitive formulation given by Kant to this "highest principle of all synthetic judgments?" It reads as follows: "the conditions of the *possibility of experience* in general are at the same time conditions of the *possibility of the objects of experience.*" [155]

The decisive content of this sentence is not so much to be found in the words italicized by Kant as in the "are at the same time." For what does this "at the same time" signify? It expresses the essential unity of the complete structure of transcendence which lies in this: the act of orientation which lets something take up a position opposite to . . . forms as such the horizon of ob-jectivity in general. The going-beyond to . . . , which in finite knowledge is necessary in advance and at every moment, is accordingly a constant ex-position [*Hinausstehen*] to . . . (*Ekstasis*). But this essential ex-position to . . . in its position [*Stehen*] forms and pro-poses to itself a horizon. Transcendence is in itself ecstatic-horizontal. This articulation of transcendence, which last in itself is conducive to unity, is expressed by the highest principle.

155. A 158, B 197, NKS, p. 194. Kemp Smith's translation omits "at the same time" [*Zugleich*] (J. S. C.).

The latter may also be grasped in the following form: that which makes the act of experience possible at the same time makes possible the content of experience, i.e., the object of experience as such. This means that transcendence makes the essent in itself accessible to a finite being. The "at the same time" in the formulation of the highest synthetic principle does not signify that the two conditions always occur together, or that if we think of the one we must also think of the other, or even that both conditions are identical. The fundamental principle is in general not a principle found by inference and one which must be held to be valid if the validity of experience is to be defended. Rather, it is the expression of the original phenomenological knowledge of the intrinsic unitary structure of transcendence. This structure has been worked out in the stages of the essential development of the ontological synthesis already presented.[156]

## § 25. Transcendence and the Laying of the Foundation of Metaphysica Generalis

The revelation of the ground of the intrinsic possibility of the essence of the ontological synthesis was defined as the task of the laying of the foundation of *metaphysica generalis*. Ontological knowledge has proved to be that which forms transcendence. The insight into the complete structure of transcendence permits us for the first time to be aware of the complete

156. The foregoing interpretation of the highest synthetic principle shows in what respect this principle also determines the essence of *a priori* synthetic judgments and, in addition, can be considered as the metaphysical principle of *sufficient reason* when the latter is correctly understood. *Cf.* on this subject: Heidegger, *Vom Wesen des Grundes, Festschrift* f. E. Husserl. (*Ergänzungsbd. z. Jahrb. f. Philos. und phänomenolog. Forsch.*, 1929, p. 71ff., esp. p. 79f.) (This study also appeared in a special printing, 3rd ed., 1949, p. 15f.)

originality of ontological knowledge—its act as well as its object.

As finite, the act of knowledge must be a receptive, reflective intuition of that which offers itself; furthermore, this intuition must be pure. It is a pure schematism. The pure unity of the three elements of pure knowledge is expressed in the concept of the transcendental schema as the "transcendental determination of time."

If ontological knowledge is schema-forming, then it creates [forms] spontaneously the pure aspect (image). Does it not follow, then, that ontological knowledge, which is achieved in the transcendental imagination, is creative? And if ontological knowledge forms transcendence which in its turn constitutes the essence of finitude, is not this finitude "overcome" by the creative character in question? Does not the finite being [man] become infinite through this "creative behavior?"

But is ontological knowledge "creative" in the manner of *intuitus originarius,* for which the essent in the act of intuition is as e-ject and never as ob-ject? In this "creative" ontological knowledge is the essent "known," i.e., created as such? Absolutely not. Not only does ontological knowledge not create the essent, it does not even relate itself directly and thematically to the essent.

But to what does it relate itself, then? What is known in ontological knowledge? A Nothing. Kant calls it an X and speaks of an "object." In what respect is this X a Nothing, and in what respect is it still "something"? A brief interpretation of the two main passages in which Kant speaks of this X should furnish the answer to the question as to what it is that is known in ontological knowledge. Characteristically, the first passage is found in the introduction to the transcendental deduction.[157] The second passage is found in the section entitled: "the Ground of

157. A 108f., NKS, p. 136f.

125

Distinction of all Objects in General into Phenomena and Noumena." [158] This section, according to the plan of the *Critique of Pure Reason,* concludes the positive laying of the foundation of *metaphysica generalis.*

The first passage reads: "Now, also, we are in a position to determine more adequately our concept of an *object* in general. All representations have, as representations, their object, and can themselves in turn become objects of other representations. Appearances are the sole objects which can be given to us immediately, and that in them which relates immediately to the object is called intuition. But these appearances are not things in themselves; they are only representations, which in turn have their object—an object which cannot itself be intuited by us, and which may, therefore, be named the non-empirical, that is, transcendental object = X."

What immediately confronts us in experience is that which is given by intuition. The appearances themselves, however, are "only representations," not things in themselves. What is represented in these presentations shows itself only in and for an act of receptive orientation. This act must "also have its object." Indeed, it must in general give something in advance which has an ob-jective character in order to form the horizon within which an autonomous essent can be encountered. This terminus [*Woraufzu*] of the precursory orientation, therefore, can no longer be intuited by us in the form of an empirical intuition. This does not exclude—on the contrary, it includes— the necessity of its being immediately perceptible in a pure intuition. This terminus of the precursory orientation, hence, can "be named the non-empirical object = X."

"All our representations are, it is true, referred by the understanding to some object; and since appearances are nothing but representations, the understanding refers them to a *something,* as the object of sensible intuition. But this something,

158. A 235ff., B 294ff., NKS, p. 257ff.

126

thus conceived, is only the transcendental object; and by that is meant a something $= X$, of which we know, and with the present constitution of our understanding can know, nothing whatsoever, but which, as a correlate of the unity of apperception, can serve only for the unity of the manifold in sensible intuition. By means of this unity the understanding combines the manifold into the concept of an object." [159]

The X is "something" of which we can know nothing. This X is not unknowable because as an essent it lies hidden "behind" a layer of appearances, but because in principle it is not able to become an object of cognition, that is, the object of a knowledge relative to the essent. It can never become such because it is a Nothing.

By a Nothing we mean not an essent but nevertheless "something." It serves only as "a correlate," i.e., according to its essence it is pure horizon. Kant calls this X the "transcendental object," that which is opposed [*Dawider*] in transcendence and is capable of being perceived by transcendence as its horizon. Now, if the X known in ontological knowledge is, in essence, horizon, this knowledge must be of such a nature that it holds this horizon open in its character as horizon. Consequently, this something may not be the direct and exclusive theme of an intention. The horizon must be unthematic but nevertheless still kept in view. Only in this way can it thrust forward [*vordrängen*] and render thematic that which is encountered within it.

The X is an "object in general," but this does not mean that it is a universal, indeterminate essent which presents itself in the form of an ob-ject. On the contrary, this expression refers to that which in advance constitutes the passing over [*Überschlag*] of all possible objects *qua* ob-jective, the horizon of an ob-jectification. If by "object" we mean an essent thematically

159. A 250, NKS, p. 268. This text has been amended by Kant himself. *Cf. Nachträge*, CXXXIV.

127

apprehended, this horizon is not an object but a Nothing. And if by "knowledge" we mean the apprehension of an essent, ontological knowledge is not knowledge.

Ontological knowledge may rightly be termed knowledge if it attains truth. However, it does not merely "possess" truth, it *is* original truth, and it is for this reason that Kant terms the latter "transcendental truth." The essence of this truth is clarified through the transcendental schematism. "All our knowledge is contained within this whole of possible experience, and transcendental truth, which precedes all empirical truth and renders it possible, consists in general relation to that experience." [160]

Ontological knowledge "forms" transcendence, and this formation is nothing other than the holding open of the horizon within which the Being of the essent is perceptible in advance. Provided that truth means: the unconcealment of [*Unverborgenheit von*] . . . , then transcendence is original truth. But truth itself must be understood both as disclosure of Being and overtness of the essent.[161] If ontological knowledge discloses the horizon, its truth lies in letting the essent be encountered within this horizon. Kant says that ontological knowledge has only "empirical use," that is, it serves to make finite knowledge possible, where by "finite knowledge" is meant the experience of the essent that manifests itself.

Hence, the question must at least remain open as to whether this knowledge, which is "creative" only on the ontological level and never on the ontic, overcomes the finitude of transcendence or whether, on the contrary, it immerses the finite "subject" in the finitude proper to it.

According to this definition of the essence of ontological knowledge, ontology is nothing other than the explicit disclosure of the systematic whole of pure knowledge so far as the latter forms transcendence.

160. A 146, B 185, NKS, p. 186.
161. *Cf. Vom Wesen des Grundes, op. cit.,* p. 75ff., 3rd ed., p. 11ff.

Kant, however, wishes to replace the "proud name of an Ontology" [162] by that of "transcendental philosophy," the object of which is the disclosure of the essence of transcendence. And he is justified, so long as the term "ontology" is taken in the sense of traditional metaphysics. This traditional ontology "claims to supply, in systematic doctrinal form, synthetic *a priori* knowledge of things in general." It seeks to raise itself to the level of ontic knowledge *a priori,* a knowledge which is the privilege only of an infinite being. If, on the contrary, this ontology abandons its "pride" and "presumption," if it undertakes to understand itself in its finitude, i.e., as an essential and necessary structure of finitude, then one may give the expression "ontology" its true essence and at the same time justify its use. It is in accordance with this meaning, first attained and secured through the laying of the foundation of metaphysics, that Kant himself uses the expression "ontology" and, indeed, in that decisive passage of the *Critique of Pure Reason* which sets forth the outline of metaphysics as a whole.[163]

By this transformation of *metaphysica generalis,* the foundation of traditional metaphysics is shaken and the edifice of *metaphysica specialis* begins to totter. However, the new problems which are thus posed will not be touched on here. Their study demands a preparation which can be achieved only through a more profound assimilation of that which Kant attained in the unity of transcendental aesthetic and logic as a laying of the foundation of *metaphysica generalis.*

162. A 247, B 303, NKS, p. 264.
163. A 845, B 873, NKS, p. 643f. *Cf.* also the use of the term "ontology" in the *Fortschritte der Metaphysik.*

# THE LAYING OF THE FOUNDATION OF METAPHYSICS IN ITS BASIC ORIGINALITY

SECTION THREE

# THE LAYING OF THE FOUNDATION OF METAPHYSICS IN ITS BASIC ORIGINALITY

Is it possible to grasp the laying of the foundation now established on an even more fundamental basis? Or is this unceasing pursuit of originality mere vain curiosity? And is it not condemned to that misery which is the fatal punishment of all who wish to know ever more and more? Above all, does it not apply a criterion to the Kantian philosophy which is foreign to it, thus leading to a critique "from without" which is always unjust?

The investigation of the problem of the originality of the Kantian laying of the foundation of metaphysics will not follow any such path. The idea of originality here in question must be taken from the Kantian laying of the foundation itself, if the discussion of originality in general is not to become a polemic but is to remain on the level of interpretation. It is a question of examining Kant's efforts to penetrate the dimension of origin and his search for the source-ground of the "fundamental sources of knowledge" by clarifying the preliminary insight which served him as a guide. In order for this examination to be successful, it is first necessary clearly to delimit the ground already established by the laying of the foundation.

# A. The Explicit Characterization of the Fundamental Ground Established in the Laying of the Foundation of Metaphysics

## § 26. The Transcendental Imagination as the Formative Center of Ontological Knowledge

The laying of the foundation of *metaphysica generalis* is the answer to the question as to the essential unity of ontological knowledge and the basis of its possibility. Ontological knowledge "forms" transcendence, i.e., it holds open the horizon which is made perceptible in advance by the pure schemata. These schemata "arise" as the "transcendental product" [1] of the transcendental imagination. The latter as the original, pure synthesis forms the essential unity of pure intuition (time) and pure thought (apperception).

But it is not only in the doctrine of the transcendental schematism that the transcendental imagination appears as the central theme; it occupies that position in the preceding stage of the laying of the foundation, in the transcendental deduction. Because the primordial act of unification is undertaken by the transcendental imagination, it is necessary that the latter be mentioned with the first characterization of the essential unity of ontological knowledge, i.e., in the second stage. The transcendental imagination is, therefore, the foundation on which the intrinsic possibility of ontological knowledge, and hence of *metaphysica generalis* as well, is constructed.

Kant introduces the pure imagination as an "indispensable function of the soul." [2] To lay bare the established ground of metaphysics, then, means to determine a faculty of the human

1. A 142, B 181, NKS, p. 183.
2. A 78, B 103, NKS, p. 112.

134

soul more precisely. That the laying of the foundation of metaphysics must finally arrive at such a task is "self-evident" provided that, in Kant's own words, metaphysics belongs to "human nature." This is why "anthropology," which Kant discussed over the years in his lectures, provides us with information about the established ground of metaphysics.[3]

"The imagination (*facultas imaginandi*) is a faculty of intuition even without the presence of an object." [3a] Hence, the imagination belongs to the faculty of intuition. The definition cited understands by "intuition" first of all the empirical intuition of the essent. As a "sensible faculty," the imagination is included among the faculties of knowledge, which last are divided between sensibility and understanding, the first representing our "lower" faculty of knowledge. The imagination is a mode of sensible intuition "even without the presence of an object." The essent intuited need not itself be present, and furthermore, unlike perception for which the object "must be represented as present," [4] the imagination does not intuit what it apprehends in its act as something actually on hand. The imagination "can" intuit, can take in an aspect, and the intuited thing concerned need not show itself as essent and need not itself provide the aspect in question.

To begin with, then, the imagination enjoys a peculiar independence with respect to the essent. It is free in its reception of

3. H. Mörchen in his Marburg dissertation, *Die Einbildungskraft bei Kant* has undertaken the task of a monographic presentation and interpretation of Kant's doctrine concerning the imagination as found in Kant's *Anthropologie, Critique of Pure Reason, Critique of Judgment,* and the other writings and lectures. The work will appear in Vol. XI of the *Jahrbuch für Philos und phän, Forschung.* The present exposition is limited to what is most essential in the light of the chief problem of the laying of the foundation of metaphysics.

3a. I. Kant, *Anthropologie in pragmatischer Hensicht,* W. W. (Cass.) VIII, § 28, p. 54.

4. Reicke, *Lose Blätter aus Kants Nachlass,* 1889, p. 102.

aspects—it is the faculty which, in a certain sense, can give itself aspects. Hence, the imagination can be termed, in a dual sense that is characteristic, a formative faculty. As a faculty of intuition it is formative in the sense that it produces an image (or aspect). As a faculty not dependent on objects of intuition, it produces, i.e., forms and provides, images. This "formative power" is at one and the same time receptive and productive (spontaneous). In this "at one and the same time" is to be found the true essence of the structure of the imagination. However, if receptivity is identified with sensibility, and spontaneity with the understanding, then the imagination falls in a peculiar way between the two.[5] This gives the imagination a remarkably ambiguous character which comes to light in the Kantian definition of this faculty. In spite of this spontaneity, when Kant divides the faculties of knowledge into two fundamental classes he lists the imagination under sensibility. As a result of this classification, the formation (the production) of images becomes the decisive element in the act of imagination, something which is also evident in the definition.

Because of its freedom, the imagination for Kant is a faculty of comparing, shaping, differentiating, and of connecting in general (synthesis). "Imagining," therefore, denotes all nonperceptive representation in the broadest sense of the term: fancying, contriving, fabricating, worrying, daydreaming, and the like. The "power of imagination" [Bildungskraft] is thus joined with wit, the power of differentiation, and the faculty of comparison in general. "The senses provide the matter for all our representations. It is from this matter that the formative faculty first derives its representations independently of the presence of objects: [first] the power of imagination, imaginatio; second, the faculty of comparison, wit, and the power of differentiation, judicum descretum; third, the faculty of combining

5. As early as Aristotle's De anima, G3, phantasia stands "between" aisthēsis and noēsis.

136

representations, not immediately with their objects, but by designating them by the mediation of a substitute." [6]

But in spite of these attempts to classify the imagination as a faculty of spontaneity, it still retains its intuitive character. It is *subjectio sub aspectum,* i.e., a faculty of intuitive presentation, of giving. The intuitive representation of an object not present can take place in two ways.

If this intuitive representation is limited to the present recollection of something perceived earlier, then the aspect which it offers is dependent on the earlier one offered by the preceding perception. This presentation which refers back to an earlier perception is one the content of which is derived from this perception (*exhibitio derivativa*).

If, on the contrary, the imagination freely invents the form of its object, then this presentation of the aspect of the object is "original" (*exhibitio originaria*). Hence, the imagination is said to be "productive." [7] This original presentation, however, is not as "creative" as *intuitus originarius,* which creates the essent in the act of intuiting it. The productive imagination only forms the aspect of a possible object, which last under certain conditions may also be realizable, i.e., capable of being made present. This realization, however, is never accomplished by the imagination itself. The formative power of the imagination is not even "productive" in the sense that it can form the content of an image absolutely from nothing, from that which has never been an object of experience either in whole or in part. It is "not capable of producing a sensible representation which has never before been given to our sensible faculty. One is always able to point out the material from which it was derived." [8]

6. Erdmann, *Reflexionen,* I, 118, *Kant's Posthumous Works in Manuscript Form,* Vol. III, 1, No. 339; *cf.* also, Pölitz, *I Kants Vorlesungen über die Metaphysik,* 2nd ed., re-edited after the edition of 1821 by K. H. Schmidt, 1924, p. 141.
7. *Anthropologie, op. cit.,* VIII, § 28.
8. *Ibid.*

Such is the essential information which the *Anthropologie* gives us with regard to imagination in general and the productive imagination in particular. The *Anthropologie* contains no more than has already been brought out by the laying of the foundation of metaphysics in the *Critique of Pure Reason*. Indeed, the discussions of the transcendental deduction and of schematism have made evident in a much more fundamental way that the imagination is an intermediate faculty between sensibility and the understanding.

Nevertheless, the definition of the imagination, according to which the latter can intuitively represent an object without its being present, does not enter into the exposition of the laying of the foundation of metaphysics provided by the *Critique of Pure Reason*. But not to mention the fact that this definition appears explicitly in the transcendental deduction (although only in the second edition),[9] has not the discussion of the transcendental schematism revealed just this character mentioned in the definition of the imagination?

The imagination forms in advance, and before all experience of the essent, the aspect of the horizon of objectivity as such. This formation of the aspect in the pure form [*Bild*] of time not only precedes this or that experience of the essent but is also prior to any such possible experience. In offering a pure aspect in this way, the imagination is in no case and in no wise dependent on the presence of an essent. It is so far from being thus dependent that its pre-formation of a pure schema, for example, substance (permanence), consists in bringing into view something on the order of constant presence [*ständige Anwesenheit*]. It is only in the horizon of this presence that this or that "presence of an object" can reveal itself. This is why the essence of the imagination, namely, the ability to intuit without a concrete presence, is grasped in the transcendental schematism in a manner which is basically more original [than that of the *An-*

9. B 151, NKS, p. 164f.

138

*thropologie*]. Finally, and again in a more original sense, the transcendental schematism also manifests the "creative" essence of the imagination. The imagination is not ontically "creative," but it is creative in the matter of the free formation of images. The *Anthropologie* stresses that the productive imagination is still dependent on sensible representations. In the transcendental schematism, on the other hand, the imagination has a function which is originally presentative and which is exercised in the pure form of time. The imagination has no need here of an empirical intuition. As compared to the *Anthropologie,* therefore, the *Critique of Pure Reason* presents the intuitive character, as well as the spontaneity, of the imagination in a more original sense.

In view of the above, it is entirely useless to attempt, by means of the study of anthropology, to comprehend the imagination as the established ground of ontology. Not only that, such an attempt is an error pure and simple in that it not only leads to a misconception of the empirical character of Kant's anthropology but also, insofar as the *Critique of Pure Reason* is concerned, fails to evaluate properly the true nature of the observations on the laying of the foundation and the efforts made in the *Critique* to uncover the origin [of the latter].

The Kantian anthropology is empirical in a double sense. First, the characterization of the faculties of the soul moves within the framework of the knowledge which ordinary experience furnishes us concerning man. Finally, the faculties of the soul, among them the imagination, are studied only with regard to the fact and the nature of their relation to the essent capable of being experienced. The productive imagination with which anthropology is concerned has to do only with the formation of the aspects of objects considered as empirically possible or impossible.

On the other hand, in the *Critique of Pure Reason* the pure productive imagination is never concerned with the imaginative

139

formation of objects but with the pure aspect of objectivity in general. It is pure productive imagination, independent of experience, which first renders experience possible. Not all productive imagination is pure, but pure imagination in the sense just described is necessarily productive. Insofar as it forms transcendence, this imagination is rightly termed transcendental.

In general, anthropology does not raise the question of transcendence. Nevertheless, the vain effort on the part of anthropology to interpret the imagination in a more original way shows that in the empirical interpretation of the faculties of the soul, which interpretation, by the way, can never be purely empirical, there is always a reference to transcendental structures. But these structures can neither be firmly established in anthropology nor derived from it through mere assumptions.

But what is the nature of that mode of knowledge which effects the disclosure of transcendence, i.e., which reveals the pure synthesis and thereby completes the explication of the imagination? When Kant terms this mode of knowledge "transcendental," the only conclusion that can be drawn from this is that the theme of the mode of knowledge in question is transcendence. But what characterizes the method of this knowledge? How does the regression to the origin take place? As long as the necessary clarity on this point is lacking, it will be impossible to take the first step toward the laying of the foundation.

It no longer seems possible at this stage of the investigation to avoid an explicit discussion of the "transcendental method." But provided that it is possible to clarify this method, the task still remains to deduce from the principles hitherto established the direction of the regression required by the dimension of origin itself. However, whether it is possible to effect an original interpretation by setting out in the new direction indicated by the principles in question depends uniquely on knowing whether Kant's laying of the foundation of metaphysics and our interpretation thereof are sufficiently original to guide us in this new course. This can only be decided by actually carrying out such an attempt. Insofar as Kant's anthropology is concerned, the way which seemed at first to be the most natural has turned out to lead to an impasse. All the more evident, then, is the necessity of keeping the interpretation focused on the phenomenon which manifests itself as the ground of the intrinsic possibility of the ontological synthesis, i.e., the transcendental imagination.

## § 27. The Transcendental Imagination as the Third Fundamental Faculty

To understand the faculties "of our soul" as transcendental faculties means, first of all, to reveal them according to the extent and the manner in which they make the essence of transcendence possible. From this point of view, the term "faculty" [*Vermögen*] does not signify a "fundamental power" actually present in the soul; rather, "faculty" here refers to what such a power is "able to do" [*vermag*] so far as it renders possible the essential structure of transcendence. "Faculty" now means "possibility" in the sense of that word discussed above.[10] Thus understood, the transcendental imagination is not merely a faculty which appears between pure intuition and pure thought, but, together with these, it is a "fundamental faculty" inasmuch as it makes possible the original unity of the other two and thereby the essential unity of transcendence as a whole. "A pure imagination, which conditions all *a priori* knowledge, is thus one of the fundamental faculties of the human soul." [11]

To say that the imagination is a fundamental faculty is also to say that it is not reducible to the other elements which together with it form the essential unity of transcendence. This is why, at the time of the decisive characterization of the essential unity of ontological knowledge, Kant specifically enu-

10. *Cf.* above, § 24, p. 119.
11. A 124, NKS, p. 146.

merates three elements: pure intuition (time), the pure synthesis constituted by the imagination, and the pure concepts of pure apperception.[12] In the same context, Kant emphasizes that "we shall see hereafter" the way in which the imagination acts as an "indispensable function of the soul without which we should have no knowledge whatsoever."

The possibility of the unity of these three elements is discussed in the transcendental deduction and established through the schematism. In introducing this idea of the pure schematism, Kant is given another opportunity to enumerate the three pure elements of ontological knowledge. And finally, the discussion of the highest principle of all synthetic judgments, i.e., the final determination of the complete essence of transcendence, is introduced by the enumeration of the three elements mentioned above "as the three sources" of the "possibility of pure synthetic judgments *a priori*."

Opposed to this unequivocal characterization of the transcendental imagination as a third fundamental faculty in addition to pure sensibility and pure understanding, a characterization derived from the intrinsic problematic of the *Critique of Pure Reason* itself, is Kant's express declaration made both at the beginning and at the end of his work.

There are, however, only "two fundamental sources of our mind, sensibility and understanding;" there are only these "two sources;" "we have no other sources of knowledge besides these two." [13] To this thesis corresponds the division of the entire transcendental investigation into transcendental aesthetic and transcendental logic. The transcendental imagination is homeless. It is not even discussed in the transcendental aesthetic, although as a "faculty of intuition" it really belongs there. On the other hand, the transcendental imagination is a theme of the transcendental logic, although as long as logic is confined to thought as such it should not be. But, this aesthetic and this

12. A 78f., B 104, NKS, p. 111f.
13. *Cf.* above § 6, p. 39.

142

logic are oriented on transcendence, which last is not merely the simple sum of pure intuition and pure thought but constitutes a unique and primordial unity within which intuition and thought function only as elements. This is why the results we attain by means of the logic and the aesthetic lead us beyond them both.

Could Kant have failed to note this consequence? Or would the suppression of the above-mentioned triplicity of fundamental faculties on behalf of the theory of the duality of stems [*Stämme*] be at all reconcilable with his way of thinking? This is so little the case that in the course of his laying of the foundation of metaphysics, in particular, at the end of the introduction to the transcendental deduction and again at the point where its development really begins, Kant speaks explicitly of "three original sources of the soul" just as if he had never established the doctrine of the duality of stems.

"There are three original sources (capacities or faculties of the soul) which contain the conditions of the possibility of all experience, and cannot themselves be derived from any other faculty of the mind, namely, *sense, imagination,* and *apperception.* . . . All these *faculties* have a transcendental (as well as an empirical) employment which concerns the form alone, and is possible *a priori.*" [14]

"We saw that there are three subjective sources of knowledge upon which rests the possibility of experience in general and of knowledge of its objects—*sense, imagination,* and *apperception.* Each of these can be viewed as empirical, namely, in its application to given appearances. But all of them are likewise *a priori* elements or foundations, which make this empirical employment itself possible." [15] In both passages it is explicitly noted that beside the empirical use of these faculties stands the transcendental. Hence, the relation to anthropology noted above is manifested anew.

Thus this triplicity of fundamental faculties and the duality

14. A 94, NKS, p. 127.
15. A 115, NKS, p. 141.

143

of the fundamental sources stand hard by one another. Yet, what about these two stems? Is it merely by accident that Kant uses this image to characterize sensibility and understanding, or is its use meant to indicate that they grow out of a "common root"?

The interpretation of the laying of the foundation of metaphysics has revealed that the transcendental imagination is not merely an external bond which fastens two extremities together. It is originally unifying, i.e., it is the specific faculty which forms the unity of the other two, which faculties themselves have an essential structural relation to it.

Is it possible that this originally unifying [*bildende*] center is that "unknown, common root" of both stems? Is it accidental that with the first introduction of the imagination Kant says that "we are scarcely ever conscious" of its existence? [16]

## B. The Transcendental Imagination as the Root of Both Stems

If the established ground does not have the character of an actual base but that of a root, then it must discharge its function in such a way as to let the stems grow out of it while lending them support and stability. Thus, we have already

16. A 78, B 103, NKS, p. 112. The specific characterization of the imagination as a fundamental faculty must have enlightened Kant's contemporaries as to the significance of this faculty. So Fichte, Schelling, and in his own way, Jacobi have attributed an essential role to the imagination. We are not able to discuss at this time the question as to whether these men recognized, maintained, or even interpreted "in a more original way" the essence of the imagination as Kant understood it. The following interpretation of the transcendental imagination proceeds from another formulation of the question and moves in a direction opposite to that of German idealism.

found the direction which we sought, with reference to which the originality of the Kantian laying of the foundation of metaphysics can be discussed within the problematic proper to it. This laying of the foundation becomes more original when it does not simply accept the established ground but reveals how this root is the root of both stems. This means nothing less than reducing pure intuition and pure thought to the transcendental imagination.

But apart from the question of its possible success, is not the doubtful character of such an undertaking obvious? Through such a reduction of the faculties of knowledge of a finite being to the imagination, would not all knowledge be reduced to the purely imaginary? Would not the essence of man dissolve into mere appearance?

However, if it is a question of showing that pure intuition and pure thought as transcendental faculties have their origin in the transcendental imagination as a faculty, this does not mean that we seek to prove that pure intuition and pure thought are simply the products of the imagination and as such mere fictions. The disclosure of the origin which has been characterized above shows, rather, that the structure of these faculties is rooted in the structure of the transcendental imagination in such a way that the latter can "imagine" something only through its structural unity with the other two.

Whether what is formed by the transcendental imagination is pure appearance in the sense of being something "merely imaginary" is a question which must remain open. To begin with, we are accustomed to call "merely imaginary" that which is not really on hand. But according to its nature, what is formed in the transcendental imagination is not something on hand, if it is true that the transcendental imagination can never be ontically creative. On the other hand, what is formed by the transcendental imagination can never be "merely imaginary" in the usual sense of that term. On the contrary, it is the

145

horizon of objectivity formed by the transcendental imagination —the comprehension of Being—which makes possible all distinction between ontic truth and ontic appearance (the "merely imaginary").

But does not ontological knowledge, the essential ground of which is supposedly the transcendental imagination, have, as essentially finite, an untruth [*Unwahrheit*] corresponding to its truth? [17] As a matter of fact, the idea of a transcendental untruth conceals within itself one of the most pressing problems relative to finitude. This problem, far from being solved, has not even been posed, because the basis for its formulation has yet to be worked out. This can only be accomplished by the revelation of the essence of transcendence and, therewith, the essence of the transcendental imagination. Pure intuition and pure thought are not to be considered merely imaginary solely because the possibility of their essence requires that they be traced back to the essential structure of the transcendental imagination. The transcendental imagination does not "imagine" pure intuition but makes it possible for pure intuition to be what it "really" can be.

But just as the transcendental imagination cannot be considered to be purely "imaginary" [*Eingebildetes*] because as a root it is "formative," so also can it not be considered to be a "fundamental power" in the soul. This regression to the essen-

17. The untruth of which Heidegger speaks here is not to be confused with "ontic" untruth, i.e., the untruth we encounter in everyday life. Transcendental untruth (or "error" or "concealment" as he sometimes terms it) is "a part of the inner structure of *Da-sein*" (*On the Essence of Truth, op. cit.,* p. 245) and is the basis of ordinary untruth or "wrong." Transcendental untruth is ultimately an essential consequence of man's relation to Being as such (or better, Being's relation to man), which last as it reveals the essent withdraws and so conceals itself. See also, *What is Metaphysics, op. cit.,* p. 340ff.; *Der Spruch des Anaximander* in *Holzwege* (Frankfurt am Main, 1950), p. 310ff.; *Über den Humanismus,* p. 19ff. (J. S. C.)

tial origin of transcendence is not at all intended to be a monistic-empirical explanation of the other faculties of the soul in terms of the imagination. Such an intention would be self-prohibitive, for, in the end, the disclosure of the essence of transcendence itself determines in what sense one may speak of the "soul" or spirit [Gemüt] and to what extent these concepts bear originally on the ontologico-metaphysical essence of man. The regression to the transcendental imagination as the root of sensibility and understanding signifies, on the contrary, only that we wish to examine [project] anew the constitution of transcendence relative to the ground of its possibility and in the light of the essential structure of the transcendental imagination which has been thrown into relief within the problematic of the laying of the foundation. This regression, which is also a laying of the foundation, moves in the dimension of "possibilities," i.e., in the dimension of that which makes possible. Consequently, the transcendental imagination as we have known it up to this point is transformed into more original "possibilities" so that even the name "imagination" becomes inadequate.

The ensuing stages of the laying of the foundation in its originality tend even less to supply an absolute basis of interpretation than do those stages of the laying bare of the foundation already set forth and examined by Kant. The strangeness of the established ground, which must have forced itself on Kant, cannot disappear but will increase as we draw nearer to the origin, since, after all, the metaphysical nature of man as a finite being is at once that which is most mysterious and most real.

The problematic of the transcendental deduction and of transcendental schematism becomes clear only if the transcendental imagination is shown to be the root of transcendence. The question as to the pure synthesis which is posed here refers to an original unification in which the unifying element must from the first be proportional to the elements to be unified. The formation of this original unity is only possible, however, if the unifying element lets the elements to be unified spring forth. The root-character of the established ground first makes comprehensible the originality of the pure synthesis, i.e., makes it comprehensible as that which lets spring forth.

Although the following interpretation will continue to be oriented according to the stages of the laying of the foundation already established, the individual stages will no longer be described. The specific interrelation of pure imagination, pure intuition, and pure thought will be revealed only to the extent indicated by the Kantian laying of the foundation itself.

### § 28. Transcendental Imagination and Pure Intuition

Kant termed the pure intuitions, space and time, "original representations." The term "original" is not to be understood here in an ontic or psychological sense and does not concern the presence or perhaps the innateness of these intuitions in the soul, but characterizes the manner in which the representations are represented. The word "original" corresponds to *originarius* and means: to let spring forth.

But for all this, these intuitions are, in a sense, formative in that they pro-pose [*vor-stellen*] in advance the aspect of space and time as multiple totalities in themselves. They receive this aspect, but the reception is in itself a formative act which gives to itself that which offers itself. The pure intuitions are essentially "originative," i.e., presentations which let the object of intuition spring forth, *exhibitio originaria*. In this act of presentation lies the essence of pure imagination. Pure intuition can only be original in the sense just noted, because, according to its essence, it is pure imagination, an imagination which in forming aspects (images) spontaneously gives them [to itself].

The enrooting of pure intuition in pure imagination becomes perfectly clear when we examine the character of what is intuited in pure intuition. Without doubt, commentators are only

148

too quick to deny that something is intuited in pure intuition for the simple reason that it is supposed to be only the "form of intuition." The fact is, however, that what is "seen" in pure intuition is in itself a unified but by no means empty totality, the parts of which are always but limitations of itself. This unified totality from the first must let itself be apprehended relative to its inclusive multiplicity, which last is generally indistinct. Pure intuition as originally unifying, i.e., giving unity, must *perceive* this unity. Therefore, Kant is justified in speaking here not of a synthesis, but of a synopsis.[18]

The totality of that which is intuited in pure intuition does not have the unity which characterizes the universality enjoyed by concepts. Hence, the unity of the totality supplied by intuition cannot arise from the "synthesis of the understanding." It is a unity perceived from the first in the act of imagination which forms the image. The "syn" of the totality of space and time pertains to a faculty of formative intuition. If the pure synopsis constitutes the essence of pure intuition, it is possible only in transcendental imagination—all the more so since the latter is in general the source of all that is "synthetic" in character.[19] The term "synthesis" must therefore be taken here in a sense broad enough to include the synopsis of intuition and the "synthesis" of the understanding.

Kant once remarked in a reflection at once striking and direct that "space and time are the pre-formative forms [*Formen der Vorbildung*] in pure intuition." [20] They form in advance the pure

18. A 94f., NKS, p. 127. Kant says here specifically that he has treated of the transcendental synopsis in the *Transcendental Aesthetic*.

19. A 78, B 103, NKS, p. 111f.

20. Erdmann, *Reflexionen*, II, 408, *Kant's Posthumous Works in Manuscript Form, op. cit.*, Vol. V, No. 5934—Adickes, referring to Erdmann's reading, erroneously in my opinion, reads "connection" [*Verbindung*] instead of "pre-formation" [*Vorbildung*]. *Cf.* below, § 32, p. 178.

aspect which serves as the horizon of that which is intuited in empirical intuition. But if, in the modality of its act, pure intuition manifests the specific essence of the transcendental imagination, is it not then true that what is pre-formed therein must also be imaginative, since it is formed by the imagination (*imaginatio*)? This characteristic of what is intuited as such in pure intuition is no formal consequence of the foregoing but lies enclosed in the essential content of that which is accessible to pure intuition. Hence, this imaginative character of space and time has nothing extraordinary or strange about it when one considers that it is a matter here of pure intuition and pure imagination. And as we have shown, what is formed in the imagination is not necessarily an ontic illusion.

Kant could have understood but little of the essential structure of pure intuition—indeed, he could have had no conception of it—had he been unable to grasp the imaginative character of what is perceived therein. He states without the slightest equivocation: "The mere form of intuition, without substance, is in itself no object, but the merely formal condition of an object (as appearance) as pure space and time (*ens imaginarium*). These are indeed something, as forms of intuition, but are not themselves objects which are intuited." [21] What is perceived in pure intuition as such is an *ens imaginarium*. Therefore, the act of pure intuition is essentially pure imagination.

The *ens imaginarium* pertains to the possible forms of "Nothing," to what is not an essent in the sense of something actually present. Pure space and pure time are "something," but they are not objects. If one says summarily that "nothing" is intuited in pure intuition and, therefore, that the latter has no object, such an interpretation is not only negative but equivocal as well, as long as it is not clearly specified that Kant is using the term "object" here in a restricted sense, according to which it is the

21. A 291, B 347, NKS, p. 195. R. Schmidt remarks that the "(*ens imaginarium*)" appears in A three lines higher, after "time."

150

essent that reveals itself in the appearance that is meant. According to this meaning, not just any "something" is an object.

Pure intuitions as "forms of intuiting" are, to be sure, "intuitions without things," [22] but nevertheless they do have a content. Space is nothing "real," that is, it is not an essent accessible to perception but "the representation of a mere possibility of coexistence." [23] However, the tendency to deny an object (in the sense of something intuited) to pure intuition is reinforced by the fact that it is possible to appeal to a character of pure intuition that is genuinely phenomenal without being able to determine this character adequately. In our cognitive relationships to given things organized "spatio-temporally" we intend only these things. Even so, however, space and time are not to be disavowed. Therefore, the positive question must read: How are space and time present in these relationships? If Kant declares they are intuitions, then the reply is immediately forthcoming: But they are never intuited. This is certainly true; they are never intuited in the sense that they become the objects of a thematic apprehension, but they are intuited according to the modality of an act which is originally form-giving [einer ursprünglich bildenden Gebung]. Precisely because what is thus intuited is what and how it is, i.e., as essentially a forming [zu Bildendes]—in accordance with the characterized dual signification of a pure aspect of creating—the act of pure intuition is not able to intuit its "object" in the manner of the thematic apprehension of something actually given.

Thus, the primordial interpretation of pure intuition as pure imagination first provides the possibility of a positive explication of what is intuited in pure intuition. As the precursory formation of a pure, unthematic, and, in the Kantian sense, unobjective aspect, pure intuition makes it possible for the act of

22. *Reflexionen*, II, 408, *Kant's Posthumous Works in Manuscript Form, op. cit.,* Vol. V, No. 5315.
23. A 374, NKS, p. 349.

151

empirical intuition exercised within its horizon not first to have to intuit space and time in the sense of an explicit apprehension of them as a multiplicity.

Hence, if it is true that the innermost essence of transcendence is grounded in pure imagination, then the transcendental character of transcendental intuition is made clear for the first time by means of this interpretation of pure intuition. Placed as it is at the beginning of the *Critique of Pure Reason,* the transcendental aesthetic is basically unintelligible. It has only an introductory character and can be truly understood only in the perspective of the transcendental schematism.

Although one cannot defend the attempt of the so-called "Marburg school" to interpret space and time as "categories" in the logical sense and to reduce the transcendental aesthetic to logic, one must admit that the attempt is inspired by a legitimate motive. This motive arises from the conviction, certainly never clearly justified, that the transcendental aesthetic taken by itself can never constitute the whole of that which lies in it as a possibility. However, from the specific "syn" character of pure intuition it does not follow that this intuition is dependent on the synthesis of the understanding. On the contrary, the correct interpretation of this "syn" character leads to the conclusion that pure intuition originates in the pure imagination. Moreover, the reduction of transcendental aesthetic to logic becomes all the more questionable when it is shown that the specific object of transcendental logic, pure thought, is itself rooted in the transcendental imagination.[24]

24. Only by means of a clear-cut separation between a synopsis of pure intuition and the synthesis of the understanding is the distinction, introduced by Kant in B § 26, p. 160, fn. (NKS, p. 170), between the "form of intuition" and "formal intuition" intelligible.

## § 29. *Transcendental Imagination and Theoretical Reason*

The attempt to show that pure thought, and hence theoretical reason in general, has its origin in the transcendental imagination seems at first sight to be futile for the simple reason that such a project appears to be absurd in itself. For one thing, Kant says specifically that the imagination is "always sensible." [25] How can a faculty essentially sensible, i.e., "inferior," be held to be the origin of a "higher" faculty? That in finite knowledge the understanding presupposes sensibility, and therefore the imagination, as a "base" is comprehensible, but the notion that the understanding itself springs essentially from sensibility is obviously absurd.

Yet, before considering any formal arguments, it must be noted that it is not a question here of the empirical derivation of a higher faculty of the soul from a lower. If, in the inquiry into the laying of the foundation of metaphysics, the faculties of the soul do not form the subject of discussion, then the order of precedence with regard to "higher" and "lower" cannot be of significance, not even insofar as the framing of objections is concerned. But first of all, what is the meaning of "sensible"?

As early as the outline of the point of departure of the laying of the foundation, we purposely delimited the essence of sensibility according to the definition provided by Kant when he spoke of it for the first time.[26] According to this definition, sensibility and finite intuition are one and the same. Finitude consists in the reception of that which offers itself. What offers itself and the way in which it offers itself remain indeterminate. Not every sensible (receptive) intuition is necessarily sensory and empirical. The "inferiority" of the affections as corporeally determined does not pertain to the essence of sensibility. Thus,

25. A 124, NKS, p. 146.
26. *Cf.* above, § 5, p. 30.

not only can the transcendental imagination be sensible, as the fundamental determination of finite transcendence it must be sensible.

The sensibility of the transcendental imagination cannot be taken as a reason for classifying it as one of the lower faculties of the soul, especially since, as transcendental, it must be the condition of the possibility of all the faculties. Thus, the most serious, because the most "natural," objection to the thesis that pure thought originates in the transcendental imagination is without foundation.

Reason can now no longer be taken as a "higher" faculty. But another difficulty immediately presents itself. That pure intuition arises from the transcendental imagination is conceivable. But that thought, which must be sharply distinguished from all forms of intuition, should have its origin in the transcendental imagination seems impossible—even if one no longer attaches any importance to the order of precedence relative to the understanding and the imagination.

But thought and intuition, though distinct, are not separated from one another like two totally different things. On the contrary, as species of representation, both belong to the same genus of re-presentation in general. Both are modes of representation of. . . . An insight into the primordially representational character of thought is not less important for our interpretation than is an exact comprehension of the sensible character of the imagination.

An original disclosure of the understanding must take account of its innermost essence, namely, its dependence on intuition. This being-dependent-on is the being-as-understanding [*Verstandsein*] of the understanding. And this "Being" is how it is and what it is in the pure synthesis of the pure imagination. But it might be objected here that although the understanding is certainly related to pure intuition "through" the pure imagination, this in no way signifies that the pure understanding is in itself transcendental imagination and not something autonomous.

That the understanding is an autonomous faculty is affirmed by logic which does not have to treat of the imagination. And in fact, Kant always introduces the understanding in a form attributed to it by a logic [which sets itself up as a science] apparently absolute. Our analysis must proceed from this autonomy of thought if the origin of the latter in the imagination is to be shown.

That traditional logic does not treat of pure imagination is indisputable. But if logic wishes to understand itself, the question as to whether or not it need be concerned with the imagination must at least remain open. It is also undeniable that Kant always borrows from logic the point of departure for the problems which he formulates. And yet it is doubtful whether logic, merely because it has made pure thought, taken in a certain sense, its only theme, offers us a guarantee that it can delimit the complete essence of pure thought or even approach it.

Does not Kant's interpretation of pure thought in the transcendental deduction and in the doctrine of schematism show that not only the functions of judgment but also the pure concepts *qua* notions represent only artificially isolated elements of the pure synthesis which, on its side, constitutes an essentially necessary "presupposition" of the "synthetic unity of apperception?" Is it not also true that even though Kant always refers to formal logic as if it were an "absolute," he merges it with what he terms "transcendental logic," which last has the transcendental imagination as its only theme. And does not the rejection of traditional logic go so far that Kant—characteristically, only in the second edition—is compelled to assert: "The synthetic unity of apperception is, therefore, the highest point to which we must ascribe all employment of the understanding, even the whole of logic, and conformably therewith, transcen-

155

dental philosophy. Indeed, this faculty of apperception is the understanding itself." [27]

The preconceptions relative to the autonomy of thought, and in the form which they owe to the existence of formal logic as a discipline apparently supreme and irreducible, cannot themselves provide the authority for a decision concerning the possibility of the origin of pure thought in the transcendental imagination. It is advisable, rather, to seek the essence of pure thought in that which the laying of the foundation itself has already revealed. We can come to a decision concerning the possible origin of the understanding only by looking to the original essence of the understanding itself and not to a "logic" which does not take this essence into account.

To characterize thought as judgment is indeed pertinent, but it is still a characterization rather far removed from the essence of thought. The description of thought as "the faculty of rules" approaches this essence "more closely" [28] because by means of this description it is possible to discover a path which leads to the fundamental determination of the understanding as "pure apperception."

The "faculty of rules" is that which, by representing them, pro-poses in advance those unities which guide all possible modes of unification in the act of representation. These unities (notions or categories) represented in their regulative function must not only be disposed in accordance with their proper affinity but must also be included in advance in an abiding [bleibenden] unity by means of an act of representation even more primordial.

The representation of this abiding unity, as the identity of the complex of the rules of unity, is the fundamental character of the act of ob-jectification. In such representational self-orientation toward . . . , the "self" is, as it were, taken out-

27. B 154, fn., NKS, p. 154.
28. A 126, NKS, p. 147.

side [*hinausgenommen*] in the act of orientation. In this act, more precisely in the "self" "exteriorized" with it, the "I" of this "self" is necessarily made manifest. It is in this way that the "I represent" "accompanies" every act of representation. But it is not a question here of a subsidiary act of knowledge which takes thought as its object. The "I" "goes with" the act of pure self-orientation. Inasmuch as this "I" is what it is only in the "I think," the essence of pure thought as well as that of the "I" lies in "pure self-consciousness." This "consciousness" of the self can only be explained by the Being of the self, not conversely. Being cannot be explained or rendered superfluous by consciousness.

Now, the "I think" is always "I think substance" or "I think causality," etc. More precisely "in" these pure unities (categories) "what we assert in them" [29] is always "I think substance, cause, etc." The ego is the "vehicle" of the categories inasmuch as in its precursory act of orientation it puts them in a position wherein, as represented, they can be regulative, unifying unities.

The pure understanding is consequently a pre-formation "by itself" representative of the horizon of unity; it is a representational, formative spontaneity which occurs in the "transcendental schematism." This schematism Kant terms specifically "the procedure of understanding in these schemata," [30] and speaks of the "schematism of our understanding." [31]

However, the pure schemata form a "transcendental product of imagination." [32] How may these theses be reconciled? The understanding does not produce the schemata but "employs" them. This employment, however, is *not* a mode of activity in which the understanding occasionally indulges. On the contrary,

29. A 343, B 401, NKS, p. 330.
30. A 140, B 179, NKS, p. 182.
31. A 141, B 180, NKS, p. 183.
32. A 142, B 181, NKS, p. 183.

this pure schematism which is grounded in the transcendental imagination constitutes original being-as-understanding, i.e., the "I think substance," etc. The apparently independent act of the understanding in thinking the unities is, as a spontaneously formative act of representation, a fundamental act of the transcendental imagination. This is all the more evident in view of the fact that this representational self-orientation does not intend this unity thematically but, as we have already indicated several times, is the unthematic pro-position of that which is represented. This pro-position, however, takes place in a formative (pro-ductive) act of representation.

If what Kant terms "our thought" is this pure self-orienting reference-to . . . , the "thinking" of such a thought is not an act of judgment but is thinking in the sense of the free, but not arbitrary, "envisioning" [*Sich-denken*] of something, an envisioning which is at once a forming and a projecting. This primordial act of "thinking" is an act of pure imagination.

The imaginative character of pure thought becomes even more apparent when we attempt, from the vantage point of the essential definition of the understanding already attained, to draw nearer to the essence of self-consciousness in order to comprehend it as reason. Here again, we should not take as authoritative the distinction, borrowed from formal logic, between the understanding which judges and reason which draws conclusions. On the contrary, it is necessary to rely on the results yielded by the transcendental interpretation of the understanding.

Kant calls the understanding "a closed unity." But from what source does the projected totality which is affinity derive its character as a totality? Insofar as it is a question of the totality of the act of representation as such, that which provides this totality must itself be an act of representation. This act of representation takes place in the formation of ideas. Because the pure understanding is the "I think," it must, on the basis of

158

its essence, have the character of a "faculty of ideas," i.e., it must be a [form of] reason, for "without reason we should have no coherent employment of the understanding." [33] Ideas "contain a certain completeness," [34] they represent "the form of a whole," [35] and, hence, in a more original sense provide rules.

Now, one might object that in the course of his analysis of the transcendental ideal which must serve "as a rule and an archetype," [36] Kant specifically states that the products of the imagination "such as painters and physiognomists profess to carry in their heads" "are of an entirely different nature." [37] Here the connection between the ideas of pure reason and those of the imagination is expressly denied. But this passage says simply that the transcendental ideal "must always rest on determinate concepts" and cannot be an arbitrary and "blurred sketch" supplied by the empirical, productive imagination. This does not prevent these "definite concepts" from being possible only in the imagination.

Now, it would be possible to agree with this interpretation of theoretical reason with regard to its kinship with the transcendental imagination insofar as the interpretation emphasizes the act of free formation proper to the representation exercised by pure thought. However, if the interpretation should conclude that the origin of pure thought is to be sought in the transcendental imagination, then one would have to raise the objection that spontaneity constitutes only one element of the imagination and that consequently, although thought is indeed related to the imagination, the two are by no means completely identical. The imagination is also and above all a faculty of intuition, i.e., receptivity. It is receptive not merely in addition to, and over

33. A 651, B 679, NKS, p. 538.
34. A 567f., B 595f., NKS, p. 485.
35. A 832, B 860, 653; *cf.* also *Vom Wesen des Grundes,* p. 28f.
36. A 570, B 598, NKS, p. 487.
37. *Ibid.*

and above, its spontaneity but in the primordial, non-composite unity of receptivity and spontaneity.

We have shown, however, that pure intuition by reason of its purity has the character of spontaneity. As pure spontaneous receptivity, it has its essence in transcendental imagination.

If pure thought is to have the same essence, it must, as spontaneity, exhibit at the same time the character of receptivity. But does not Kant identify understanding and reason with spontaneity pure and simple?

However, if Kant identifies the understanding with spontaneity, this no more rules out a receptivity on the part of the understanding than the identification of sensibility—finite intuition—with receptivity rules out a corresponding spontaneity. But perhaps the exclusive consideration of empirical intuition tends to emphasize the receptivity of this intuition just as, correlatively, the consideration of the "logical" function of the understanding within empirical knowledge leads to an emphasis of its spontaneity and [connective] function.

On the other hand, in the domain of pure knowledge, i.e., that which has to do with the problem of the possibility of transcendence, pure receptivity, the mode of receptivity which gives to itself (spontaneously) that which offers itself, cannot remain concealed. Therefore, must not the transcendental interpretation of pure thought, while insisting on the spontaneity of the latter, just as vigorously set forth a pure receptivity? Without doubt. This receptivity has already been affirmed in the course of the preceding interpretation of the transcendental deduction and of schematism.

In order to comprehend the essentially intuitive character of pure thought, it is necessary only to understand and retain the true essence of finite intuition as a reception of that which offers itself. Now, it has been established that the fundamental character of the "unity" of transcendental apperception is that, as constantly unifying in advance, it is opposed to all that is haphazard. This is why in the representative act of orientation only this opposition is received and nothing more. The free formative projection which develops affinity while submitting to it is in itself a receptive act of representation. The rules which are represented in the understanding, taken as the faculty of rules, are not apprehended as actually given "in consciousness" but as rules of connection (synthesis) which compel as they connect. If a rule exercises its function only in the receptive act which lets it rule, then the "idea" as the representation of rules can itself represent only in the mode of receptivity.

In this sense, pure thought is in itself—not merely accessorially—pure intuition. Consequently, this spontaneity, which in the very unity of its structure is receptive, must have its origin in the transcendental imagination in order that it can be what it is. As pure apperception, the understanding has the "ground of its possibility" in a faculty which "contemplates an infinity of representations and concepts which it has made itself." [38] Forming it in advance, the transcendental imagination pro-jects the complex of possibilities which it "contemplates," thus proposing the horizon within which the knowing self, and not only this, acts. This is why Kant is able to assert: "Human reason is by its nature architectonic. This is to say, it regards all our knowledge as belonging to a possible system." [39]

The intuitive character inherent in pure thought does not appear so strange to us when we consider that the pure intuitions, space and time, are just as "unintuitive" (as long as "intuitive" is taken to mean "perceptible by organs of sense") as the categories, provided that we understand them correctly, i.e., as pure schemata. The necessity which manifests itself in the ob-jectification of a horizon of ob-jectivity can only be encountered as that which constrains, if the being which encounters it is free to accept it as such. Insofar as freedom implies

38. *Über die Fortschritte der Metaphysik, op. cit.,* VIII, p. 249.
39. A 474, B 502, NKS, p. 429.

placing oneself under a necessity which is self-imposed, it is inherent in the essence of the pure understanding, pure theoretical reason. The understanding and reason are not free because they have the character of spontaneity but because this spontaneity is a receptive spontaneity, i.e., is transcendental imagination.

As the reduction of pure intuition and pure thought to transcendental imagination is accomplished, we become aware that by this reduction the transcendental imagination manifests itself more and more as a structural possibility of transcendence—as that which makes transcendence as the essence of the finite self possible. Thus, the imagination not only ceases to be an empirical faculty of the soul, and one which is discoverable as such; it also is free from that restriction which hitherto has limited its essence to being only the source of the theoretical faculty. And so we must now hazard the last step in the revelation of the "basic originality" of the established ground.

## § 30. Transcendental Imagination and Practical Reason

In the *Critique of Pure Reason,* Kant declares: "By 'the practical' I mean everything that is possible through freedom." [40] However, insofar as the possibility of theoretical reason depends upon freedom, it is in itself, as theoretical, practical. But if finite reason is receptive even in its spontaneity and, therefore, arises from the transcendental imagination, then practical reason must also be based on the latter. However, the origin of practical reason cannot be "deduced" by means of such arguments, no matter how sound they may seem to be, but requires an explicit revelation through an elucidation of the essence of the "practical self."

According to what has been said concerning the ego of

40. A 800, B 828, NKS, p. 632.

pure apperception, the essence of the self lies in "self-consciousness." However, the mode according to which the self exists and the form in which it exists in this "consciousness" is determined through the "Being" of the self. The self is always overt to itself, and this overtness is what it is only insofar as it co-determines the Being of the self. Now, in order to examine the practical self relative to the basis of its possibility, it is necessary first of all to delimit this self-consciousness which makes the self *qua* self possible. In considering this practical, i.e., moral, self-consciousness, we must seek to determine the respect in which its essential structure refers back to the transcendental imagination as its origin.

The moral ego, the self, the true essence of man, Kant also terms the *person*. In what does the essence of the personality of the person consist? "Personality itself is . . . the idea of the moral law and the respect which is inseparable from it." [41] Respect is "susceptibility" to the law, that which renders us capable of responding to it as a moral law. If respect constitutes the essence of the person as the moral self, then according to what has been said, it must be a mode of self-consciousness. In what way is it such?

Can respect function as a mode of self-consciousness when, according to Kant's own designation, it is a "feeling"? The feelings as effective states of pleasure or displeasure belong to sensibility. But since this last is not necessarily determined by bodily states, there remains open the possibility of a pure feeling, one which is not necessarily determined by the affections but "produced by the subject itself." [42] It is necessary, therefore, to examine the essence of feeling in general. The elucidation of this essence will enable us to decide in what way

41. *Religion Within the Limits of Reason Alone,* trans. Theodore M. Greene and Hoyt Hudson (Chicago, 1934), p. 22f.
42. *Fundamental Principles of the Metaphysic of Morals,* trans. Thomas Abbott (New York, 1949), p. 19.

"feeling" in general, and therewith respect as a pure feeling, can constitute a mode of self-consciousness.

Even in the "lower" feelings of pleasure, a fundamental structure that is characteristic is revealed. Pleasure is not only pleasure in something but also a state of enjoyment—a way in which a man experiences joy, in which he is happy. Thus, in every sensible (in the narrow sense of the term) and non-sensible feeling, the following structure is to be found: feeling is a feeling-for . . . and as such is also a way of feeling oneself. The modality according to which this feeling renders the self manifest, i.e., lets it be, is always and essentially co-determined by the nature of the object for which the subject in feeling himself experiences a feeling. How is this structure realized in respect and why is the latter a pure feeling?

Kant presents the analysis of respect in the *Critique of Practical Reason*.[43] The following interpretation will deal only with the essentials of this analysis.

As such, respect is respect for . . . the moral law. It does not serve as a criterion by which to judge our actions, and it does not first appear after a moral act has been carried out—perhaps as a way of adopting an attitude toward this act. On the contrary, respect for the moral law first constitutes the possibility of such an act. Respect for . . . is the way in which the law first becomes accessible to us. It follows, then, that this feeling of respect does not, as Kant expresses it, serve as a "foundation" of the law. The law is not what it is because we have a feeling of respect for it but conversely: this feeling of respect for the law and, hence, the way in which the law is made manifest through it, determines the manner in which the law is as such capable of affecting us.

Feeling is having feeling for . . . so that the ego which experiences this feeling at the same time feels itself. Accord-

43. *Critique of Practical Reason*, trans. L. W. Beck (Chicago, 1949), p. 180ff.

ingly, in respect for the law, the ego which experiences this respect must also, in a certain sense, become manifest to itself. This manifestation is neither subsequent [to the acts] nor is it something that takes place only occasionally. Respect for the law—this specific way of making the law manifest as the basis of the determination of action—is in itself a revelation of myself as the self that acts. That for which the respect is respect, the moral law, the reason as free gives to itself. Respect for the law is respect for oneself as that self which does not let itself be determined by self-conceit and self-love. Respect, in its specific mode of manifestation, has reference to the person. "Respect is always directed toward persons, never things." [44]

In having respect for the law, I submit to it. This specific feeling for . . . which is characteristic of respect is a submission. In having respect for the law, I submit to myself. I am myself in this act of submitting to myself. What, or more precisely who, is the self manifested to myself in this feeling of respect?

In submitting to the law, I submit myself to myself *qua* pure reason. In submitting to myself, I raise myself to myself as a free being capable of self-determination. This raising the self by submitting to the self reveals the ego in its "dignity." Negatively expressed: in having respect for the law which I give to myself as a free being, I am unable to despise myself. Consequently, respect is that mode of being-as-self of the ego which prevents the latter from "rejecting the hero in his soul." Respect is the mode of being responsible for the Being of the self; it is the authentic being-as-self.

The projection of the self, in submission, on the total, fundamental possibility of authentic existence, this possibility being given by the law, is the essence of the self, i.e., practical reason.

The preceding interpretation of the feeling of respect not only reveals to what extent this feeling constitutes practical

44. *Ibid.*, p. 186.

reason but also makes it clear that the concept of feeling in the sense of an empirical faculty of the soul is eliminated and replaced by a transcendental, fundamental structure of the transcendence of the moral self. The expression "feeling" must be understood in this ontologico-metaphysical sense if we are to do justice to what Kant means by his characterization of respect as a "moral feeling" and as the "feeling of my existence." No further steps are now required in order to see that this essential structure of respect lets the primordial nature of the transcendental imagination appear as it is in itself.

The self-submissive, immediate surrender to . . . is pure receptivity; the free self-imposition of the law is pure spontaneity. In themselves, the two are originally one. Furthermore, only by understanding that the origin of practical reason is to be found in the transcendental imagination are we able to understand why it is that in the feeling of respect neither the law nor the active self is objectively apprehended but that both are made manifest therein in a more original, unthematic and unobjective way as duty and action, and form the non-reflective, active mode of being-as-self.

## § 31. The Basic Originality of the Established Ground and Kant's Recoil from Transcendental Imagination

The "highest principle of all synthetic judgments" delimits the complete essence of the transcendence of pure knowledge. The transcendental imagination is manifested as the essential ground of this essence. The more primordial interpretation of the essence of this essential ground which has been given above first reveals the true significance of the highest principle. This principle speaks of the essential constitution of human beings in general insofar as it is defined as finite pure reason.

This fundamental constitution of the essence of man, "rooted"

166

in the transcendental imagination, is the "unknown" of which Kant must have had an intimation when he spoke of "the root unknown to us"; for the unknown is not that of which we know absolutely nothing but that of which the knowledge makes us uneasy. However, Kant did not carry out the primordial interpretation of the transcendental imagination; indeed, he did not even make the attempt, despite the clear indications he gave us concerning such an analytic.

Kant recoiled from this unknown root.

In the second edition of the *Critique of Pure Reason* the transcendental imagination, as it was described in the vigorous language of the first edition,[45] is thrust aside and transformed —to the benefit of the understanding. But at the same time, if he is not to undo the entire laying of the foundation, Kant in the second edition must uphold all that in the first constitutes the transcendental function of the imagination with respect to the establishment of the foundation.

We cannot discuss here the sense in which the pure imagination reappears in the *Critique of Judgment* or whether, in particular, it reappears in that specific relation to the laying of the foundation of metaphysics which was described above.

Kant begins by striking out in the second edition the two principal passages in the preceding edition which specifically present the imagination as a third fundamental faculty beside sensibility and the understanding. The first passage [46] is replaced by a critical discussion of the analyses by Locke and Hume of the understanding, just as if Kant—although mistakenly—looked upon his conception in the first edition as being still too close to the empirical.

The second passage [47] disappears because of the reworking of the transcendental deduction as a whole.

45. See above, §§ 24 and 25.
46. A 94, NKS, p. 127.
47. A 115, NKS, p. 141.

Indeed, even the passage in the first edition of the *Critique of Pure Reason* wherein Kant first introduced the imagination as an "indispensable function of the soul," [48] he later modified, although only in the author's copy, in a way which is highly significant.[49] In place of "function of the soul," he substituted "function of the understanding." Thus, the pure synthesis is assigned to the pure understanding. The pure imagination is no longer indispensable as a faculty in its own right. Thus the possibility of making it the essential basis of ontological knowledge is apparently eliminated, even though the chapter on schematism, wherein this thesis is presented clearly enough, remains unaltered in the second edition.

However, the transcendental imagination is not first revealed as the formative center of pure knowledge in the chapter on schematism (the fourth stage); it is already revealed as such in the transcendental deduction (the third stage). If in the second edition, therefore, the transcendental imagination is to be set aside insofar as its central function as a fundamental faculty is concerned, then the transcendental deduction must first be completely reworked. The transcendental imagination is the disquieting unknown which supplies the motive for the new conception of the transcendental deduction. Through this motive also, the objective of the new treatment of the transcendental deduction first becomes visible.[50] This objective first provides the proper guide for a more penetrating interpretation of the reworking in question. Such an interpretation cannot be presented here. We must be satisfied to indicate the change in position with respect to the transcendental imagination.

The substitution, cited above, of the expression "function of the understanding" for "function of the soul" characterizes Kant's new position with regard to the transcendental imag-

48. A 78, B 103, NKS, p. 112.
49. *Cf. Nachträge*, XLI.
50. *Cf.* below, p. 172.

168

ination. It is no longer a "function" in the sense of an autonomous faculty, but is now a "function" only in the sense of an operation of the faculty of understanding. While in the first edition, all synthesis, i.e., synthesis as such, arises from the imagination as a faculty not reducible either to sensibility or understanding, in the second edition the understanding alone assumes the role of origin for all synthesis.

At the very beginning of the transcendental deduction as presented in the second edition, Kant states that "synthesis" "is an act of spontaneity of the faculty of representation . . . [which] . . . to distinguish it from sensibility, must be entitled understanding." [51] One should notice here the neutral expression "faculty of representation."

"Synthesis" is, in general, the name given to an "act of understanding." [52] The "faculty of combining *a priori*" is the "understanding." [53] This is why Kant now speaks of the "pure synthesis of understanding." [54]

However, Kant is not content only implicitly to attribute the function of synthesis to the understanding; he also states explicitly that "the *transcendental synthesis* . . . is an action of the understanding on the sensibility." [55] "The transcendental act of imagination" is conceived as "the synthetic influence of the understanding upon inner sense." [56]

But does not this passage also indicate that, in spite of everything, the transcendental imagination is retained? Certainly, for its complete elimination in the second edition would have been much too strange, especially since the "function" of the imagination remains indispensable for the problematic. More-

51. B 130, NKS, p. 151.
52. *Ibid.*
53. B 135, NKS, p. 154.
54. B 140, 153; NKS, pp. 158, 166.
55. B 152, NKS, p. 165.
56. B 154, NKS, p. 167.

over, the term continues to figure in those unreworked parts of the *Critique of Pure Reason* which come before and after the transcendental deduction.

Nevertheless, in the second edition the transcendental imagination is present only in name. "It is one and the same spontaneity, which in the one case, under the title of imagination, and in the other case, under the title of understanding, brings combination into the manifold of intuition." [57] Imagination is now only the name of the empirical synthesis, i.e., the synthesis as relative to intuition. This synthesis, as the passages cited above show clearly enough, still belongs *qua* synthesis to the understanding. "Synthesis" is termed "imagination" only insofar as it refers to intuition; fundamentally, however, it is [a product of the] understanding.[58]

The transcendental imagination no longer functions as an autonomous fundamental faculty, mediating between sensibility and understanding in their possible unity. This intermediate faculty disappears and only two fundamental sources of the mind are retained. The function of the transcendental imagination is transferred to the understanding. And when, in the second edition, Kant provides a proper name, apparently descriptive, for the imagination, namely, *synthesis speciosa*,[59] he shows by this expression that the transcendental imagination has lost its former autonomy. It receives this name only because in it the understanding is referred to sensibility and without this reference would be *synthesis intellectualis*.

But why did Kant recoil from the transcendental imagination? Did he perhaps fail to see the possibility of a more primordial laying of the foundation? On the contrary, the preface to the first edition defines the task of such a laying of the foundation with great clarity. In it Kant distinguishes two "sides" of the

57. B 162, NKS, p. 171f.
58. B 151, NKS, p. 164.
59. *Ibid.*

170

transcendental deduction, one "objective," the other "subjective." [60]

This implies, if one holds to the preceding interpretation of the transcendental deduction, that this deduction poses the question of the intrinsic possibility of transcendence and by its answer reveals the horizon of objectivity. The analysis of the objectivity of possible objects is the "objective" side of the deduction.

Objectivity is formed in the self-orienting act of ob-jectification. The question of knowing what faculties are involved in this act and under what conditions it is possible is the question of the subjectivity of the transcending subject as such. It is the "subjective" side of the deduction.

For Kant, what matters above all is the revelation of transcendence in order thus to elucidate the essence of transcendental (ontological) knowledge. This is why he says of the objective deduction: "It is therefore essential to my purposes. The other seeks to investigate the pure understanding itself, its possibility, and the cognitive faculties upon which it rests, and so deals with it in its subjective aspect. Although this latter exposition is of great importance for my chief purpose, it does not form an essential part of it. For the chief question is always simply this: what and how much can the understanding and reason know apart from all experience? not—how is the faculty of thought itself possible?" [61]

The transcendental deduction is in itself objective-subjective and at one and the same time. For this deduction is the revelation of transcendence which first produces the essential orientation of finite subjectivity toward all objectivity. The subjective side of the deduction, then, can never be lacking; however, its explicit elaboration may well be deferred. If Kant has decided on such a course, he is able to do so only because

60. A XVIff., NKS, p. 11ff.
61. A XVII, NKS, p. 12.

of his clear insight into the essence of such an elaboration of the subjective side of the laying of the foundation of metaphysics.

In the description of the transcendental deduction cited above, it is clearly stated that the deduction must lead back to "the cognitive faculties" "upon which [the understanding] rests." Furthermore, Kant sees very clearly that this regression to the origin cannot be an investigation which is psychologically and empirically explicative and which "hypothetically" posits a ground. Now, this task of a transcendental revelation of the essence of the subjectivity of the subject (the "subjective deduction") is not introduced into the preface as an afterthought. On the contrary, even in the preparation of the deduction, Kant speaks of an "enterprise never before attempted" which is necessarily veiled in "obscurity." He does not intend to give an "elaborate" theory of subjectivity even though the "deduction of the categories" "compels" us to enter "deeply into the first grounds of the possibility of our knowledge in general." [62]

Thus, Kant was aware of the possibility and the necessity of a more primordial laying of the foundation, but it formed no part of his immediate purpose. However, this cannot justify the elimination of the transcendental imagination, since it is the latter which forms the unity and ob-jectivity of transcendence. The transcendental imagination itself must have provided the motive which led Kant to turn away from it as an autonomous and transcendental fundamental faculty.

Not having carried out the subjective deduction, Kant continued to be guided by the notions of the composition and characterization of the subjectivity of the subject provided by traditional anthropology and psychology. To these disciplines, the imagination was a lower faculty within sensibility. In fact, the result of the transcendental deduction and the doctrine of schematism, i.e., the insight into the transcendental essence of

62. A 98, NKS, p. 131.

172

pure imagination which they provide, was not in itself enough to permit the subjectivity of the subject as a whole to be seen in a new light.

How can sensibility as a lower faculty be said to determine the essence of reason? Does not everything fall into confusion if the lower is put in place of the higher? What is to happen to the honorable tradition according to which, in the long history of metaphysics, *ratio* and the *logos* have laid claim to the central role? Can the primacy of logic disappear? Can the architectonic of the laying of the foundation of metaphysics, i.e., its division into transcendental aesthetic and logic, be preserved if the theme of the latter is basically the transcendental imagination?

Does not the *Critique of Pure Reason* deprive itself of its own theme if pure reason is transformed into transcendental imagination? Does not this laying of the foundation lead to an abyss?

By his radical interrogation, Kant brought the "possibility" of metaphysics before this abyss. He saw the unknown; he had to draw back. Not only did the imagination fill him with alarm, but in the meantime [between the first and second editions] he had also come more and more under the influence of pure reason as such.

Through the laying of the foundation of metaphysics in general, Kant first acquired a clear insight into the character of the "universality" of ontologico-metaphysical knowledge. Now, for the first time, he had the means to undertake a critical exploration of the domain of "moral philosophy" and to replace the vague, empirical generality of the ethical doctrines of popular philosophy by those essential and primordial ontological analyses which alone are capable of securing a metaphysic of morals and the foundation thereof. In the struggle against the superficial and palliative empiricism of the reigning moral philosophy, Kant attached increasing importance to the dis-

173

tinction which he established between the *a priori* and the empirical. And since the essence of the subjectivity of the subject is to be found in personality, which last is identical with moral reason, the rationality of pure knowledge and of [moral] action must be affirmed. All pure synthesis, indeed, all synthesis in general, must as relevant to spontaneity depend on that faculty which in the strictest sense is free, the active reason.

The purely rational character of the personality, which becomes even more obvious, cannot, even for Kant, cast doubt upon the finitude of man if it is true that a being determined by morality and duty [*Sittlichkeit und Sollen*] neither is nor can become "infinite." Rather, it awoke Kant to the realization that finitude must be sought in the purely rational being itself and not first in the circumstance that this being is determined by "sensibility." Only through this realization can morality be conceived as pure, i.e., as neither conditioned nor created by the empirical individual.

This ontological problem of the person as finite pure reason cannot be formulated with reference to anything peculiar to the constitution and mode of existence of a particular type of finite, rational being. Such, however, is the imagination which is not only regarded as a specifically human faculty but also as a sensible one.

Being thus self-reinforcing, the problematic of a pure reason must inevitably thrust the imagination into the background, thus concealing its transcendental nature completely.

It is incontestable that the distinction between a finite rational being in general and man as a particular example of such a being comes to the fore in the transcendental deduction as the latter appears in the second edition. Indeed, even Kant's first "correction," appearing on the first page of the second edition, makes this clear. To the characterization of finite knowledge, more precisely, to that of finite intuition, he adds: "to man at least." [63] This is intended to show that although all

63. B 33, NKS, p. 65.

174

finite intuition is receptive, this receptivity does not necessarily, as is the case with man, require the mediation of sense organs.

The "strangeness" and obscurity of the transcendental imagination as it appears in its capacity as the established ground in the first attempt to lay the foundation, on the one hand, and the luminous power of pure reason on the other, combine to obscure anew that prospect of the primordial essence of the transcendental imagination which, as it were, opened up only for an instant.

Considered in the light of the basic problem of the *Critique of Pure Reason,* such is the fundamental import of an observation long made by Kant's commentators, an observation usually expressed as follows: Kant has turned from the "psychological" interpretation of the first edition to the more "logical" interpretation of the second.

It should be noted, in truth, that the laying of the foundation is no more "psychological" in the first edition than it is "logical" in the second. On the contrary, both are transcendental, i.e., necessarily "objective" as well as "subjective." All that takes place so far as the subjective transcendental deduction is concerned is that in order to preserve the supremacy of reason the second edition has decided for the pure understanding as opposed to the pure imagination. In the second edition, the subjective "psychological" deduction does not disappear. On the contrary, because it is oriented on the pure understanding as the faculty of synthesis, the subjective side becomes even more prominent. To attempt to trace the understanding back to a more primordial "faculty of knowledge" is, henceforth, superfluous.

The interpretation of the stages of the laying of the foundation of metaphysics presented above is oriented exclusively on the first edition and always keeps the finitude of human transcendence in the center of the problematic. In the second edition, Kant has enlarged the concept of a rational finite being to the point where it no longer coincides with the con-

175

cept of man and thus has posed the problem of finitude with greater comprehensiveness. Is this not reason enough for an essential interpretation of the *Critique* to adhere to the second edition? According to what has been said, it is evident that this edition is not "better" because it proceeds in a more logical manner. On the contrary, when correctly understood, this edition is even more "psychological" simply because it is oriented exclusively on pure reason as such.

But are not these considerations enough to condemn the present interpretation and, above all, the primordial explication of the transcendental imagination which it proposes?

But why, from the beginning, has the finitude of pure knowledge been placed at the center [of our interpretation]? Because metaphysics, with the laying of the foundation of which we are concerned, belongs to "human nature." Consequently, the specific finitude of human nature is decisive for the laying of this foundation. This question, apparently superficial, as to whether, in the interpretation of the *Critique of Pure Reason,* the second edition deserves to be ranked over the first or conversely is only the pale reflection of a question which is decisive insofar as the Kantian laying of the foundation is concerned: Is the transcendental imagination as the established ground solid enough to determine primordially, i.e., in its unity and its totality, the finite essence of the subjectivity of the human subject? Or, on the contrary, with the elimination of the transcendental imagination does the problem of a finite, human pure reason assume a more comprehensible form and thus approach nearer to a possible solution? As long as this question is not decided, the more primordial interpretation of the transcendental imagination, attempted here, remains necessarily incomplete.

## C. The Transcendental Imagination and the Problem of Human Pure Reason

To begin with, we will show by a decisive argument that the *Critique of Pure Reason* as a laying of the foundation of metaphysics from the first treats only of human pure reason. The formulation of the problem of the possibility of *metaphysica generalis* reads: "How are *a priori* synthetic judgments possible?" Kant's solution of the problem is set forth as follows:

"The problem mentioned above may be solved only relative to those faculties which permit man to enlarge his knowledge *a priori*. These faculties constitute in man what may be *properly termed his pure reason*. For, if we understand by the pure reason of a being in general the faculty of knowing things independently of experience and therefore of sensible representations, we by no means determine thereby the manner in which such knowledge is possible for the being in question (for example, for God or for any other higher spirit), and the problem, therefore, remains undecided. On the other hand, *insofar as man is concerned,* all knowledge is composed of two elements: concept and intuition." [64]

This passage is to be found in the treatise entitled *On the Progress of Metaphysics*. The composition of this treatise shows that Kant was fully and immediately conscious of the problems inherent in metaphysics as such. In a laying of the foundation of metaphysics, therefore, the problem is the "specific" finitude of human subjectivity. And this finitude cannot be introduced merely as a possible "case" of a finite rational being.

Human finitude necessarily involves sensibility in the sense of receptive intuition. As pure intuition (pure sensibility) it is

---

64. *Über die Fortschritte der Metaphysik, op. cit.,* VIII, p. 312 (italics are Heidegger's).

a necessary element of the structure of transcendence characteristic of finitude. Human pure reason is necessarily pure sensible reason. This pure reason must be sensible in itself and not become so merely because it is connected with a body. Rather, the converse is true; man as a finite rational being can in a transcendental, i.e., metaphysical, sense "have" his body only because transcendence as such is sensible *a priori*.

Now, if transcendental imagination is to be the primordial ground of human subjectivity taken in its unity and totality, then it must also make possible a faculty on the order of pure sensible reason. But pure sensibility, according to the universal signification in which it must be taken for the laying of the foundation of metaphysics, is time.

How can time as pure sensibility form a primordial unity with the "I think"? Is the pure ego which, according to the interpretation generally accepted, Kant conceived to be extratemporal and opposed to time, to be considered as "temporal"? And all this on the basis of the transcendental imagination? How, in general, is the latter related to time?

## § 32. The Transcendental Imagination and Its Relation to Time

We have shown how the transcendental imagination is the origin of pure sensible intuition.[65] Thus, we have proved essentially that time as pure intuition arises from the transcendental imagination. However, a specific, analytical explication of the precise manner in which time is based upon the transcendental imagination is necessary.

As the pure succession of the *now*-series, time is "in constant flux."[66] Pure intuition intuits this succession unobjectively. To intuit means: to receive that which offers itself. Pure intuition

65. See above, § 28, p. 148.
66. B 291, NKS, p. 255.

178

gives to itself, in the receptive act, that which is capable of being received.

Reception of . . . is usually understood as the act of receiving something given or present. But this limited conception of the receptive act, a conception inspired by empirical intuition, must not be applied to pure intuition and its characteristic receptivity. It is easy to see that the pure intuition of the pure succession of *nows* cannot be the reception of something actually present. If it were, then it could at most only "intuit" the actual *now* but never the *now*-sequence as such and the horizon which it forms. Strictly speaking, the simple act of receiving something actually present could not even intuit a single *now,* since each *now* has an essentially continuous extension in a *just passing* and *just coming* [*Soeben und Sogleich*]. The receptive act of pure intuition must in itself give the aspect of the *now* in such a way that it looks ahead to the *just coming* and back to the *just passing.*

We now discover, and in a more concrete way, why it is that pure intuition, which is the subject of the transcendental aesthetic, cannot be the reception of something "present." Pure intuition which, as receptive, gives itself its object is by nature not relative to the presence of something, least of all to [the presence of] an essent actually given.

If the act of pure intuition has this character, does it not follow from this that it is "at bottom" pure imagination? This follows only insofar as pure intuition itself forms [*bildet*] that which it is able to receive. But that this originally formative act should be in itself, and at one and the same time, an act of looking at, looking ahead, and looking back—certainly this has nothing to do with the transcendental imagination!

If only Kant himself had not *specifically* set forth the three-fold way in which the act of imagination is formative!

In his lectures on metaphysics and, in particular, those having to do with rational psychology, Kant analysed the "formative power" as follows: this faculty "produces representations relative to the present, the past, or the future. Consequently, the faculty of imagination consists of:

(1) the faculty of forming images [*Abbildung*], the representations of which are of the present: *facultas formandi,*

(2) the faculty of reproducing images, the representations of which are of the past: *facultas imaginandi,*

(3) the faculty of anticipating images, the representations of which are of the future: *facultas praevidendi.*" [67]

The expression "forming images" requires a brief explanation. This expression does not signify the making of a reproduction in the sense of a copy but signifies the aspect which is immediately taken of the object, itself present. This forming of an image does not mean reproducing an image in the likeness of the object but putting into an image in the sense of the immediate apprehension of the appearance [*Aussehen*] of the object itself.

Although in this passage, Kant does not speak of the transcendental imagination, it is clear that the "formation of of images" by the imagination is *in itself* relative to time. Pure imagination, thus termed because it forms its images [*Gebilde*] spontaneously, must, since it is itself relative to time, constitute [form] time originally. Time as pure intuition is neither only what is intuited in the pure act of intuition nor this act itself deprived of its "object." Time as pure intuition is *in one* the formative act of intuiting and what is intuited therein. Such is the complete concept of time.

Pure intuition can form the pure succession of the *now*-sequence only if, in itself, it is imagination as that which forms, reproduces, and anticipates. Hence it follows that time, above

67. Politz, *Vorlesungen über die Metaphysik, op. cit.,* p. 88, *cf.* p. 83.

180

all in the Kantian sense, should not be thought of as an indifferent field of action which the imagination enters, as it were, in order to further its own activity. Although, on the ordinary plane of experience where "we take account of time," we must consider it to be a pure succession of *nows,* this succession by no means constitutes primordial time. On the contrary, the transcendental imagination as that which lets time as the *now*-sequence spring forth is—as the origin of the latter—primordial time.

But can such a radical interpretation of the imagination, i.e., as primordial time, be justified by Kant's infrequent references to the subject? The important consequences which result from this interpretation demand that it be more concretely and securely established.

### § 33. The Inherently Temporal Character of the Transcendental Imagination

In the first edition of the *Critique* the imagination is termed the faculty of "synthesis in general." Therefore, if we wish to exhibit the inherently temporal character of the imagination we must examine the passage wherein Kant expressly treats of the nature of synthesis. This passage is found in the section which prepares the way for the carrying out of the transcendental deduction according to the two ways previously considered. The section is entitled: *"The* a priori *Grounds of the Possibility of Experience."* [68]

The location in the text of the thematic analysis of the notion of synthesis is not arbitrary. And if, in particular, Kant presents the discussion of this notion in the form of a *Preliminary Remark,*[68a] one should not take it to be a casual and, at bottom, superfluous observation. On the contrary, the content of this

68. A 95ff., NKS, p. 129ff.
68a. A 98, NKS, p. 131.

181

passage insofar as its bearing on the transcendental deduction and the transcendental schematism is concerned must be kept in view from the first. In this connection, it will be recalled that the transcendental deduction as the third stage of the laying of the foundation has as its object the demonstration of the intrinsic possibility of the essential unity of the ontological synthesis.

The three elements of pure knowledge are: pure intuition, pure imagination, and pure understanding. The possibility of their unity, i.e., the essence of their original unification (synthesis) is the problem. For this reason, an elucidation of the synthesis relative to these three elements is required.

Kant divided his preliminary remark into three sections: "I. *The Synthesis of Apprehension in Intuition;* II. *The Synthesis of Reproduction in Imagination;* III. *The Synthesis of Recognition in Concepts.*"

But are these modes of synthesis three in number because the essential unity of knowledge requires three elements? Or has the fact that there are three modes of synthesis a more fundamental ground, one which explains why these modes as modes of pure synthesis are unified and hence capable, on the basis of this original unity, of "forming" the essential unity of the three elements of pure knowledge?

Or again, are there three modes of synthesis because time appears in them, and they express the threefold unity of time as past, present, and future? Now, if the original unification of the essential unity of ontological knowledge takes place through time and if, on the other hand, the basis of the possibility of knowledge is the transcendental imagination, is it not obvious that the latter is primordial time? And yet, in the course of enumerating the three modes of synthesis does not Kant, by designating the second as "the synthesis of reproduction in imagination," say in effect that the imagination is only one element among others and in no way the root of concept and intuition? Yes, he does.

But the transcendental deduction which is to be provided with a foundation by this analysis of the threefold synthesis shows just as indisputably that the imagination is not merely one faculty among others but their formative center. That the transcendental imagination is the root of sensibility and understanding first became evident through the more primordial interpretation that has been given it. We may not make use of this result here. Rather, the working out of the inherently temporal character of the three modes of synthesis should provide the ultimate and decisive proof that the interpretation of the transcendental imagination as the root of the two stems is not only possible but necessary.

In order to be generally understood, the Kantian analysis of the three modes of synthesis requires clarification on several points which must be kept in view in what follows.

First of all, Kant's mode of expression needs to be made more precise. In particular, what is meant by the synthesis "of" apprehension, the synthesis "of" reproduction, the synthesis "of" recognition? The meaning of this "of" is not that apprehension, reproduction, and recognition are subjected to a synthesis, or that they effect a synthesis, but that synthesis as such has the character of apprehension, reproduction, or recognition. In other words, these expressions mean respectively: synthesis in the modes of apprehension, reproduction, and recognition; or again, synthesis as apprehending, reproducing, or recognizing. Thus, Kant treats of synthesis, i.e., of the faculty of synthesis, relative to these three modes, each of which characterize it in a specific way.

On the other hand, it should be noted that in the individual paragraphs of the transcendental deduction the explication of the modes of synthesis begins by describing the way in which

183

they function in empirical intuition, empirical imagination, and empirical thought. This preliminary characterization is also intended to show that in pure intuition, pure imagination, and pure thought there are to be found corresponding modes of pure synthesis constitutive of each. At the same time, Kant shows that these modes of pure synthesis constitute the condition of the possibility of the empirical synthesis in the cognitive relation to the essent.

Furthermore, it should be noted that the true objective of the interpretation of the three modes of synthesis—although not always formulated with sufficient clarity—is the exhibition of the internal and essential interrelatedness which these modes enjoy in virtue of their common inherence in the essence of pure synthesis as such.

And finally, as Kant himself specifically requested, we must not forget that "throughout what follows this must be borne in mind as being quite fundamental": "all our representations . . . are subject to time." Therefore, if all representation, whether intuitive, imaginative, or reflective, is governed by the threefold synthesis, does not this imply that all representation is unified in advance through its subjection to the temporal character of this synthesis?

### a) PURE SYNTHESIS AS PURE IMAGINATION [69]

Empirical intuition as the immediate reception of a "this-here" [Dies-da] always reveals something manifold. Therefore, the aspect obtained by this intuition "contains" a manifold. This manifold can be "represented as a manifold only insofar as the mind distinguishes the time in the sequence of one impression upon another." In distinguishing time, the mind must constantly and in advance say "now and now and now" in order to be able to encounter "now this" and "now that" and

69. A 98–100, NKS, pp. 131–2.

"now all this at once." Only by distinguishing the *now's* in this way is it possible to "run through" the impressions and hold them together.

Intuition is a representation of a manifold—a *repraesentatio singularis*—only if, as receptive, it takes up and comprehends "directly" and at once the manifold which presents itself. Intuition is "synthetic" in itself. This synthesis is unique in that it "directly" takes an aspect (image) of the impressions which present themselves in the horizon of the succession of *now's*. It is, in the sense described, an immediate forming of an image.

It is also necessary that we have a pure synthesis of apprehension, because without it we could not have the representation of time, i.e., the pure intuition itself. This pure synthesis of apprehension does not first take place within the horizon of time; rather, it is this synthesis itself which first forms the *now* and the *now*-sequence. Pure intuition is "original receptivity," an act of receiving that which it spontaneously lets come forth. Its mode of presentation is a productive one, and what the pure intuitive presentation (as that which procures an aspect) produces (creates) is the immediate aspect of the *now* as such, that is, it produces at each instant the aspect of the actual present as such.

Empirical intuition is directly concerned with the essent present in the *now;* the synthesis of apprehension, however, is concerned with the *now* (the present itself), but in such a way that this concern with . . . in itself forms that with which it is concerned. The pure synthesis as apprehension is, as presentative of the "present in general," time-forming.

Now, Kant states specifically: "there must therefore exist in us an active faculty for the synthesis of this manifold. To this faculty I give the title imagination. Its action, when immediately directed upon perceptions, I entitle apprehension." [70]

Synthesis in the mode of apprehension arises from the

70. A 120, NKS, p. 144; *cf.* also Kant's note.

imagination; hence, the pure synthesis of apprehension must be considered as a mode of the transcendental imagination. Now, if this synthesis is time-forming, then the transcendental imagination itself possesses a pure temporal character. Inasmuch as pure imagination is an "ingredient" of pure intuition and that, accordingly, a synthesis of the imagination is to be found in intuition, that which Kant later designates as "imagination" cannot be identical with the transcendental imagination.

### b) PURE SYNTHESIS AS PURE REPRODUCTION [71]

Kant again begins his analysis with a reference to the reproductive synthesis in empirical representation. The "mind" can represent the essent, i.e., something previously perceived, "even in the absence of the object." Such representation, or as Kant says, "imagination," presupposes, however, that the mind has the possibility of bringing back [*beibringen*] in the form of a representation the essent previously represented, in order to represent it in its real [*seiend*] unity with the essent actually perceived. This act of bringing-back-again (reproduction) is thus an act of unification.

However, this reproductive synthesis can only unify if the mind in its act of bringing-back-again does not "drop out of thought" [72] that which it brings back. Hence, such a synthesis necessarily includes the power of retention. Essents experienced earlier can be retained only if the mind "distinguishes time" and, therefore, grasps such temporal determinations as "earlier" and "in the past." An essent experienced earlier would be completely lost with each additional *now* if it were not capable of being retained. Therefore, if the empirical synthesis is to be possible, the no-longer-now *as such* must, in advance and before all experience, be capable of being brought back to the present and united with the actual *now*. This occurs in pure

71. A 100–103, NKS, pp. 132–3.
72. A 102, NKS, p. 133.

186

reproduction as a mode of pure synthesis. And if the empirical synthesis of reproduction belongs primarily to empirical imagination, then pure reproduction is a pure synthesis of pure imagination.

But is not pure imagination supposed to be essentially productive? Why should a reproductive synthesis pertain to it? Pure reproduction—does not this imply a productive reproduction, a square circle?

But is pure reproduction truly a productive act of reproduction? This act forms, in fact, the possibility of reproduction in general, and in this way: it brings the horizon of the earlier in view and holds it open as such in advance.[73] Pure synthesis in the mode of reproduction forms the past as such. This signifies, however, that pure imagination, relative to this mode of synthesis, is time-forming. It can be termed "re-production" not because it looks back to an essent which has disappeared or which has been previously experienced but because, in general, it discloses the horizon of a possible looking-back-to, i.e., the past, and thus "forms" "posteriority" and the [movement] "back-to" that which was.

But in this formation of time according to the mode of "the

73. Kant asserts (A 102, NKS, p. 133): "a reproductive synthesis of the imagination is to be counted among the transcendental acts of the mind." Now, Kant usually terms the non-transcendental imagination (i.e., the empirical) reproductive imagination. If one takes "reproductive" in the sense of "empirical" then the statement cited above becomes meaningless. For this reason, Riehl (*Korrekturen zu Kant, Kantstudien,* Vol. V [1901], p. 268) proposes to read "productive" in place of "reproductive." This would undoubtedly avoid the alleged inconsistency, but it would also set aside what Kant intended to express in this sentence, namely, that the productive, i.e., here, pure, imagination is purely productive in that it makes reproduction in general possible. The insertion of "productive" makes sense only if it is not intended to replace the term "reproductive" but to determine it more precisely. This, however, is made superfluous by the whole context. If the context is to be amended at all, it is necessary to read "pure reproductive synthesis."

187

past" where are we to find the pure synthesis? The act which originally retains "the past" is in itself an act which forms and retains the no-longer-now. This act of formation is as such united with a *now*. Pure reproduction is essentially one with the pure synthesis of intuition as that which forms the present. "The synthesis of apprehension is therefore inseparably bound up with the synthesis of reproduction," [74] for every *now* is now already past. In order to provide the present aspect directly in the form of an image, the synthesis of apprehension must be able to retain the manifold which it has just run through and, at the same time, function as a pure synthesis of reproduction.

However, if the pure synthesis of apprehension as well as that of reproduction is an activity of the transcendental imagination, then this last must be understood as a faculty of "synthesis in general" which "inseparably" functions synthetically according to these two modes. In this original unity of both modes, therefore, the imagination can also be the origin of time (as the unity of the present and the past). If this original unity of both modes of synthesis did not exist, "not even the purest and most elementary representations of space and time could arise." [75]

Nevertheless, if time is the tri-unitary totality of present, past, and future, and if Kant adds a third mode to the two modes of synthesis which we have just shown to be time-forming, and finally, if all representation, including thought itself, must be subject to time, then this third mode of synthesis must be that which "forms" the future.

c) PURE SYNTHESIS AS PURE RECOGNITION [76]

The analysis of the third mode of synthesis is much more extensive than either of the other two, although at first sight it seems fruitless to seek therein what, according to the "com-

74. A 102, NKS, p. 133.
75. *Ibid.*
76. A 103–110, NKS, pp. 133–8.

188

pelling" argumentation just given, one should expect to find. The synthesis of pure recognition is to constitute the third element of pure knowledge, namely, pure thought. But what has recognition to do with the production of the future? How is pure thought, the ego of pure apperception, to have a temporal character when Kant specifically sets the "I think" and reason in general opposite to all temporal relation?

"Pure reason as a purely intelligible faculty is not subject to the form of time, nor consequently to the conditions of succession of time." [77] And immediately after the chapter on schematism, in the introduction to the determination of the highest principle of all synthetic judgments, does not Kant show that all temporal characteristics must be excluded from the "highest principle of all analytic judgments," the law of non-contradiction, which circumscribes the essence of pure thought? The "at one and the same time" (*ama*) can have no place in the formulation of this principle. Otherwise, the proposition would be "modified by the condition of time." [78] "The principle of contradiction, however, as a merely logical principle, must not in any way limit its assertions to time-relations. The above formula is therefore completely contrary to the intention of the principle." [79]

Is it surprising, then, that one finds nothing in Kant about the temporal character of the third mode of synthesis? It is fruitless, however, to indulge in mere supposition or to let the matter be decided by what can be discovered by a superficial reading of Kant's discussion of this third synthesis.

Kant begins the exposition of the third mode of synthesis with a characterization of empirical recognition. He proceeds from synthesis as reproduction: "If we were not conscious that what we think is the same as what we thought a moment before, all reproduction in the series of representations would be use-

77. A 551, B 579, NKS, p. 475.
78. A 152, B 191, NKS, p. 191.
79. A 152f., B 192, NKS, p. 191.

less." [80] The reproductive synthesis must effect and maintain the unification of what it brings back with the essent actually manifest in perception.

But when the mind, returning from its regression into the past, turns again to the essent now present, what assurance does it have that this essent now present is the same as the one which, as it were, it previously abandoned in order to effect this representation? The reproductive synthesis, according to its nature, comes upon something which it holds to be the essent experienced before, during, and after its work in the present perception. This perception itself, however, intends only the essent in its immediate presence.

But does not the whole succession of representations break up into isolated representations so that the synthesis of reproduction when it returns [from the past to the present] must at every instant unite that which it brings back with the essent actually at hand, which last, therefore, is always other [than what is brought back]? What must the unity of intuition, which apprehends, and imagination, which reproduces, be like if what they would present to us as one and the same is, as it were, placeless?

Or, can we say that this place is first created after the achievement of the perception and the recollection associated with it, a recollection which would unite its object with the reality present in "the actual state"? Or are both of these modes of synthesis oriented in advance on the essent as present in its identity?

This is obviously the case. For at the basis of both syntheses and determining them there lies an act of unification (synthesis) of the essent relative to its identity. The synthesis intending this identity, i.e., that which pro-poses the essent as identical, Kant terms, and justly so, synthesis "in concepts," for a concept is indeed a representation of unity which in its identity "applies to

80. A 103, NKS, p. 133.

190

many." "For this unitary consciousness is what combines the manifold, successively intuited and thereupon also reproduced, into one representation." [81]

The synthesis which, according to the description of the empirical genesis of concepts, is the third is precisely the first, i.e., the one which governs the other two described above. It anticipates them, as it were. Kant gives this synthesis of identification a name which is most appropriate. Its mode of unification is a recognition. It pro-spects [*erkundet*] and "investigates" [82] that which must be pro-posed in advance as identical, in order that the syntheses of apprehension and reproduction can find a closed field of essents within which they can fix and receive as essent that which they bring back or encounter.

As empirical, this prospective synthesis of identification necessarily presupposes a pure identification. This means that just as pure reproduction constitutes the possibility of a bringing-back-again, so, correlatively, must pure recognition provide the possibility for all identification. However, if the function of this pure synthesis is recognition, this does not mean that its prospecting is concerned with an essent which it can pro-pose to itself as identical but that it prospects the horizon of pro-position in general. As pure, its prospecting is the pure formation of that which makes all projection [*Vorhaften*] possible, i.e., the future. Thus, the third mode of synthesis also proves to be essentially time-forming. And inasmuch as Kant attributes the modes of forming, reproducing, and pre-forming [*Ab- Nach- und Vorbildung*] images to the empirical imagination, the act of forming the prospective horizon as such, pure pre-formation, is an act of pure imagination.

Although it first appeared fruitless, even absurd, to attempt to explain the internal formation of pure concepts by considering them as being essentially determined by time, we have now

81. *Ibid.*, NKS, p. 134.
82. A 126, NKS, p. 147.

not only brought to light the temporal character of the third mode of pure synthesis but have also shown that this mode of pure pre-formation, insofar as its internal structure is concerned, enjoys a priority over the other two, with which last, nevertheless, it is essentially connected. Is it not evident, then, that the Kantian analysis of pure synthesis in concepts, despite the fact that it apparently has nothing to do with time, in reality reveals the most primordial essence of time, that is, that it temporalizes itself primarily out of the future?

Be that as it may, we have succeeded in showing the intrinsically temporal character of the transcendental imagination. If the transcendental imagination as the pure formative faculty in itself forms time, i.e., lets it spring forth, then the thesis stated above, that transcendental imagination is primordial time, can no longer be avoided.

The universal character of pure sensibility, i.e., time, has now also been revealed. The transcendental imagination, therefore, is capable of forming and sustaining the unity and primordial totality of the specific finitude of the human subject which last has been presented as pure, sensible reason.

But do not pure sensibility (time) and pure reason remain absolutely heterogeneous? And is not the concept of a pure, sensible reason self-contradictory? The objections raised against the attempt to understand the selfhood of the self as intrinsically temporal, i.e., not limited in its temporal character to the way in which it is empirically apprehended, seem invincible.

But if the attempt to prove that the self is temporal will not succeed, perhaps the opposite procedure will have a better chance of success. In short, what about a proof that time as such has the character of selfhood? The chance of its being unsuccessful is the less because it is incontestable that time "apart from the subject, is nothing," [83] and this implies that in the subject it is all.

83. A 35, B 51, NKS, p. 78.

192

But what is the meaning of the expression "in the subject"? Time is not contained in the subject as cells are contained in the brain. Hence there is little to be gained by constantly invoking the subjectivity of time. Is Kant limited then to this negative insight, that time "apart from the subject, is nothing"? Has he not shown in the transcendental deduction and in the chapter on schematism that time is essentially involved in the intrinsic structure of transcendence? And does not transcendence determine the being-as-self of the finite self? Must not this aspect of subjectivity be kept in view if one aspires to an investigation of the much discussed "subjective" character of time? If Kant has come upon time in the "depths" of the essential foundation of transcendence, is what is said about time by way of introduction in the transcendental aesthetic to be taken as the last word on the matter? Or is what is there discussed only a reference to the more primordial nature of time? All things considered, cannot the temporal character of the subject be elucidated only from the subjective character of time—provided, of course, that the latter is correctly understood?

### § 34. Time as Pure Self-affection and the Temporal Character of the Self

In the passage wherein he first describes the essential unity of knowledge (the second stage of the laying of the foundation), Kant remarks that "space and time . . . must also always affect the concept" [84] of our representations of objects. What is the meaning of this seemingly obscure thesis, i.e., that time affects a concept, in particular, the concept of the representations of objects?

We will begin the interpretation with a clarification of the expression "concept of our representations of objects." This

84. A 77, B 102, NKS, p. 111.

expression refers, first of all, to the "universality" which characterizes all representation of objects as such, i.e., the objectification of. . . . This act, the thesis asserts, is necessarily affected by time. But hitherto, observations concerning time were limited to the assertion that time and also space form the horizon within which the affections of sense are able to get through to and solicit us [uns treffen und angehen]. Now, it is time itself which affects us. But all affection is a manifestation by which an essent already on hand gives notice of itself. Time, however, is neither on hand nor is it "outside" us. Where does it come from if it is to affect us?

Time is pure intuition only in that it spontaneously preforms the aspect of succession and, as an act both receptive and formative, pro-poses this aspect as such to itself. This pure intuition solicits itself [geht sich an] by that which it intuits (forms) and without the aid of experience. Time is, by nature, pure affection of itself. But more than this, it is that in general which forms something on the order of a line of orientation which going from the self is directed toward . . . in such a way that the objective thus constituted springs forth and surges back along this line.[85]

As pure self-affection, time is not an active affection concerned with the concrete self; as pure, it forms the essence of all auto-solicitation. Therefore, if the power of being solicited as a self belongs to the essence of the finite subject, time as pure self-affection forms the essential structure of subjectivity.

---

85. *Ja, noch mehr, sie ist gerade das, was überhaupt so etwas wie das "Von-sich-aus-zu-auf . . ." bildet, dergestalt, dass das so sich bildende Worauf-zu zurückblickt und herein in das Vorgenannte Hin-zu . . .*

For an understanding of this passage, familiarity with Heidegger's analysis of "decisiveness running ahead of itself" *vorlaufende Entschlossenheit,* i.e., to death as a possibility, is helpful. See *Sein und Zeit,* p. 298ff., p. 324ff. (J. S. C.).

Only on the basis of this selfhood can a finite being be what it must be: a being dependent on receptivity.

Now we are in a position to clarify the meaning of the statement: Time necessarily affects the concept of the representations of objects. To affect *a priori* the act of ob-jectification as such, i.e., the pure act of orientation toward . . . means: to bring up against it something on the order of an opposition, "It"—the pure act of ob-jectification—being pure apperception, the ego itself. Time is implicated in the internal possibility of this act of ob-jectification. As pure self-affection, it originally forms finite selfhood in such a way that the self can become self-consciousness.

In working out the presuppositions which are decisive insofar as the intrinsic problematic of the *Critique of Pure Reason* is concerned,[86] we accorded a central importance to the finitude of knowledge. This finitude of knowledge depends upon the finitude of intuition, on receptivity. Consequently, pure knowledge, in other words, knowledge of the ob-jective as such, the pure concept, is based on a receptive intuition. Pure receptivity is [found in a subject] affected in the absence of experience, i.e., [in a subject which] affects itself.

Time as pure self-affection is that finite, pure intuition which sustains and makes possible the pure concept (the understanding) as that which is essentially at the service of intuition.

Hence, it is not in the second edition that Kant first introduces the idea of pure self-affection, which last, as has now become clear, determines the innermost essence of transcendence. It is simply that the idea is formulated more explicitly in this edition and, characteristically enough, appears [at the beginning of the work] in the transcendental aesthetic.[87] To be sure, this passage must remain obscure as long as the interpretation lacks that perspective assured by the more primordial

86. *Cf.* above, § 4, p. 27.
87. B 67f., NKS, p. 87f.

comprehension of the laying of the foundation of metaphysics made possible by the preceding presentation of the stages of this foundation. But given this perspective, the passage is almost "self-evident."

"Now that which, as representation, can be antecedent to any and every act of thinking anything, is intuition; and if it contains nothing but relations, it is the form of intuition. Since this form does not represent anything save insofar as something is posited in the mind, it can be nothing but the mode in which the mind is affected through its own activity (namely, through this positing of [their] representation), and so is affected by itself; in other words, it is nothing but an inner sense in respect of the form of that sense." [88]

"Sense" means "finite intuition." The form of sense, therefore, is pure receptivity. The internal sense does not receive "from without" but from the self. In pure receptivity, internal affection must arise from the pure self, i.e., be formed in the essence of selfhood as such, and therefore must constitute the latter. Pure self-affection provides the transcendental ground-structure [*Urstruktur*] of the finite self as such. Therefore, it is absolutely untrue that the mind exists in such a way that, among other beings, it relates certain things to itself and in so doing posits itself [*Selbstsetzungen ausübt*]. Rather, this line of orientation from the self toward . . . and back to [the self] first constitutes the mental character of the mind as a finite self.

It is at once obvious, therefore, that time as pure self-

88. *Ibid.* The proposed change of "their representation" [*Ihrer Vorstellung*] to "its representation" [*seiner Vorstellung*] is the result of a misunderstanding of the essential sense of the text. The "their" is not meant to express that the representation is a representation of the mind, but, posited by the mind, re-presents the "pure relations" of the succession of the *now*-sequence as such and pro-poses them to receptivity.

affection is not found "in the mind" "beside" pure apperception. On the contrary, as the basis of the possibility of selfhood, time is already included in pure apperception and first enables the mind to be what it is.

The pure finite self has in itself a temporal character. Therefore, if the ego, i.e., pure reason, is essentially temporal, the fundamental determination which Kant provides for transcendental apperception must first become intelligible through this temporal character.

Time and the "I think" are no longer opposed to one another as unlike and incompatible; they are the same. Thanks to the radicalism with which, in the laying of the foundation of metaphysics, Kant for the first time subjected time and the "I think," each taken separately, to a transcendental interpretation, he succeeded in bringing them together in their primordial identity —without, to be sure, having seen this identity expressly as such.

Can one still consider it to be of no importance that in speaking of time and the "I think," Kant used the same essential predicates?

In the transcendental deduction, the transcendental nature (i.e., that which makes transcendence possible) of the ego is thus described: "The abiding and unchanging 'I' (pure apperception) forms the correlate of all our representations." [89] And in the chapter on schematism wherein the transcendental essence of time is brought to light, Kant says: "The existence of what is transitory passes away in time but not time itself." [90] And further on: "Time . . . does not change." [91]

Naturally, it could be objected that this coincidence of essential predicates is not surprising, for Kant in making use of this terminology intends only to assert that neither the ego

89. A 123, NKS, p. 146.
90. A 143, B 183, NKS, p. 184.
91. A 182, B 225, NKS, p. 213.

nor time is "in time." Certainly, but does it follow from this that the ego is not temporal? Rather, is it not necessary to conclude that the ego is so temporal that it is time itself and that only as such in its very essence is it possible at all?

What does it mean to say that the "abiding and unchanging 'I' forms the correlate of all our representations"? First of all, that the "abiding and unchanging" ego carries out the act of ob-jectification, which act forms not only the relation of from-the-self-toward . . . [*Hin-zu-auf* . . . ], but also the correlation of back-to [the self], and as such constitutes the possibility of opposition. But why does Kant assert that the "abiding and unchanging" ego accomplishes [*bilde*] this act of ob-jectification? Does he mean to emphasize that the ego is always found at the basis of all mental events and "persists" as something unaffected by the vicissitudes which characterize such events? Could Kant have meant by the "abiding and unchanging" ego something on the order of mental substance—Kant who, relying on his own laying of the foundation of ontology, worked out the paralogism of substantiality? [92] Or did he merely wish to affirm that this ego is not temporal but, in a certain sense, infinite and eternal although not *qua* substance? But why does this supposed affirmation appear precisely where it does—there where Kant delimits the finitude of the ego, i.e., its act of ob-jectification? For the simple reason that the permanence and immutability of the ego belong essentially to this act.

The predicates "abiding" and "unchanging" are not ontic assertions concerning the immutability of the ego but are transcendental determinations. They signify that the ego is able to form an horizon of identity only insofar as *qua* ego it pro-poses to itself in advance something on the order of permanence and immutability. It is only within this horizon that an object is capable of being experienced as remaining the same through change. The "abiding" ego is so called because

92. A 348ff., B 406ff., NKS, p. 333ff.

as the "I think," i.e., the "I represent," it pro-poses to itself the like of subsistence and persistence. *Qua ego*, it forms the correlative of subsistence in general.

The provision of a pure aspect of the present in general is the very essence of time as pure intuition. The description of the ego as "abiding and unchanging" means that the ego in forming time originally, i.e., as primordial time, constitutes the essence of the act of ob-jectification and the horizon thereof.

Nothing has been decided, therefore, concerning the atemporality and eternity of the ego. Indeed, the transcendental problematic in general does not even raise this question. It is only as a finite self, i.e., as long as it is temporal, that the ego is "abiding and unchanging" in the transcendental sense.

If the same predicates are attributed to time, they do not signify only that time is not "in time." Rather, they also signify that if time as pure self-affection lets the pure succession of the *now*-sequence arise, that which thus arises, although it is considered in the ordinary experience of time as subsisting in its own right, is by no means sufficient to determine the true essence of time.

Consequently, if we are to come to a decision concerning the "temporality" or "atemporality" of time, the primordial essence of time as pure self-affection must be taken as our guide. And wherever Kant justly denies a temporal character to pure reason and the ego of pure apperception, he merely states that reason is not subject to "the form of time."

In this sense alone is the deletion of "at the same time" justified.[93] On this subject, Kant argues as follows: If the

93. *Cf.* above, § 33c, p. 181. A passage in the dissertation of 1770 shows that Kant changed his opinion on the subject of this "at the same time": *Tantum vero abest, ut quis unquam temporis conceptum adhuc rationis ope aliunde deducat et explicet, ut potius ipsum principium contradictionis eundem praemittat ac sibi conditionis loco*

"principle of contradiction" required the "at the same time" and hence "time" itself, then the principle would be limited to intra-temporal reality, i.e., to the essent accessible to experience. However, this fundamental principle governs all thought no matter what its content. Therefore, there is no place in it for temporal determination.

But, although the "at the same time" is undoubtedly a determination of time, it is not necessarily relative to the intra-temporality of the essent. Rather, the "at the same time" designates that temporal character which as precursory "recognition" ("pre-formation") pertains to all identification as such. The latter in turn is essentially at the basis of the possibility, as well as the impossibility, of contradiction.

Because of his orientation on the non-original essence of time, Kant is forced to deny all temporal character to "the principle of contradiction." It would be contrary to sense to try to effect an essential determination of primordial time itself with the aid of what is derived from it. The ego cannot be conceived as temporal, i.e., intra-temporal, precisely because the

*substernat. A enim et non A non repugnant, nisi simul (h.e. tempore eodem) cogitata de eodem . . . De mundi sensibilis atque intelligibilis forma et principiis."* § 14, 5. *Works* (Cass.) II, p. 417. Kant demonstrates here the impossibility of the "rational" deduction of time, i.e., of its intuitive character, by alluding to the fact that all *ratio,* including the fundamental principle of thought in general, presupposes "time." To be sure, the temporal meaning of *tempore iodem* intended remains obscure. If it is interpreted as signifying "in the same now," then Moses Mendelsohn was right when, with reference to the subject of this passage, he wrote in a letter to Kant:
"I do not believe the condition *eodem tempore* to be absolutely necessary for the law of contradiction. Insofar as it is a question of the same subject, both A and non-A cannot be predicated of it even at different times, and nothing more is required for the concept of impossibility than that the same subject be provided with two predicates, A and non-A. One can also say: *impossibile est, non A praedicatum de subjecto A."* Kant, *Works* (Cass.), IX, p. 93.

200

self originally and in its innermost essence is time itself. Pure sensibility (time) and pure reason are not only homogeneous, they belong together in the unity of the same essence which makes possible the finitude of human subjectivity in its totality.

## § 35. The Basic Originality of the Established Ground and the Problem of Metaphysics

Kant's laying of the foundation of metaphysics seeks the ground of the intrinsic possibility of the essential unity of ontological knowledge. The ground which it discovers is the transcendental imagination. In opposition to the disposition of the mind into two fundamental sources (sensibility and understanding) the imagination compels recognition as an intermediate faculty. However, the more primordial interpretation of this established ground has revealed that this intermediate faculty is not only a central element and one which is originally unifying but also the root of both stems.

Thus a way is opened to the original source-ground of the two fundamental sources. The interpretation of the transcendental imagination as a root, i.e., the disclosure of the manner in which the pure synthesis puts forth and sustains the two stems, leads naturally back to that in which this root is rooted, primordial time. The latter alone, as the original tri-unitary formation of future, past, and present, makes possible the "faculty" of pure synthesis and with it that which it is capable of producing, i.e., the unification of the three elements of ontological knowledge, the unity of which forms transcendence.

The modes of pure synthesis—pure apprehension, pure reproduction, pure recognition—are not three in number because they are relative to the three elements of pure knowledge but because, originally one, they are time-forming and thus constitute the temporalization of time itself. Only because these modes of pure synthesis are originally one in the three-

201

fold unity of time do they constitute the ground of the possibility of the original unification of the three elements of pure knowledge. This is why the primordially unifying element, the transcendental imagination, apparently only a mediating, intermediate faculty, is nothing other than primordial time. Only because the transcendental imagination is rooted in time can it be the root of transcendence.

Primordial time makes transcendental imagination, which in itself is essentially spontaneous receptivity and receptive spontaneity, possible. Only in this unity can pure sensibility as spontaneous receptivity and pure apperception as receptive spontaneity belong together and form the essential unity of pure sensible reason.

However, if, as takes place in the second edition, the transcendental imagination is eliminated as an autonomous fundamental faculty and its function is taken over by the understanding as pure spontaneity, then the possibility of comprehending the unity of pure sensibility and pure thought in finite human reason is lost. Indeed, it cannot even be entertained as an hypothesis. The first edition is more faithful to the innermost character and development of the problematic which characterizes the laying of the foundation of metaphysics because, by virtue of its indissoluble primordial structure, the transcendental imagination opens up the possibility of a laying of the foundation of ontological knowledge and, hence, of metaphysics. Therefore, relative to the problem which is central to the whole work, the first edition is essentially to be preferred to the second. All transformation of the pure imagination into a function of pure thought—a transformation accentuated by German idealism following the second edition—is the result of a misunderstanding of the true nature of the pure imagination.

Primordial time lets the pure formation of transcendence take place. Through the fundamental disclosure of the established ground which has just been presented, we now under-

202

stand for the first time the necessary course of development of the five stages of the laying of the foundation and the significance which has been accorded to the central part of this laying of the foundation, i.e., the transcendental schematism.

Ontological knowledge is made up of "transcendental determinations of time" because transcendence is temporalized in primordial time.

This necessary central function of time is usually expressed in Kant through his definition of it as the universal form of every act of representation. However, what is essential is the consideration of the conditions under which this representation takes place. The "preliminary remark" which precedes the transcendental deduction is intended to show in what respect the three modes of pure synthesis are in themselves essentially one. To be sure, Kant does not succeed in showing explicitly that they are time-forming or how they are one in primordial time. Nevertheless, the fundamental function of time is emphasized, particularly in connection with the analysis of the second mode of synthesis, that of reproduction in the imagination.

What is it that constitutes "the *a priori* ground of a necessary synthetic unity" capable of reproducing the essent no longer present in the form of a representation by linking it to the actual present? "What that something is we soon discover, when we reflect that appearances are not things in themselves but are the mere play of our representations, and in the end reduce to determinations of inner sense." [94]

Does this mean that in itself the essent is nothing and dissolves in a play of representations?

Not at all. What Kant means to say is this: The encountering of the essent takes place, for a finite being, in an act of representation whose pure representations of objectivity are mutually compatible [*eingespielt*]. This compatibility is determined in ad-

94. A 101, NKS, p. 132.

vance in such a way that it can come into play in a free-space which is formed by the pure determinations of the internal sense. This pure internal sense is pure self-affection, i.e., primordial time. The pure schemata as transcendental determinations of time form the horizon of transcendence.

Because from the first, Kant saw the problem of the internal possibility of the essential unity of ontological knowledge in this perspective and held fast to the central function of time, he was able, in presenting the unity of transcendence according to the two ways of the transcendental deduction, to forego an explicit discussion of time.

It is true that in the second edition, Kant apparently refuses to acknowledge the transcendental priority of time in the formation of transcendence as such, i.e., he disavows the essential part of the laying of the foundation of metaphysics, the transcendental schematism.

In the second edition, a *General Note on the System of the Principles,*[95] on ontological knowledge as a whole, was added. It begins with the sentence: "That the possibility of a thing cannot be determined from the category alone, and that in order to exhibit the objective reality of the pure concept of understanding we must always have an intuition, is a very noteworthy fact." Here in a few words is expressed the essential necessity of a sensibilization of the notions, i.e., their presentation in the form of a "pure image." But it is not stated that this pure image must be pure intuition *qua* time.

The next paragraph begins with an explicit reference to the sentence quoted above: "But it is an even more noteworthy fact that in order to understand the possibility of things in conformity with the categories, and so to demonstrate the *objective reality* of the latter, we need not merely intuitions but intuitions that are in all cases *outer intuitions.*"[96] Here appears the transcendental function of space, which unmistakably opens up a

95. B 288ff., NKS, p. 252ff.
96. B 291, NKS, p. 154.

new perspective for Kant. Space enters into pure schematism. It is true that in the second edition the chapter on schematism has not been modified to take this into account. But is it not necessary to conclude, nevertheless, that the primacy of time has disappeared? This conclusion would not only be premature, but to attempt to infer from this passage that it is not time alone which forms transcendence would also be a complete misunderstanding of the whole interpretation as carried out thus far.

But, one might object, if transcendence is not based on time alone, is it not only natural for Kant, in limiting the primacy of time, to thrust aside the pure imagination? In reasoning thus, however, one forgets that pure space as pure intuition is no less rooted in the transcendental imagination than is "time," insofar as the latter is understood as that which is formed in pure intuition, namely, the pure succession of the *now*-sequence. In fact, in a certain sense, space is always and necessarily identical with time thus understood.

However, it is not in this form but as pure self-affection that time is the primordial ground of transcendence. As such, it is also the condition of the possibility of all formative acts of representation, for example, the making manifest of space. It does not follow, then, that to admit the transcendental function of space is to reject the primacy of time. Rather, this admission obligates one to show how space, like time, also belongs to the self as finite and that the latter, precisely because it is based on primordial time, is essentially "spatial."

The acknowledgment in the second edition that space in a certain sense also belongs to the transcendental schematism only makes it clear that this schematism cannot be grasped in its innermost essence as long as time is conceived as the pure succession of the *now*-sequence. Time must be understood as pure self-affection; otherwise its function in the formation of schemata remains completely obscure.

We encounter here a peculiarity inherent in the Kantian laying of the foundation of metaphysics. Although that which is uncovered by the regression to the source-ground is revealed in its true nature, i.e., as being constitutive of transcendence, the faculties of the mind involved therein, and with them time as pure intuition, are not explicitly and primordially defined in the light of this transcendental function. Rather, throughout the course of the laying of the foundation and even in its conclusion, they are presented according to the provisional conception of the first point of departure. And because Kant, at the time of his presentation of the transcendental schemata, had not worked out an interpretation of the primordial essence of time, his elucidation of the pure schemata as transcendental determinations of time is both fragmentary and obscure, for time taken as the pure *now*-sequence offers no possible means of access to the "temporal" interpretation of the notions.[97]

Nevertheless, an interpretation limited to a recapitulation of what Kant explicitly said can never be a real explication, if the business of the latter is to bring to light what Kant, over and above his express formulation, uncovered in the course of his laying of the foundation. To be sure, Kant himself is no longer able to say anything concerning this, but what is essential in all philosophical discourse is not found in the specific propositions of which it is composed but in that which, although unstated as such, is made evident through these propositions.

The fundamental purpose of the present interpretation of the *Critique of Pure Reason* is to reveal the basic import of this work by bringing out what Kant "intended to say." Our interpretation is inspired by a maxim which Kant himself wished to see applied to the interpretation of philosophical works and which he formulated in the following terms at the end of his reply to the critique of the Leibnizian, Eberhard.

"Thus, the *Critique of Pure Reason* may well be the real apology for Leibniz, even in opposition to his partisans whose

97. *Cf.* above, § 22, p. 106.

206

words of praise hardly do him honor. It can also be an apology for many older philosophers about whom certain historians of philosophy, for all the praises they bestow, speak the purest nonsense. They do not understand the intentions of these philosophers when they neglect the key to all explication of the works of pure reason through concepts alone, namely, the critique of reason itself (as the common source of all concepts), and are incapable of looking beyond the language which these philosophers employ to what they intended to say." [98]

It is true that in order to wrest from the actual words that which these words "intend to say," every interpretation must necessarily resort to violence. This violence, however, should not be confused with an action that is wholly arbitrary. The interpretation must be animated and guided by the power of an illuminative idea. Only through the power of this idea can an interpretation risk that which is always audacious, namely, entrusting itself to the secret élan of a work, in order by this élan to get through to the unsaid and to attempt to find an expression for it. The directive idea itself is confirmed by its own power of illumination.

Kant's laying of the foundation of metaphysics leads to the transcendental imagination. This is the common root of both stems, sensibility and understanding. As such, it makes possible the original unity of the ontological synthesis. This root itself, however, is implanted in primordial time. The primordial ground which is revealed in the Kantian laying of the foundation is time.

Kant's laying of the foundation of metaphysics begins with *metaphysica generalis* and so becomes a question as to the possibility of ontology in general. This question concerns the essence of the ontological constitution of the essent, i.e., Being in general.

The laying of the foundation of metaphysics is based on

98. *Über eine Entdeckung, op. cit.,* VI, p. 71.

time. The question as to Being, the fundamental question of a laying of the foundation of metaphysics, is the problem of *Sein und Zeit.*

This title contains the directive idea of the present interpretation of the *Critique of Pure Reason* as a laying of the foundation of metaphysics. This idea, to which the interpretation bears witness, provides an indication of the problem of a fundamental ontology. Fundamental ontology should not be viewed as something which is supposedly "new" in contrast to what is reputed to be "old." Rather, it is the expression of an attempt to assimilate the essentials of a laying of the foundation of metaphysics, thus aiding this foundation, by a repetition, to realize its own primordial possibility.

# THE LAYING OF THE FOUNDATION OF
# METAPHYSICS IN A REPETITION

# THE LAYING OF THE FOUNDATION OF METAPHYSICS IN A REPETITION

By a repetition of a fundamental problem we understand the disclosure of the primordial possibilities concealed in it. The development of these possibilities has the effect of transforming the problem and thus preserving it in its import as a problem. To preserve a problem means to free and to safeguard its intrinsic powers, which are the source of its essence and which make it possible as a problem.

The repetition of the possibilities of a problem, therefore, is not a simple taking up of that which is "in vogue" with regard to this problem and concerning which "one may reasonably expect to make something." In this sense, the possible is the all-too-real which is at the disposal of everyone. The possible, thus understood, in fact hinders all genuine repetition and thereby all relation to history [*Geschichte*].

When correctly understood, a repetition of the laying of the foundation of metaphysics must begin by making sure of the authentic result of the previous—in this case the Kantian—laying of the foundation. At the same time, what is sought as the "result" of the laying of the foundation of metaphysics in the *Critique of Pure Reason* and the way in which this result

211

is determined will decide how far the understanding of the possible which governs all repetition extends and whether it is equal to that which is repeatable.

# A. The Laying of the Foundation of Metaphysics as Anthropology

## § 36. The Established Ground and the Result of Kant's Laying of the Foundation

In going through the individual stages of the Kantian laying of the foundation, we have discovered how it leads to the transcendental imagination as the ground of the intrinsic possibility of the ontological synthesis, i.e., transcendence. Is the establishment of this ground, in other words, its primordial explication as temporality, the [true] result of the Kantian laying of the foundation? Or does the latter yield something else? Certainly, in order to establish the aforesaid result there was no need of following with so much effort the internal development of the laying of the foundation in each of its stages. It would have been sufficient to cite the texts relative to the central function of the transcendental imagination in the transcendental deduction and the transcendental schematism. But if the result does not consist in the knowledge that the transcendental imagination constitutes the foundation, what other result can the laying of the foundation be expected to yield?

If the result of the laying of the foundation does not lie in its "actual conclusion," then we must ask ourselves what the development of the laying of the foundation reveals insofar as the problem of the establishment of metaphysics is concerned. What takes place in the Kantian laying of the foundation? Nothing less than this: The establishment of the intrinsic possibility

212

of ontology is accomplished as the disclosure of transcendence, i.e., the subjectivity of the subject.

The question as to the essence of metaphysics is the question of the unity of the fundamental faculties of the human "mind." The Kantian laying of the foundation yields this conclusion: The establishment of metaphysics is an interrogation of man, i.e., it is anthropology.

However, did not the first attempt to grasp the Kantian laying of the foundation more originally, the attempt to reduce it to anthropology, miscarry? [1] Certainly, insofar as it revealed that what anthropology offers as an explication of knowledge and its two sources is brought out in a more fundamental way by the *Critique of Pure Reason* itself. But all that can be inferred from this is that the anthropology presented by Kant is empirical and not an anthropology which can satisfy the requirements of the transcendental problematic, i.e., that it is not a pure anthropology. Thus, the necessity of an adequate, that is, a "philosophical" anthropology to further the ends of a laying of the foundation of metaphysics becomes even more pressing.

That the outcome of the Kantian laying of the foundation lies in the insight into the necessary connection between anthropology and metaphysics is affirmed unequivocally by Kant's own statements. Kant's laying of the foundation of metaphysics has as its goal the establishment of "metaphysics in its final purpose," *metaphysica specialis,* to which belong the three disciplines: cosmology, psychology, and theology. As a critique of pure reason, this laying of the foundation must understand these disciplines in their innermost essence, provided that metaphysics is to be grasped in its possibility and its limits as a "natural disposition of mankind." The fundamental essence of human reason manifests itself in those "interests" with which, because it is human, it is always concerned. "The whole interest

1. *Cf.* above § 26, p. 134.

of my reason, whether speculative or practical, is concentrated in the three following questions:
1. What can I know?
2. What ought I do?
3. What may I hope?" [2]
These three questions, however, are those with which the three disciplines of true metaphysics, i.e., *metaphysica specialis,* are concerned. Man's knowledge is concerned with nature, with that which is actually given in the broadest sense of the term (cosmology); man's activity concerns his personality and freedom (psychology); finally, man's hope is directed toward immortality as bliss, as union with God (theology).

These three fundamental interests do not determine man as a natural being but as a "citizen of the world." They constitute the object of philosophy as a "matter of world citizenship," that is, they define the domain of philosophy. Hence, Kant states in the introduction to his course of lectures on logic wherein he develops the concept of philosophy in general: "The field of philosophy as pertaining to world citizenship can be reduced to the following questions:
1. What can I know?
2. What should I do?
3. What may I hope?
4. What is man?" [3]
Here, a fourth question is added to the three previously cited. But when we consider that *psychologia rationalis* as a discipline of *metaphysica specialis* already treats of man, are we not constrained to believe that this fourth question relative to man is only superficially added to the other three and is, therefore, superfluous.

However, Kant does not simply add this fourth question to the other three, for he says: "Basically, all these can be classified

2. A 804, B 832f., NKS, p. 635.
3. *Works* (Cass.), VIII, p. 343.

214

under anthropology, since the first three are related to the last." [4]

With this, Kant states unequivocally the real result of the laying of the foundation of metaphysics. The attempt to repeat the laying of the foundation also receives thereby a clear indication of the task involved. To be sure, Kant mentions anthropology only in a very general way. However, in the light of what has been said above, it seems true beyond a doubt that only a philosophical anthropology can undertake the laying of the foundation of true philosophy, i.e., *metaphysica specialis*. Is it not necessary to conclude, therefore, that a repetition of the Kantian laying of the foundation pursues as its specific task the development of a "philosophical anthropology" and hence that the idea of such an anthropology must be determined beforehand?

## § 37. The Idea of a Philosophical Anthropology

What does a philosophical anthropology include? What is anthropology in general and how does it become philosophical? "Anthropology" denotes the science of man. It comprises all the information that can be obtained about the nature of man as a being composed of a body, a soul, and a mind. The domain of anthropology includes not only those given verifiable properties which distinguish the human species from plants and animals but also man's latent abilities and the differences of character, race, and sex. And inasmuch as man not only appears as a natural being but also as a being that acts and creates, anthropology must also seek to know what man as an active being can and should "make of himself." His powers and obligations depend finally on certain basic attitudes which man as such is always capable of adopting. These attitudes are called *Weltanschauungen* and the "psychology" of these includes the whole of the science of man.

4. *Ibid.*, p. 344.

215

Since anthropology must consider man in his somatic, biological, and psychological aspects, the results of such disciplines as characterology, psychoanalysis, ethnology, pedagogic psychology, the morphology of culture, and the typology of *Weltanschauungen* must converge in it. Hence, the content of such a science is not only vast but also fundamentally heterogeneous because of basic differences in the manner of formulating questions, the necessity of justifying the results acquired, the mode of presentation of the facts, the form of communication, and finally the essential presuppositions [of each of the component disciplines]. Insofar as all of these differences and, in certain respects, the totality of the essent as well can be related to man and thus classified under anthropology, anthropology becomes so comprehensive that the idea of such a science loses all precision.

Anthropology today, therefore, is not only the name of a discipline; the term denotes a fundamental tendency characteristic of the present position of man with regard to himself and to the totality of the essent. According to this tendency, a thing is known and understood only when it receives an anthropological explanation. Today, anthropology not only seeks the truth concerning man but also claims to have the power of deciding the meaning of truth as such.

No other epoch has accumulated so great and so varied a store of knowledge concerning man as the present one. No other epoch has succeeded in presenting its knowledge of man so forcibly and so captivatingly as ours, and no other has succeeded in making this knowledge so quickly and so easily accessible. But also, no epoch is less sure of its knowledge of what man is than the present one. In no other epoch has man appeared so mysterious as in ours.[5]

5. *Cf.* Max Scheler, *Die Stellung des Menschen im Kosmos*, 1928, p. 13f.

However, is not the very fact that the problems of anthropology are characterized by this breadth and uncertainty conducive to the formation of a philosophical anthropology and to the encouragement of its further development? With the idea of a philosophical anthropology do we not acquire that discipline in which the whole of philosophy must be concentrated?

Several years ago, Max Scheler said of philosophical anthropology: "In a certain sense, all the central problems of philosophy can be reduced to the question of man and his position and metaphysical situation within the totality of Being, the world, and God." [6] But Scheler also saw, and with great clarity, that the many determinations relative to the essence of man cannot be simply packed together, as it were, in a common definition. "Man is so broad, motley, and various a thing that the definitions of him all fall a little short. He has too many sides." [7] This is why Scheler's efforts, which in his last years became more intense and more fruitful, were directed not only to the attainment of a unitary idea of man but also to the working out of the essential difficulties and complications connected with this task.[8]

Perhaps the fundamental difficulty of a philosophical anthropology lies not in the problem of obtaining a systematic unity insofar as the essential determinations of this multifarious being, man, are concerned, but in the concept of anthropology itself. This is a difficulty which even the most abundant and "spectacular" knowledge can no longer explain away.

How, then, does an anthropology become philosophical? Is it only because its knowledge acquires a degree of generality

6. *Cf. Zur Idee des Menschen, Abhandlungen und Aufsätz,* Vol. I (1915), p. 319. In the second and third editions, the volumes have been published under the title *Vom Umsturz der Werte.*
7. *Ibid.*
8. *Cf. Die Stellung des Menschen im Kosmos.*

which differentiates it from empirical knowledge, although we are never able to determine precisely the degree of generality at which knowledge stops being empirical and becomes philosophical?

Certainly, an anthropology may be said to be philosophical if its method is philosophical, i.e., if it is pursued as an inquiry into the essence of man. In this case, anthropology strives to distinguish the essent we call man from plants, animals, and every other type of essent, and by this delimitation it attempts to bring to light the specific essential constitution of this particular region of the essent. Philosophical anthropology then becomes a regional ontology of man, coordinated with other ontologies with which it shares the whole domain of the essent. Thus understood, philosophical anthropology cannot be considered without further explication as the center of philosophy; above all, this last pretension cannot be based on the internal problematic of this anthropology.

It is also possible for anthropology to be philosophical if, as anthropology, it determines either the objective of philosophy or its point of departure or both at once. If the objective of philosophy lies in the development of a *Weltanschauung,* then anthropology must define the "position of man in the cosmos." And if man is accepted as that essent which, in the order of establishing an absolutely certain knowledge, is absolutely the first given and the most certain, then it is inevitable that, following the plan of a philosophy thus conceived, human subjectivity be placed at the very center of the problem. The first task is compatible with the second, and both, as modes of anthropological inquiry, can avail themselves of the method and the results of a regional ontology of man.

But just these diverse possibilities of defining the philosophical character of an anthropology are sufficient in themselves to show the indeterminateness of this idea. This indeterminateness is increased if one takes into account the diversity of the empirical-anthropological knowledge on which, at least in the beginning, every philosophical anthropology relies.

As natural and self-evident as the idea of a philosophical anthropology may appear in spite of its ambiguity, and as irresistible as the urge to reaffirm it may be in spite of these objections, still it is inevitable that "anthropologism" in philosophy will always be combated. The idea of philosophical anthropology is not only insufficiently determined, its role within philosophy as a whole remains obscure and indecisive.

The reason for these deficiencies is to be found in the limitations inherent in the idea of a philosophical anthropology. This discipline has not been explicitly justified with respect to the essence of philosophy but only with respect to the object and point of departure of philosophy as seen from without. Thus, the delimitation of this idea ends by reducing anthropology to a kind of dumping-ground for all basic philosophical problems. It is obvious that this way of considering anthropology is both superficial and, from the standpoint of philosophy, highly questionable.

But even if, in a certain sense, anthropology gathers to itself all the central problems of philosophy, why may these be reduced to the question: What is man? Is this reduction possible only if someone decides to undertake it or, on the contrary, must these problems lead back to this question? And if the latter is true, what is the basis of this necessity? Is it perhaps that the central problems of philosophy have their source in man, not only in the sense that man propounds them but also that in their intrinsic content they bear a relation to him? In what respect do all central philosophical problems find their abode in the essence of man? And, in general, which problems are essential and wherein lies their center? What is the meaning of the expression "to philosophize" if the philosophical problematic is such that it finds its abode and its center in the essence of man?

219

As long as these questions are not developed systematically and made precise, it will not be possible to determine the essential limits of the idea of a philosophical anthropology. Only the discussion of these questions furnishes the basis for a possible discussion of the essence, right, and function of a philosophical anthropology within philosophy.

Again and again there appear new attempts to present plausible arguments for a philosophical anthropology and to defend the central role of this discipline without, however, basing the latter on the essence of philosophy. Again and again the opponents of anthropology are able to appeal to the fact that man is not at the center of reality and that there is an "infinity" of essents "in addition" to him—a rejection of the central role of philosophical anthropology which is no more philosophical than its affirmation.

Thus, a critical reflection on the idea of a philosophical anthropology not only reveals its indefiniteness and its intrinsic limitations but also makes clear that we have at our disposal neither the basis nor the frame of reference for a thorough examination of its essence.

Although Kant traced the three questions of true metaphysics back to a fourth, i.e., the question as to the essence of man, it would be premature on that account to consider this question as anthropological and to entrust the laying of the foundation of metaphysics to a philosophical anthropology. Anthropology, simply because it is anthropology, cannot provide a foundation for metaphysics.

But is not the discovery of this connection between the question of the essence of man and the establishment of metaphysics the real result of the Kantian laying of the foundation? Must not this connection serve as a guide in the repetition of the laying of the foundation?

However, the critique of the idea of philosophical anthropology shows that it is not enough simply to formulate this

220

fourth question: What is man? On the contrary, the indefiniteness of this question indicates that even now we are not yet in possession of the decisive result of the Kantian laying of the foundation.

## § 38. The Question of the Essence of Man and the True Result of Kant's Laying of the Foundation

It becomes more and more obvious that we will not discover the true result of the Kantian laying of the foundation as long as we rely on a definition or a fixed thesis. The manner of philosophizing peculiar to Kant will become accessible to us only if, with greater resolution than heretofore, we examine not what he says but what is achieved in his laying of the foundation. The primordial explication of the *Critique of Pure Reason* as we have given it above has as its only objective the revelation of this achievement.

But what is the true result of the Kantian laying of the foundation? It is not that the transcendental imagination is the established ground, not that this laying of the foundation becomes a question as to the essence of human reason, but that, with the revelation of the subjectivity of the subject, Kant recoiled from the ground which he himself had established.

Does not this recoil also belong to the result? What takes place therein? Is it something inconsequent for which Kant should be reproached? Is this recoil and this refusal to go the whole way only something negative? On the contrary, it makes obvious that in pursuing his laying of the foundation, Kant undermined the base [*Boden*] on which in the beginning he set his *Critique*. The concept of pure reason and the unity of a pure sensible reason become problems. Kant's profound study of the subjectivity of the subject, "the subjective deduction," leads us into obscurity. It is not only because Kant's anthropology is empirical and not pure that he does not refer to it but also be-

221

cause, in the course of the laying of the foundation, our mode of questioning man itself is brought into question. It is not the answer to the question of the essence of man which must be sought; rather, it is a matter first of all of asking how in the laying of the foundation of metaphysics it is possible to bring man into question and why it is necessary to do this.

The questionable character of the interrogation relative to man is precisely what is illuminated in the development of the Kantian laying of the foundation of metaphysics. It now appears that Kant's recoil from the ground which he himself revealed, namely the transcendental imagination, is—relative to his intention of preserving pure reason, i.e., of holding fast to the base which is proper to it—that movement of philosophical thought which makes manifest the destruction of this base and thus places us before the abyss [*Abgrund*] of metaphysics.

It is by this result that the primordial explication of the Kantian laying of the foundation as given above first acquires its justification and establishes its necessity. All the effort expended in this interpretation has been inspired not by a vain pursuit of the primordial and not by a drive to know ever more and more but only by the task of laying bare the internal character and development of the laying of the foundation and the problematic proper to it.

However, if the laying of the foundation seeks neither to evade the question as to the essence of man nor to supply a clear-cut answer thereto but only to bring its questionable character to light, then what becomes of Kant's fourth question, namely, that to which *metaphysica specialis* and with it true philosophy is to be reduced?

We will succeed in asking this fourth question as it should be asked only if we forego a premature answer and develop it as a question through the understanding we have now attained of the result of the laying of the foundation.

It is now a matter of asking why the three questions—1.

222

What can I know? 2. What should I do? 3. What may I hope? —"admit of being related" to the fourth? Why can "all these be classified under anthropology"? What do these three questions have in common? In what respect are they one and, hence, capable of being reduced to the fourth? How must this fourth question itself be formulated in order to include the other three and sustain them in its unity?

The most profound interest of human reason forms the connecting link between these three questions. In them are brought into question a power, a duty, and a hope of human reason.

Where there is a question concerning a power and one delimits its possibilities, there is revealed at the same time a non-power [Nicht-Können]. An omnipotent being need not ask, "What am I able to do"?, i.e., "What am I not able to do"? Not only does such a being have no need to ask such a question; it is contrary to its nature to be able to ask it. This not-being-able is not a deficiency but the absence of all deficiency and all "negativity." Whosoever asks, "What am I able to do"? betrays thereby his own finitude. And whosoever is concerned in his innermost interests by such a question reveals a finitude in his innermost nature.

When an obligation is brought into question, the being who raises the question hesitates between a "yes" and a "no," thus finding himself tormented by the question of what he should do. A being fundamentally concerned with his duty understands himself through a not-yet-having-fulfilled, so that he is driven to ask himself what he should do. This not-yet of the fulfillment of something still indeterminate reveals a being who, because his duty is his most intimate interest, is basically finite.

Whenever a hope is brought into question, it is a matter of something which can be granted or denied to the one who asks. What is asked for is such that it can be expected or not expected. All expectation, however, reveals a privation, and if this privation involves the most intimate interest of human reason then the latter is affirmed to be essentially finite.

Thus, not only does human reason betray its finitude by these questions, but also its innermost interest is concerned with this finitude. It is not a question of eliminating the power, the obligation, and the hope in order to evade the finitude but, conversely, it is a question of becoming certain of this finitude in order to hold oneself in it.

Hence, finitude is not merely an accidental property of human reason; the finitude of human reason is finitization [*Verendlichung*], i.e., "concern" [9] [*Sorge*] about the ability to be finite.

It follows that human reason is not finite only because it propounds these three questions, but, on the contrary, it propounds these three questions because it is finite and so radically finite, indeed, that in its rationality this finitude itself is at stake. It is because these three questions concern this unique [object], i.e., finitude, that their relation admits of being established to the fourth question: What is man?

But these three questions do not have a merely accidental relationship to the fourth. In themselves they are nothing other than this fourth question, that is, according to their essence they must be reducible to it. But this relation is necessary and

9. In the pages that follow, Heidegger makes increasing use of the "existentials" of *Sein und Zeit,* an existential being a determination of the Being of man in contrast to a category which is a determination of the Being of essents. Because of their importance insofar as an understanding of Heidegger's thought is concerned, a brief explanation of these existentials as they appear has been included.

"Concern," according to *Sein und Zeit,* is the Being of *Dasein* and as such has a significance which is wholly ontological, every "ontic characteristic of man in the sense of an ethical and ideological evaluation of 'human life'" being excluded. (See below, p. 243.) The structure of *concern* is characterized by Heidegger as "being-already-ahead-of-itself [itself-*Dasein*] as-in- (the-world) as being-among (the things which are found in the world)" (*Sein und Zeit,* p. 192). As being-ahead, already-in, and among, *concern* has a three-fold structure, corresponding to the three dimensions of time. (J. S. C.)

224

essential only if the fourth question is stripped of its generality and indeterminateness and acquires the univocal character of an interrogation of the finitude in man.

In this form this question is not subordinate to the other three but is transformed into the first, from which the others are derived.

In spite of this result, in spite of the determinateness of the question as to man, or rather because of it, the problem which this question poses is rendered even more acute. It would be well now to ask what kind of question this question as to man is, and if in general it can be an anthropological question. The result of the Kantian laying of the foundation is thus clarified to the point that we are now able to see in it an authentic possibility of repetition.

The laying of the foundation of metaphysics is rooted in the question of the finitude of man in such a way that this finitude itself can first become a problem. The laying of the foundation of metaphysics is a "dissociation" (analytic) of our knowledge, i.e., of finite knowledge, into its elements. Kant terms it "a study of our inner nature." [10] Such a study ceases to be an arbitrary, disorderly interrogation of man and becomes a "matter of duty" [11] to the philosopher only if the problematic which governs it is grasped with sufficient originality and comprehensiveness and so leads us to examine the "inner nature" of "our" self as the problem of the finitude in man.

However diverse and important the knowledge which "philosophical anthropology" may supply concerning man, it can never pretend to be a fundamental discipline of philosophy, solely because it is anthropology. On the contrary, it runs the constant risk of concealing from us the necessity of developing the question of man as a problem and of connecting this problem with a laying of the foundation of metaphysics.

10. A 703, B 731, NKS, p. 570.
11. *Ibid.*

We are not able to discuss here if and how "philosophical anthropology"—above and beyond the problem of a laying of the foundation of metaphysics—yet has a task which is proper to it.

## B. The Problem of the Finitude in Man and the Metaphysics of *Dasein*

We have undertaken the present interpretation of the *Critique of Pure Reason* in order to bring to light the necessity, insofar as a laying of the foundation of metaphysics in concerned, of posing the fundamental problem of the finitude in man. This is the reason that finitude has been constantly stressed at the beginning of the interpretation as well as in the course of its development. And if in his laying of the foundation Kant undermines the base which he himself established, this signifies for us that the question of the "presuppositions" implicit in the *Critique,* presuppositions which were indicated at the beginning of this interpretation [12] and which are relative to the essence of knowledge and its finitude, now assume the importance of a decisive problem. Finitude and the singularity of the question which it raises radically determine the internal form of a transcendental "analytic" of the subjectivity of the subject.

### § 39. The Problem of a Possible Determination of the Finitude in Man

How is the finitude in man to be examined? Is this in general a serious problem? Is not the finitude of man evident always, everywhere, and in a thousand different ways?

In order to uncover the finitude of man is it not enough to

12. *Cf.* Section Two, p. 25ff.

226

adduce at random any one of his many imperfections? But in this way we obtain at best only a proof that man is a finite being. We learn neither in what the essence of man's finitude consists nor yet how this finitude determines man to be the essent that he basically is.

And even if we succeeded in adding together the sum of all human imperfections and "abstracting" what is common to them, we could understand thereby nothing of the essence of finitude. We would not be able to know in advance whether the imperfections of man enable us to obtain a direct insight into his finitude, or whether, on the contrary, these imperfections are merely a simple consequence of this finitude and, hence, are understandable only through it.

And even if we succeeded in doing the impossible, if we succeeded in proving rationally that man is a created being, the characterization of man as an *ens creatum* would only point up the fact of his finitude without clarifying its essence and without showing how this essence constitutes the fundamental nature of the essence of man.

Thus, how the question of the finitude in man—the most common manifestation of his essence—is to be approached is not at all self-evident. The sole result of our inquiry, therefore, is that the question of the finitude in man is no arbitrary exploration of the properties of this being. On the contrary, the question arises as soon as one begins the task of a laying of the foundation of metaphysics. As a fundamental question it is required by this problem itself. Consequently, the problematic of a laying of the foundation of metaphysics must include an indication as to the direction in which the question of the finitude of man must advance.

Finally, if the task of a laying of the foundation of metaphysics admits of an authentic repetition, then the essential connection between the problem of a laying of the foundation and the question inspired by it, namely, that of the finitude in

227

man, must be exhibited more clearly and with greater precision.

The Kantian laying of the foundation of metaphysics begins with a justification of *metaphysica generalis* as that which is at the basis of true metaphysics, i.e., *metaphysica specialis*. But *metaphysica generalis*—under the name "ontology"—is the fixed form of that which in antiquity, and finally with Aristotle, was established as the problem of *prōtē philosophia,* philsophizing in the true sense of the term. However, the question of the *on ē on* (of the essent as such) is mingled in a very confused way here with that of the essent in totality (*theion*).

The term "metaphysics" denotes a conception of the problem in which not only the two fundamental dimensions of the question of the essent but also their possible unity become debatable. This is quite apart from the further question as to whether these two dimensions are sufficient in themselves to exhaust the whole of the problematic of a fundamental knowledge of the essent.

If the question of the finitude in man is to be determined through an authentic repetition of a laying of the foundation of metaphysics, then it is advisable to turn the Kantian question from its orientation on the rigid discipline and fixed system of the metaphysics of the schools and set it on that course which is suitable to its own problematic. This also implies that the Aristotelian formulation of the problem cannot be accepted as definitive.

With the *ti to on* [what is the essent?], the question of the essent is posed, but to pose a question does not necessarily mean that one is capable of mastering and working out the problematic which animates it. The extent to which the problem of metaphysics is still enveloped in the question *ti to on* can be understood if we realize that the formulation of this question does not enable us to determine how it embodies the problem of the finitude in man. Still less can we obtain an indication as to how the finitude in man is to be made the object of

228

our questioning merely by a reiteration of this question. The repetition of the problem of a laying of the foundation of *metaphysica generalis* is not equivalent, therefore, to a simple echoing [*nachsprechen*] of the question: What is the essent as such? The repetition must develop as a problem the question which, in brief, we term the question of Being. The purpose of this development is to show in what respect the problem of the finitude in man and the inquiries which it calls for necessarily contribute to our mastery of the question of Being. Basically it is a matter of bringing to light the essential connection between Being as such (not the essent) and the finitude in man.

## § 40. The Primordial Elaboration of the Question of Being as the Means of Access to the Problem of the Finitude in Man

The fundamental question of the ancient *physiologoi* [13] concerning the essent in general (the *logos* of the *physis*) is developed —and such is the significance of the internal evolution of ancient metaphysics from its beginning to Aristotle—from a general idea, indeterminate but rich in content, and leads to the determinateness of the two types of problems which, according to Aristotle, constitute philosophy in the true sense of the term.

As obscure as the connection between these two types may be, still it is possible to establish, at least from one point of view, an order of precedence with regard to them. Insofar as the question of the essent in totality and in its principal divisions presupposes a certain understanding of what the essent as such is, then the question of the *on ē on* must take precedence over the question of the essent in totality. Relative to the possibility of acquiring a fundamental knowledge of the essent in totality,

13. *Cf.* Aristotle, *Physics,* G 4, 203 b 15: Kant, moreover, speaks in the *Critique of Pure Reason* (A 845, B 873, NKS, p. 662) of the "physiology of pure reason."

then, the question of knowing what the essent is as such is primary. Whether this priority also holds when it is a question of the self-establishment of metaphysics is a matter which we must be content only to mention here.

But is not the general question *ti to on* so vague that it no longer has an object and offers no clue as to how and where an answer is to be sought?

When we ask what the essent as such is, we wish to know what determines the essent *qua* essent. We call it the Being of the essent, and the question which is concerned with it is the question of Being.

The object of this question is that which determines the essent as such. This determining [element] must be known in the *how* of its determining and interpreted (i.e., understood) as such and such. However, in order to be able to understand the essential determination of this essent through Being, the determining element itself must be understood with sufficient clarity. It is necessary, therefore, first to comprehend *Being as such,* and this comprehension must precede that of the essent as such. Thus, the question *ti to on* (what is the essent) implies a more original question: *What is the significance of Being which is pre-comprehended* [vorverstandene] *in this question?*

But if the question *ti to on* is itself very difficult to grasp how can a question which is more original and at the same time more "abstract" be admitted as the source of a concrete problematic?

That such a problematic exists can be verified by referring to a situation which has always existed in philosophy but which has been accepted all too easily as self-evident. It is first relative to its what-being [*Was-sein*] (*ti estin*) that we define and examine the essent which is manifest to us in every mode of comportment we exhibit toward it. In the language of philosophy, this what-being is termed *essentia* (essence). It renders the essent possible in that which it is. This is why what constitutes

230

the thing-ness [*Sachheit*] of a thing (*realitas*) is designated as its *possibilitas* (intrinsic possibility). The appearance (*eidos*) of an essent informs us as to what it is. Consequently, the what-being of an essent is termed *idea*.

In connection with every essent there arises the question, unless it has already been answered, as to whether it—the essent having this determinate what-being—is or is not. Therefore, we also determine an essent relative to the fact "that it is" [*Dass-sein*] (*oti eotin*) which in the usual terminology of philosophy is expressed as *existentia* (reality).

In every essent "there is" what-being and that-being [*Dass-sein*], *essentia* and *existentia*, possibility and reality. Has "being" the same meaning in these expressions? If not, why is it that Being is divided into what-being and that-being? Does this distinction between *essentia* and *existentia*, a distinction which is accepted as self-evident, resemble that between cats and dogs, or is there a problem here which must finally be posed and which can be posed only by asking what Being as such is?

Is it not true that if we fail to develop this question, the attempt to "define" the essentiality of essence and to "explain" the reality of the real will be deprived of a horizon?

And is not the distinction between what-being and that-being, a distinction whose basis of possibility and mode of necessity remain obscure, entwined with the notion of Being as being-true [*Wahr-sein*]? And does not this last notion come to light in the "is" of every proposition—and not only there—whether expressed or not? [14]

Considering what lies concealed in this problem-word "Being," have we not reason enough to attempt to clarify it? Is it necessary that this question of Being remain indeterminate, or should we venture an even more primordial course of action in order to work this question out?

How is the question, "What is the meaning of Being?" to

14. *Cf. Vom Wesen des Grundes,* first section.

231

find an answer if the direction from which the answer can be expected remains obscure? Must we not first ask in what direction it is advisable to look in order from this perspective to be able to determine Being as such and thus obtain a concept of Being with reference to which the possibility and necessity of its essential articulation will become comprehensible? So the question of "first philosophy," namely, "What is the essent as such?" must force us back beyond the question "What is Being as such?" to the still more fundamental question: *Whence are we to comprehend a notion such as that of Being, with the many articulations and relations it includes?*

Therefore, if there exists an internal connection between the laying of the foundation of metaphysics and the question of the finitude in man, the more primordial elaboration of the question of Being now attained will exhibit in a more elemental way the essential relation of this question to the problem of finitude.

But at first sight, this connection remains obscure, above all since one is not generally inclined to attribute such a relation to the question under consideration. This relation is certainly evident in Kant's questions cited above, but how can the question of Being, particularly in the form in which it is now developed, i.e., as a question of the possibility of the comprehension of Being, have an essential relation to the finitude in man? Within the framework of the abstract ontology inspired by the metaphysics of Aristotle, the question of Being may acquire a certain sense and so be presented with some justification as a special problem, a problem that is scholarly but more or less artificial. But there seems to be no evidence of an essential relation between this problem and that of the finitude in man.

If up to this point we have endeavored to clarify the original form of the problem of Being by orienting it on the Aristotelian question, this does not imply that the origin of this problem is to be found in Aristotle. On the contrary, authentic philosophical thinking will be able to come upon the question of Being only if this question belongs to the innermost essence of philosophy, which in turn exists only as a fundamental possibility of human *Dasein*.

When we raise the question as to the possibility of understanding a notion such as that of Being, we do not thereby invent this notion and artificially make a problem of it in order merely to take up again a question characteristic of philosophical tradition. Rather, we are raising the question of the possibility of comprehending that which, as men, we already understand and have always understood. The question of Being as a question of the possibility of the concept of Being arises from the preconceptual comprehension of Being. Thus, the question of the possibility of the concept of Being is once again forced back a step and becomes the question of the possibility of the comprehension of Being in general. The task of the laying of the foundation of metaphysics, grasped in a more original way, becomes, therefore, that of the explication of the intrinsic possibility of the comprehension of Being. The elaboration of the question of Being thus conceived first enables us to decide if, and in what way, the problem of Being in itself bears an intrinsic relation to the finitude in man.

### § 41. The Comprehension of Being and the Dasein in Man

That we, as men, have a comportment [*Verhalten*] to the essent is evident. Faced with the problem of representing the essent, I can always refer to some particular essent or other— whether it be such that I am not and which is not my like, or such that I am myself, or such that I am not but because it is a self is my like. The essent is known to us—but Being? Are we not seized with vertigo when we try to determine it or even to consider it as it is in itself? Does not Being resemble Nothing? In fact,

233

no less a person than Hegel has said it: "Pure Being and pure Nothing are, then, the same." [15]

With the question of Being as such we are poised on the brink of complete obscurity. Yet we should not turn away prematurely but should seek to bring this comprehension of Being in all its singularity closer to us. For despite the seemingly impenetrable obscurity which envelops Being and its signification, it remains incontestable that at all times and wherever the essent appears to us, we have at our disposal a certain comprehension of Being. We concern ourselves with the what-being and thus-being of the essent, acknowledge or dispute its that-being and, at the risk of deceiving ourselves, come to decisions concerning its being-true [*Wahr-sein*]. The assertion of every proposition, e.g., "Today is a holiday," implies an understanding of the "is" and, hence, a certain comprehension of Being.

In the cry "Fire!" we understand that there *is* a fire, that help *is* necessary, that everyone must save himself, i.e., secure his being as best he can. And even when we do not say anything about an essent, even when in silence we assume an attitude toward it, we understand, although implicitly, its mutually compatible what-being, that-being, and being-true.

In every mood wherein "things are this or that way" with us, our own *Da-sein* is manifest to us. We have, therefore, an understanding of Being even though the concept is lacking. This pre-conceptual comprehension of Being, although constant and far-reaching, is usually completely indeterminate. The specific mode of Being, for example, that of material things, plants, animals, men, numbers, is known to us, but what is thus known is not recognized as such. Furthermore, this preconceptual comprehension of the Being of the essent in all its constancy, amplitude, and indeterminateness is given as something completely

15. *Science of Logic,* trans. W. H. Johnston, L. G. Struthers (London, 1921) Vol. I, p. 94.

234

beyond question. Being as such is so little in question that apparently it "is" not.

This comprehension of Being, such as we have briefly sketched it, remains on the level of the purest, most assured, and most naïve patency [*Selbstverständlichkeit*], and yet if *this comprehension of Being did not occur,* man could never be the essent that he is, no matter how wonderful his faculties. Man is an essent in the midst of other essents in such a way that the essent that he is and the essent that he is not are always already manifest to him. We call this mode of Being *existence,*[16] and only on the basis of the comprehension of Being is existence possible.

In his comportment to the essent which he himself is not, man finds it to be that by which he is sustained, on which he is dependent, and over which, for all his culture and technique, he never can be master. Furthermore, dependent on the essent that he is not, man is, at bottom, not even master of himself.

With the existence of man there occurs an irruption into the totality of the essent such that, by this event, the essent becomes manifest in itself, i.e., manifest as essent—this manifestation being of varying amplitude and having different degrees of clarity and certitude. However, this prerogative [*Vorzug*] of not being simply an essent among other essents, which last are not manifest to one another, but, in the midst of essents, of *being delivered up to them as such* [an es als ein solches ausgelie-

16. *Existence* (or *Ex-sistence,* as Heidegger later terms it), like *concern,* is another of Heidegger's "existentials." This term "existence" "is not identical with the traditional concept of *existentia"* which "signifies reality as opposed to *essentia* as the possibility of something" (*Über den Humanismus,* p. 15). Existence is "The Being to which *Dasein* can and always does dispose itself" (*Sein und Zeit,* p. 12). It is a "standing forth into the truth of Being;" hence, to assert that "Man ex-sists is not to answer the question as to whether man is real or not but the question as to his essence" (*Über den Humanismus,* p. 16). (J. S. C.)

fert] *and of being answerable to oneself as essent,* in short, this prerogative of existing, involves in itself the necessity of a comprehension of Being.

Man would not be able to be, *qua* self, an essent thrown [*geworfene*] into the world if he could not let the essent as such be.[17] However, in order to let the essent be what and how it is, the existent essent [man] must always have already projected that which it encounters as essent. Existence implies being dependent on the essent as such so that man as essent is given over to the essent on which he is thus dependent.

As a mode of Being, existence is in itself finitude and, as such, is only possible on the basis of the comprehension of Being. There is and must be such as Being only where finitude has become existent. [*Dergleichen wie Sein gibt es nur und muss es geben, wo Endlichkeit existent geworden ist.*] The comprehension of Being which dominates human existence, although man is unaware of its breadth, constancy, and indeterminateness, is thus manifest as the innermost ground of human finitude. The comprehension of Being does not have the harmless generality which it would have were it just another human property. Its

17. The notion of letting-be (*sein-lassen*) adumbrated in *Sein und Zeit* and discussed in this passage in connection with man's situation in the world of essents, later becomes an important factor in Heidegger's conception of what distinguishes the activity of the artist from that of the ordinary man. Although never clearly stated as such, this conception seems to be that the artist differs from the ordinary man who looks upon essents only as objects having value for him as tools, etc., in that the artist lets the essent be what it is in itself. This letting-be, accomplished through restraint (*Verhaltenheit*) and a tarrying by the essent *qua* work of art, is a preservation of it. (See *Der Ursprung des Kunstwerkes, Holzwege,* p. 7ff.) (It is interesting to compare this notion with Keats' "negative capability.")

There is also a suggestion in Heidegger that the activity of the thinker (the true philosopher) is not unlike that of the artist in that the thinker "lets Being be" (*Über den Humanismus,* p. 42). (J. S. C.)

"generality" is the basic originality of the innermost ground of the finitude of *Dasein*. Only because the comprehension of Being is the most finite in the finite, can it make possible even the so-called "creative" faculties of finite human beings. And only because it takes place in the very bosom of finitude is the comprehension of Being characterized by obscurity as well as by the breadth and constancy which have been noted.

It is on the basis of his comprehension of Being that man is *presence* [*Da*], with the Being of which takes place the revelatory [*eröffnende*] irruption into the essent. It is by virtue of this irruption that the essent as such can become manifest to a self. *More primordial than man is the finitude of the* Dasein *in him.*

The elaboration of the basic question of *metaphysica generalis,* i.e., the question *ti to on,* has been thrown back upon the more fundamental question of the intrinsic essence of the comprehension of Being as that which sustains, actuates, and orients the specific question concerning the concept of Being. This more primordial interpretation of the basic problem of metaphysics has been developed with the intention of bringing to light the connection of the problem of the laying of the foundation of metaphysics with the question of the finitude in man. It now appears that we do not even have to ask ourselves about the relation of the comprehension of Being to the finitude in man. This comprehension of Being itself is the innermost essence of finitude. We have thus acquired a concept of finitude which is fundamental to the problematic of the laying of the foundation of metaphysics. If this laying of the foundation depends upon the question of knowing what man is, the indefiniteness of this question is in part overcome, since the question as to the nature of man has become more determinate.

If man is only man on the basis of the *Dasein* in him, then the question as to what is more primordial than man can, as a

237

matter of principle, not be an anthropological one. All anthropology, even philosophical anthropology, always proceeds on the assumption that man is man.

The problem of the laying of the foundation of metaphysics is rooted in the question of the *Dasein* in man, i.e., in the question of his ultimate ground, which is the comprehension of Being as essentially existent finitude. This question relative to *Dasein* asks what the essence of the essent so determined is. Insofar as the Being of this essent lies in existence, the question as to the essence of *Dasein* is an existential one. Every question relative to the Being of an essent—and, in particular, the question relative to the Being of that essent to whose constitution finitude as the comprehension of Being belongs—is metaphysics.

Hence, the laying of the foundation of metaphysics is based upon a metaphysics of *Dasein*. But is it at all surprising that a laying of the foundation of metaphysics should itself be a form of metaphysics, and that in a pre-eminent sense?

Kant, who in his philosophizing was more alert to the problem of metaphysics than any other philosopher before or since, would not have understood his own intention had he not perceived this connection. He expressed his opinion concerning it with the clarity and serenity which the completion of the *Critique of Pure Reason* bestowed on him. In the year 1781, he wrote to his friend and disciple, Marcus Herz, concerning this work: "An inquiry of this sort will always remain difficult, for it contains the metaphysics of metaphysics." [18]

This remark once and for all puts an end to all attempts to interpret, even partially, the *Critique of Pure Reason* as theory of knowledge. But these words also constrain every repetition of a laying of the foundation of metaphysics to clarify this "metaphysics of metaphysics" enough to put itself in a position to open up a possible way to the achievement of the laying of the foundation.

18. *Works* (Cass.), IX, p. 198.

## C. The Metaphysics of *Dasein* as
## Fundamental Ontology

No anthropology which understands its own mode of inquiry and its own presuppositions can claim even to develop the problem of a laying of the foundation of metaphysics, to say nothing of carrying it out. The question necessary for a laying of the foundation of metaphysics, namely, the question of the essence of man, belongs to the metaphysics of *Dasein*.

The expression "metaphysics of *Dasein*" is, in a positive sense, ambiguous. The metaphysics of *Dasein* not only treats of *Dasein,* it is also the metaphysics which necessarily is realized as *Dasein*. It follows, then, that this metaphysics cannot be "about" *Dasein* as, for example, zoology is about animals. The metaphysics of *Dasein* is in no sense an "organon" fixed and ready at hand. It must constantly be reconstructed by the transformation which its idea undergoes because of the development of the possibility of metaphysics.

Its destiny remains bound to the secret coming-to-be [*Geschehen*] of metaphysics in *Dasein* in virtue of which man first numbers or forgets the hours, days, years, and centuries which he has devoted to his endeavors.

The internal exigencies of a metaphysics of *Dasein* and the difficulty of defining this metaphysics have been brought to light clearly enough by the Kantian endeavor. When clearly understood, the true result of this endeavor lies in the disclosure of the bond which unites the problem of the possibility of metaphysics with that of the revelation of the finitude in man. Thus is brought to light the necessity of a reflection concerning the way in which a metaphysics of *Dasein* should be concretely developed.

## § 42. *The Idea of a Fundamental Ontology*

In the presentation of its problem as well as in the point of departure, course of development, and final objective, the laying of the foundation of metaphysics must be guided solely and rigorously by its fundamental question. This fundamental question is the problem of the internal possibility of the comprehension of Being, from which all specific questions relative to Being arise. The metaphysics of *Dasein* when guided by the question of the laying of the foundation reveals the structure of Being proper to *Dasein* in such a way that this structure is manifest as that which makes the comprehension of Being possible. The disclosure of the structure of Being of *Dasein* is ontology. So far as the ground of the possibility of metaphysics is established in ontology—the finitude of *Dasein* being its foundation—ontology signifies fundamental ontology. Under the designation fundamental ontology is included the problem of the finitude in man as the decisive element which makes the comprehension of Being possible.

However, fundamental ontology is only the first stage of the metaphysics of *Dasein*. We are able to discuss here neither this metaphysics as a whole nor the way in which it is rooted historically in concrete *Dasein*. Rather, we are now faced with the task of clarifying the idea of fundamental ontology, which idea has guided the present interpretation of the *Critique of Pure Reason*. Furthermore, only the basic outline of the characterization of fundamental ontology will be given here in order thus to call to mind the principal stages of a preceding attempt.[19]

The structure of Being of every essent and that of *Dasein* in particular is accessible only through the understanding insofar as this has the character of projection [*Entwurf*]. As fundamental ontology reveals, the understanding is not simply a

19. *Cf. Sein und Zeit.*

mode of cognition but a fundamental moment of existence. Hence, the specific achievement of projection, above all when it is a matter of ontological comprehension, is necessarily construction.

However, the term "construction" does not have here the sense of free invention. Rather, it is a projection in which the precursory orientation as well as the trajection must be predetermined and made secure. *Dasein* must be constructed in its finitude and with regard to that which makes the comprehension of Being intrinsically possible. All construction relevant to fundamental ontology is verified by that which its projection makes manifest, i.e., by the way in which this projection brings *Dasein* to its own overtness and renders its intrinsic metaphysic present to it [*seine innere Metaphysik da-sein lässt*].

The construction proper to fundamental ontology is distinguished by the fact that it lays bare the internal possibility of that which holds sway over *Dasein*. This dominating element is not only that which is most familiar to *Dasein* but is also that which is most indeterminate and self-evident. This construction can be understood as an effort on the part of *Dasein* to grasp in itself the primordial metaphysical fact which consists in this, that the most finite in its finitude is known without being understood.

The finitude of *Dasein*—the comprehension of Being—*lies in* forgetfulness [*Vergessenheit*].[20]

This forgetfulness is nothing accidental and temporary but is constantly and necessarily renewed. All construction relevant

20. The "forgetfulness" of which Heidegger speaks here does not refer to a mental state but to "an essential relation of man to Being" (*Über den Humanismus*, p. 21). Both as an individual engaged in the ordinary business of living and as a philosopher, i.e., a "metaphysician," man is concerned with objects and the "is-ness" [*Seiendheit*] of objects and "forgets" about Being, this forgetfulness being "something fated" (*Geschick*) by Being itself. (J. S. C.)

to fundamental ontology, construction which strives toward the disclosure of the internal possibility of the comprehension of Being, must in its act of projection wrest from forgetfulness that which it thus apprehends. The basic, fundamental-ontological act of the metaphysics of *Dasein* is, therefore, a remembering [*Wiedererinnerung*].

But true remembrance must always interiorize what is remembered, i.e., let it come closer and closer in its most intrinsic possibility. This signifies, relative to the development of a fundamental ontology, that this remembrance must let itself be guided constantly, uniquely, and effectively by the question of Being in order thus to keep the existential analytic of *Dasein,* the development of which is the responsibility of fundamental ontology, on the right path.

## § 43. The Inception and Course of Development of Fundamental Ontology [21]

The *Dasein* in man characterizes him as that essent who, placed in the midst of essents, comports himself to them as such. This comportment determines man in his Being and makes him essentially different from all other essents which are manifest to him.

An analytic of *Dasein* must, from the beginning, strive to uncover the *Dasein* in man according to that mode of Being which, by nature, maintains *Dasein* and its comprehension of Being, i.e., primordial finitude, in forgetfulness. This mode of Being of *Dasein*—decisive only from the point of view of a

21. For an adequate understanding of this and the following paragraphs, a study of *Sein und Zeit* is indispensable. We refrain here from taking a position with regard to the criticism which has been expressed up to this point. This position—insofar as the rather confused "objections" which have been presented remain within the limits of the problem—will be the object of a special publication.

242

fundamental ontology—we call "everydayness" [*Alltäglichkeit*].²²
The analytic of everydayness must take care not to allow the
interpretation of the *Dasein* in man to become confused with
an anthropo-psychological description of the "experiences"
and "faculties" of man. This anthropo-psychological knowledge
is not declared thereby to be "false," but it is necessary to show
that, despite its exactitude, such knowledge is incapable of
coming to grips with the problem of the existence of *Dasein,*
i.e., the problem of its finitude. A grasp of this problem, however, is required by the decisive question, namely, that of Being.

The existential analytic of existence does not have as an
objective a description of how we manage a knife and fork.
It is intended to show how all commerce with essents—even
when it seems to concern only the latter—presupposes the transcendence of *Dasein,* namely, being-in-the-world. With this
transcendence is achieved the projection, hidden and, for the
most part, indeterminate, of the Being of the essent in general.
By means of this projection, the Being of the essent becomes
manifest and intelligible, although, at first and ordinarily, only
in a confused way. In this mode of comprehension the difference
between Being and the essent remains concealed, and man himself is presented as an essent among other essents.

Being-in-the-world cannot be reduced to a relation between
subject and object. It is, on the contrary, that which makes
such a relation possible, insofar as transcendence carries out

22. Everydayness and the associated concepts, "lapsing" (*Ver-
fallen*), "the one" (*das Man*), and "unauthenticity" (*Uneigent-
lichkeit*), which are the subject of an extended analysis in *Sein und
Zeit* are, as Heidegger is at pains to point out here and elsewhere, in
no way to be considered as ethical concepts (although that they are
often so considered is, in part, Heidegger's own fault—he need not
have chosen terms which have such obvious moral and religious overtones). Rather, these concepts refer to a mode of existence which
is characterized by that "forgetfulness" of Being discussed above.
(J. S. C.)

the projection of the Being of the essent. The existential analytic illuminates this projection (this act of understanding) within the limits imposed by its point of departure. It is not so much a question of pursuing a study of the intrinsic constitution of transcendence as of elucidating its essential unity with feeling [*Befindlichkeit*] and dereliction [*Geworfenheit*].[23]

All projection—and, consequently, even man's "creative" activity—is *thrown* [*geworfener*], i.e., determined by the dependence of *Dasein* on the essent in totality, a dependence to which *Dasein* always submits. This fact of being thrown [dereliction] is not restricted to the mysterious occurrence of the coming-into-the-world of *Dasein* but governs being-present [*Da-sein*] as such. This is expressed in the movement which has been described as a lapsing. This idea of lapsing does not refer to certain negative events of human life which a critique of culture would be disposed to condemn but to an intrinsic character of the transcendental finitude of man, a character which is bound to the nature of projection as "thrown."

The development of existential ontology, which begins by the analysis of everydayness, has as its sole objective the explication of the primordial transcendental structure of the *Dasein* in man. In transcendence, *Dasein* manifests itself as need of the comprehension of Being. This transcendental need assures [*sorgt*] the possibility of something on the order of *Dasein*. This need is nothing other than finitude in its most intrinsic form as that which is the source of *Dasein*.

The unity of the transcendental structure of this need,

23. Feeling is one of the two ways (the other being understanding [*Verstehen*], which for Heidegger is essentially projection) in which man becomes aware of himself and his world. What is disclosed by feeling in particular is man's dereliction, i.e., that man in the world finds himself cast or thrown into a situation not of his own choosing and among things over which he is not master. (J. S. C.)

characteristic of the *Dasein* in man, has been termed "concern." The word itself is of little consequence, but it is essential to understand what the analytic of *Dasein* seeks to express by means of it. If one takes the expression "concern"—despite the specific directive that the term has nothing to do with an ontic characteristic of man—in the sense of an ethical and ideological evaluation of "human life" rather than as the designation of the structural unity of the inherently finite transcendence of *Dasein,* then everything falls into confusion and no comprehension of the problematic which guides the analytic of *Dasein* is possible.

In any case, there is reason to believe that the explication of the essence of finitude required for the establishment of metaphysics must itself always be basically finite and never absolute. It follows that this reflection on finitude, which is always to be renewed, cannot succeed by exchanging and adjusting various points of view in order finally and in spite of everything to give us an absolute knowledge of finitude, a knowledge which is surreptitiously posited as being "true in itself." It remains, therefore, only to develop the problematic of finitude as such. Finitude becomes manifest to us in its intrinsic essence if we approach it in the light of the fundamental question of metaphysics as primordially conceived, a method of approach which, to be sure, cannot claim to be the only one possible.

It is clear from the above that the metaphysics of *Dasein* as a laying of the foundation of metaphysics has its own truth, which in its essence is as yet all too obscure. No one dominated by an attitude inspired by a *Weltanschauung,* i.e., an attitude which is popular and ontic, and particularly no one dominated by an attitude—whether approving or disapproving—inspired by theology, can enter the dimension of the problem of a metaphysics of *Dasein.* For, as Kant says, "the critique of reason

245

. . . can never become popular, and indeed there is no need that it should." [24]

Hence, whoever would institute a critique of the transcendental interpretation of "concern" as the transcendental unity of finitude—a critique the possibility and necessity of which no one would deny—must show, first, that the transcendence of *Dasein* and consequently the comprehension of Being, do not constitute the finitude in man, second, that the establishment of metaphysics does not have that essential relation to the finitude of *Dasein* of which we have spoken, and finally, that the basic question of the laying of the foundation of metaphysics is not encompassed by the problem of the intrinsic possibility of the comprehension of Being.

Before presenting an interpretation of transcendence as "concern," the fundamental-ontological analytic of *Dasein* purposely seeks first to provide an explication of "anxiety" [*Angst*] as a "decisive fundamental feeling" in order to show concretely that the existential analytic is constantly guided by the question from which it arises, namely, the question of the possibility of the comprehension of Being. Anxiety is declared to be the decisive fundamental faculty not in order to proclaim, from the point of view of some *Weltanschauung* or other, a concrete existence-ideal but *solely with reference to the problem of Being as such.*

Anxiety is that fundamental feeling which places us before the Nothing. The Being of the essent is comprehensible—and in this lies the innermost finitude of transcendence—only if *Dasein* on the basis of its essence holds itself into Nothing. Holding oneself into Nothing is no arbitrary and casual attempt to "think" about this Nothing but an event which underlies all feeling oneself [*Sichbefinden*] in the midst of essents already on hand. The intrinsic possibility of this event must be clarified in a fundamental-ontological analytic of *Dasein*.

24. B XXXIV, NKS, p. 31.

246

"Anxiety" thus understood, i.e., according to fundamental ontology, prohibits us from interpreting "concern" as having the harmlessness of a categorical structure. It gives concern the incisiveness necessary to a fundamental existential and thus determines the finitude in *Dasein* not as a given property but as the constant, although generally veiled, precariousness [*Erzittern*] which pervades all existence.

But the explication of concern as the transcendental, fundamental constitution of *Dasein* is only the first stage of fundamental ontology. For further progress toward the goal, we must let ourselves be guided and inspired with ever increasing rigor by the question of Being.

## § 44. The Goal of Fundamental Ontology

The next and decisive stage of the existential analytic is the concrete explication of concern as temporality. Since the problematic of the laying of the foundation of metaphysics has an intrinsic relation to the finitude in man, it might seem that the development of "temporality" serves as a concrete determination of the finitude in man as a "temporal" being. For the "temporal" is commonly held to be the finite.

But the fact that not only man but all finite essents are considered to be "temporal" in the ordinary sense of the term —a sense which, within its limits, is justified—is enough to indicate that the interpretation of *Dasein* as temporality cannot move within the field of the ordinary experience of time.

One should also not be led to believe that the sense of "temporal" in question is that which inspires modern philosophy (Bergson, Dilthey, Simmel) in its attempt to obtain a more searching and a more intuitive understanding of the "liveliness" of life by determining its temporal character.

On the contrary, if the interpretation of *Dasein* as temporality is the goal of fundamental ontology, then it must be motivated

247

exclusively by the problem of Being as such. In this way, is first revealed the fundamental-ontological sense of the question of time, i.e., the only sense that it has in *Sein und Zeit*.

The fundamental-ontological laying of the foundation of metaphysics in *Sein und Zeit* must be understood as a repetition. The passage from Plato's *Sophist* does not serve as a decoration but as an indication that the *Gigantomachia* [war of the giants] relative to the Being of the essent first broke out in ancient metaphysics. Through this struggle, the way in which *Being as such*—no matter with what generality and ambiguity the question of Being may yet be enveloped—is understood must become apparent. But inasmuch as in this struggle the question of Being as such is first won but not yet developed in the manner indicated as a problem of the intrinsic possibility of the comprehension of Being, neither the explication of Being as such nor the horizon necessary for this explication can come to light. This is why, in attempting the repetition of this problem, it is imperative that we be attentive to the way in which philosophical thought in this first struggle expressed itself spontaneously, as it were, concerning Being.

To be sure, the present study cannot provide a thematic exposition of this *gigantomachia,* to say nothing of an interpretation of its basic tendencies. An indication of its salient characteristics must suffice.

What is the significance of the fact that ancient metaphysics defined the *ontōs on*—the essent which is essent to the highest degree—as *aei on?* The Being of the essent obviously is understood here as permanence and subsistence. What projection lies at the basis of this comprehension of Being? A projection relative to time, for even eternity, taken as the *nunc stans,* for example, is as a "permanent" *now* conceivable only through time.

What is the significance of the fact that the essent in the proper sense of the term is understood as *ousia, parousia,* i.e., basically as "presence" [*Anwesen*], the immediate and always present possession, as "having" [*Habe*]? ²⁵ This projection reveals that "Being" is synonymous with *permanence in presence*.

In this way, therefore, i.e., in the spontaneous comprehension of Being, temporal determinations are accumulated. Is not the immediate comprehension of Being developed entirely from a primordial but self-evident *projection of Being relative to time?*

Is it not then true that from the first this struggle for Being takes place within the horizon of time?

Is it surprising, then, that the ontological interpretation of the what-being of the essent is expressed in the *to ti ēn einai?* Does not this "that which has always been" include the moment of permanent presence and even in the sense of a certain anticipation [*Vorgängigkeit*]?

Can the *a priori* which in the tradition of ontology is held to be a characteristic of the determination of Being be explained by asserting that the "earlier" which it implies "naturally" has nothing to do with "time"? Certainly, it has nothing to do with the "time" recognized by the ordinary comprehension of time. But is this "earlier" positively determined thereby, and is this annoying temporal character pushed aside? Or does it not reappear as a new and more difficult problem?

Is it therefore simply a habit, more or less fortunate and formed no one knows where or when, that in the classification of the essent, i.e., in the differentiation of the essent relative to its Being, we "spontaneously" determine it as temporal, atemporal, or supratemporal?

What is the basis of this spontaneous and "self-evident" comprehension of Being through time? Has anyone even attempted,

25. *Anwesen*, "presence," commonly signifies the goods and possessions, e.g., real estate, which collectively form an adjunct to the person. The term *Habe*, derived from the verb *haben*, "to have," has a similar meaning. (J. S. C.)

by posing this problem explicitly, to ask why this is so and why it must happen thus?

The essence of time as it was fixed—and, as it turned out, decisively—for the subsequent history of metaphysics by Aristotle does not provide an answer to this question. On the contrary, it would be easy to show that it is precisely Aristotle's conception of time that is inspired by a comprehension of Being which—without being aware of its action—interprets Being as permanent presence and, consequently, determines the "Being" of time from the point of view of the *now,* i.e., from the character of time which in itself is constantly present and, hence, (in the ancient sense of the term) really *is.*

Now it is true that time is also considered by Aristotle as something which takes place in the "soul" and in the "mind." However, the determination of the essence of the soul, the mind, the spirit, and the consciousness of man is not guided directly and primarily by the problematic of the laying of the foundation of metaphysics, nor is time interpreted in the light of a preliminary insight into the problematic, nor, finally, is the explication of the transcendental structure of *Dasein* as temporality understood and developed as a problem.

The philosophical "remembrance" of the hidden projection of Being on time as the central event in the history of the metaphysical comprehension of Being in antiquity and beyond assigns a task to the repetition of the basic problem of metaphysics: it is necessary that the regression toward the finitude in man required by this problematic be carried out in such a way that in *Da-sein* as such temporality is made manifest as a transcendental primordial structure.

The attainment of this objective of fundamental ontology insofar as it is accomplished by the explication of the finitude in man makes an existential interpretation of conscience, guilt, and death necessary.

The transcendental exposition of historicity [*Geschichtlichkeit*]

250

on the basis of temporality will at the same time provide a pre-conception of the mode of Being of that becoming [*Geschehen*] which takes place [*geschieht*] in the repetition of the question of Being. Metaphysics is not something which is simply "created" by man in systems and doctrines; rather the comprehension of Being, its projection and rejection, takes place in *Dasein* as such. "Metaphysics" is the fundamental event which comes to pass with the irruption into the essent of the concrete existence of man.

The metaphysics of *Dasein* which is developed in fundamental ontology does not claim to be a new discipline within the framework of an established order but seeks only to awaken the insight that philosophical thought takes place as the explicit transcendence of *Dasein*.

If the problematic of the metaphysics of *Dasein* is designated as that of *Being and Time* [*Sein und Zeit*] the explication which has been given concerning the idea of a fundamental ontology makes it clear that it is the conjunction "and" in the above title which expresses the central problem. Neither Being nor time need be deprived of the meanings which they have had until now, but a more primordial explication of these terms must establish their justification and their limits.

### § 45. The Idea of Fundamental Ontology and the Critique of Pure Reason

Kant's laying of the foundation of metaphysics, which for the first time subjects the internal possibility of the overtness of the Being of the essent to a decisive examination, must necessarily encounter time as the basic determination of finite transcendence if, indeed, it is true that the comprehension of Being in *Dasein* spontaneously projects Being on time. But at the same time this laying of the foundation must go beyond the ordinary conception of time to the transcendental comprehension of it as pure self-affection. This self-affection is essentially one with pure apperception and in this unity makes possible the total structure of pure sensible reason.

It is not because time serves as the "form of intuition" and is interpreted as such at the beginning of the *Critique of Pure Reason* that in its essential unity with the transcendental imagination it acquires a central metaphysical function. On the contrary, it acquires this function because, by virtue of the finitude of the *Dasein* in man, the comprehension of Being must be projected on time.

The *Critique of Pure Reason* thus threatens the supremacy of reason and the understanding. "Logic" is deprived of its traditional primacy relative to metaphysics. Its basic idea is brought into question.

If the essence of transcendence is based on pure imagination, i.e., originally on time, then the idea of a "transcendental logic" becomes non-sensical especially if, contrary to Kant's original intention, it is treated as an autonomous and absolute discipline.

Kant must have had an intimation of this collapse of the primacy of logic in metaphysics when, speaking of the fundamental characteristics of Being, "possibility" (what-being) and "reality" (which Kant termed "existence"), he said: "So long as the definition of possibility, existence, and necessity is sought solely in pure understanding, they cannot be explained save through an obvious tautology." [26]

And yet, in the second edition of the *Critique* did not Kant re-establish the supremacy of the understanding? And as a result of this did not metaphysics, with Hegel, come to be identified with "logic" more radically than ever before?

What is the significance of the struggle initiated in German idealism against the "thing in itself" except a growing forgetfulness of what Kant had won, namely, the knowledge that

26. A 244, B 302, NKS, p. 262.

252

the intrinsic possibility and necessity of metaphysics, i.e., its essence, are, at bottom, sustained and maintained by the original development and searching study of the problem of finitude?

What is the outcome of Kant's effort if Hegel defines metaphysics in these terms: "Logic is consequently to be understood as the system of Pure Reason, as the Realm of Pure Thought. *This realm is the Truth as it is, without husk in and for itself* —one may therefore express it thus: that this content *shows forth God as He is in His eternal essence before the creation of Nature and of a finite Spirit.*" [27]

Can there be a more convincing proof that neither metaphysics "which belongs to human nature" nor human nature itself is "self-evident"?

In interpreting the *Critique of Pure Reason* from the standpoint of fundamental ontology, are we justified in believing that we are wiser than our illustrious predecessors? Or do our own efforts, if we dare compare them with those of our predecessors, evidence a secret withdrawal before something which we—and certainly not by accident—no longer see?

Has not our interpretation of the *Critique of Pure Reason*, an interpretation inspired by fundamental ontology, made the problematic of a laying of the foundation of metaphysics more precise even though it stops short of the decisive point? Therefore, there is only one thing to do: we must hold open the questions posed by our inquiry.

Moreover, is not the *Transcendental Analytic,* taken in the broad sense to which our interpretation is limited, followed by a *Transcendental Dialectic?* And if the substance of the latter consists only in the critical application of the insight attained relative to the essence of *metaphysica generalis* to the rejection of *metaphysica specialis,* must we not conclude that this apparently negative content of the *Transcendental Dialectic* also conceals a positive problematic?

27. *Science of Logic,* p. 60.

And could it not be that this problematic is concentrated in the question which up to the present has guided, although in a veiled and implicit manner, every problematic of metaphysics, namely, the question of the finitude of *Dasein?*

Kant says that "transcendental appearance," to which traditional metaphysics owes its possibility, is necessary. Must not this transcendental untruth be positively established in its original unity with transcendental truth on the basis of the intrinsic essence of the finitude in *Dasein?* Does not the dis-essence [*Unwesen*] of this appearance pertain to the essence of finitude?

Is it not advisable, then, to free the problem of "transcendental appearance" from that architectonic into which Kant—oriented as he is on traditional logic—forces it, especially since the position of logic as the possible ground and guide for the problematic of metaphysics is threatened by the Kantian laying of the foundation?

What is the transcendental essence of truth? How, on the basis of the finitude of *Dasein,* are the essence of truth and the dis-essence of untruth originally united with man's fundamental need, as an essent thrown in the midst of essents, to comprehend Being?

Does it make sense and is it justifiable to think that man, because his finitude makes an ontology, i.e., a comprehension of Being necessary to him, is "creative" and therefore "infinite" when nothing is so radically opposed to ontology as the idea of an infinite being?

But is it possible to develop the finitude in *Dasein* even as a problem without "presupposing" an infinitude? What is the nature of this "presupposition" in *Dasein?* What is the significance of the infinitude thus "posed"?

Will the problem of Being succeed in recovering its elementary force and amplitude through all these questions? Or, at this point, are we so much the fools of organization, bustle, and speed that we are no longer able to be friends of the essen-

254

tial, the simple, and the stable? This "friendship" (*philia*) alone turns us toward the essent as such, a movement from which springs the question of the concept of Being (*sophia*)—the basic question of philosophy.

Or for this also do we first need remembrance?

Let Aristotle speak:

> *Kai dē kai to palai te kai nun kai aei zētoumenon kai aei aporhoumenon ti to on . . .*

(Metaphysics Z1, 1028, b 2 sqq.)